Putin's Totalit

Kate C. Langdon • Vladimir Tismaneanu

Putin's Totalitarian Democracy

Ideology, Myth, and Violence
in the Twenty-First Century

palgrave
macmillan

Kate C. Langdon
Crofton, MD, USA

Vladimir Tismaneanu
University of Maryland
College Park, MD, USA

ISBN 978-3-030-20581-2   ISBN 978-3-030-20579-9 (eBook)
https://doi.org/10.1007/978-3-030-20579-9

© The Editor(s) (if applicable) and The Author(s), under exclusive licence to Springer Nature Switzerland AG 2020
This work is subject to copyright. All rights are solely and exclusively licensed by the Publisher, whether the whole or part of the material is concerned, specifically the rights of translation, reprinting, reuse of illustrations, recitation, broadcasting, reproduction on microfilms or in any other physical way, and transmission or information storage and retrieval, electronic adaptation, computer software, or by similar or dissimilar methodology now known or hereafter developed.
The use of general descriptive names, registered names, trademarks, service marks, etc. in this publication does not imply, even in the absence of a specific statement, that such names are exempt from the relevant protective laws and regulations and therefore free for general use.
The publisher, the authors and the editors are safe to assume that the advice and information in this book are believed to be true and accurate at the date of publication. Neither the publisher nor the authors or the editors give a warranty, express or implied, with respect to the material contained herein or for any errors or omissions that may have been made. The publisher remains neutral with regard to jurisdictional claims in published maps and institutional affiliations.

This Palgrave Macmillan imprint is published by the registered company Springer Nature Switzerland AG
The registered company address is: Gewerbestrasse 11, 6330 Cham, Switzerland

In memory of both

*Walter Laqueur,
historian and critical intellectual
(26 May 1921–30 September 2018),*

and

*Jacob L. Talmon,
political scientist and critical intellectual
(14 June 1916–16 June 1980),*

and to

*the victims of totalitarian domination
and those who fight against it.*

Acknowledgments

Our book owes a substantial debt to several mentors, friends, and family. First, I, Kate C. Langdon, maintain a profound appreciation and admiration for Dr. Mark Hoffman, who went above and beyond his professorial duties as my thesis advisor at Vassar College. Without his trust and encouragement, I would not have pursued my unorthodox research on the topic of Putinism and authoritarianism in Russia. I thank Dr. Stephen Rock from Vassar College as well; not only did he agree to act as the second reader for my tome of a thesis, but he also offered criticisms that have much improved the themes of the original text. Both Vassar professors encouraged me to expand it into a book for publication.

Much gratitude must be expressed to my co-author Dr. Vladimir Tismaneanu. His passion for truth and humanity is boundless, as is his wealth of knowledge. To study under someone for whom scholarship is a way of life, not just a career, is truly humbling. Dr. Tismaneanu's work heavily influenced my original project, and I found it an amazing experience to revamp that work into a professional publication alongside his active collaboration over the past year. Likewise, I convey my deep thanks to Dr. Piotr Kosicki from the University of Maryland, College Park, who volunteered to read 200 pages written by a student he hardly knew at the time. His genuine interest in students' ideas, in what others might write off as "just undergraduate" work, is sorely absent from so many educational institutions.

As for Jordan Luber, no words are fit to describe his contributions. Like the number of hours he spent reviewing and helping to conceptualize my contribution to this co-authored work, his belief in both the cause of human dignity and me is endless.

Second, I, Vladimir Tismaneanu, wish to pay tribute here to my friends Karen Dawisha (1949–2018) and Alvin Z. Rubinstein (1927–2001), both distinguished scholars of Soviet and post-Soviet affairs as well as models of intellectual acumen and moral intelligence. Additionally, I would like to share that co-authoring this book with Kate Langdon and benefitting from Jordan Luber's insightful suggestions have been enriching experiences. There is nothing a professor can find more rewarding than sharing and elaborating ideas in collaboration with such young and truly brilliant students. Moreover, 2018 was quite a difficult year for me in terms of health. It was first and foremost thanks to my wife, Mary Sladek, and our son, Adam Volo Tismaneanu, that I managed to overcome the vexing circumstances and return to my normal life as a teacher, a scholar, and—to use Raymond Aron's formulation—an engaged spectator.

Contents

1	**Recentering Putinism**	1
	Debunking the "Putin Phenomenon" and Recentering Putinism	4
	Challenges to Putinism and the Survival of Historical Trends	17
	Brief Chapter Outline	22
	References	30
2	**The Inheritance of an Autocratic Legend**	35
	The Basis of Tsarist Rule: Absolute Power in Exchange for Border Protection	36
	Leninism Continues the Autocratic Legacy	40
	The Ghost of Autocracy Haunts Modern Russia	44
	References	50
3	**Enter "the Hero"**	55
	The Dresden Connection	58
	After the Soviet Fall	61
	Apartment Bombings and the Need for a National Savior	63
	War as a Distracting and Mobilizing Force	65
	Recognizing the Need for the People's Approval	67
	Shaking the Unshakeable: Crises of the Economy and Legitimacy	71
	References	77

4 The Intellectual Origins of Putinism — 83
What Is Ideology? — 85
Ideology and Blurring: The Progression into Totalitarianism — 88
Intellectual Origins of Putinism and Beyond — 90
Putin the Opportunist, or Putin the Believer? — 97
References — 108

5 Putinism as a Culture in the Making — 113
The Security Imaginary: A Domestic Tool for Defining the Russian National Identity — 115
Nostalgia for the Soviet Paradise — 117
A One-Sided State of Perpetual War — 121
Russia as a Victim — 123
Rewriting History Around Russian Exceptionalism — 125
Russia as the Superior Culture — 128
Biopolitics and Racism: Self-Other Distinctions and Identity — 131
Putinism and the Specter of Homo Sovieticus — 137
References — 148

6 Russian Nationalism in Education, the Media, and Religion — 153
Ideology and Youth Education in Russia — 155
Ideology and the Media in Russia — 157
Ideology and Religion in Russia — 161
How Individuals Reproduce the Kremlin's Ideology — 165
References — 183

7 Russian Foreign Policy: Freedom for Whom, to Do What? — 189
Putin's Foreign Policy, the "Near Abroad," and Beyond — 192
The Case of Ukraine and Expanding Biopolitics — 195
The Case of Syria and Exaggerating Russia's Role in Global Anti-Terrorism — 201
Foreign Policy and the Internal Policing of the Enemy — 205
References — 219

8 The New Dark Times — 225
References — 242

Index — 245

About the Authors

Kate C. Langdon is an Erasmus Mundus scholar. She has studied in the United States, Russia, the Czech Republic, the Netherlands, and Poland. She holds an M.A. from the European Politics and Society: Václav Havel Programme, led by Charles University in Prague. Previously, she received her Bachelor of Arts degree in both Political Science and Russian Studies at Vassar College, New York, and was inducted into Phi Beta Kappa. Langdon also interned for the U.S. Department of State in Kyiv, Ukraine, and Budapest, Hungary, during the summers of 2015 and 2016, respectively.

Vladimir Tismaneanu is a professor in the Department of Government and Politics at the University of Maryland, College Park, United States, and a Global Fellow at the Woodrow Wilson International Center for Scholars. In addition to regularly contributing to the Romanian-Moldovan branch of Radio Free Europe/Radio Liberty, he has authored numerous books, including *The Devil in History: Communism, Fascism, and Some Lessons of the Twentieth Century* (2012). Together with Romanian political scientist Marius Stan, he most recently co-authored *Romania Confronts Its Communist Past: Democracy, Memory, and Moral Justice* (2018).

CHAPTER 1

Recentering Putinism

Today, we are living in an updated version of the dark times first perceived by German poet Bertolt Brecht and best described by German philosopher Hannah Arendt. These new dark times, in which ordinary citizens fail to illuminate the wrongdoing—or do-gooding—of civilization and its leaders and hence allow for lies to degrade truth and human dignity,[1] are defined by the current age of Bashar al-Assad's genocidal Syrian regime, of Poland's Law and Justice, of Marine Le Pen's National Front, of Viktor Orbán's Hungary, of Nicolás Maduro's Venezuela, of Daniel Ortega's Nicaragua, of Recep Tayyip Erdoğan's Turkey, of Vladimir Putin's Russia, and of Donald Trump's America. The list of what Arendt and other defenders of liberty would condemn as threats to a healthy and free society rattles on; worst of all, it only appears to be growing, as more and more populations across the world vote for exclusionary parties whose policies would result in economic disaster, isolationism, press censorship, and other impediments to the best interests of diversity, plurality, liberty, and human rights.

Under such precarious conditions, it is imperative for scholars, policymakers, and voters alike to examine how it is possible for any political leader to command extensive control over a supposedly democratic nation-state. It is especially important to understand power dynamics when a leader's power is granted mostly on the basis of popularity, rather than dragooned by force. Vladimir Putin's Russia presents a prime source of research on this paradox. On a basic level, this is because Putin's name is plastered in newspapers and magazines across the globe on a daily basis. Most importantly, however, this is because Putin, as the leader of the Russian nation-state, has come to embody a genuine ideological movement that erodes faith in liberal values of democracy and the public on a scale unmatched in other states as of 2019. Putin's Russia is arguably the most active perpetuator and exponent of these new dark times—not only because of its physical body count and its moral body count, but also because of its audacious, genocidal-utopian ideology, as conceived of by the Russian government and people.

While a plethora of scholars and books[2] have been published in recent years to provide insight as to the enigma that Putin the man is, little analysis exists of the Russian population's behaviors or their history as forces themselves. The bulk of such research—conducted by scholars including Ian McAllister, Richard Sakwa, and Stephen White—centers only on Putin and portrays him as little more than a disproportionately powerful opportunist seeking as much money and glory for himself (and, by extension, Russia) as he possibly can. This approach is perilous because it pays no heed to the issue of the population's complicity or desire for an authoritarian leader. It neglects the Russian people's reactions, thereby providing a misleading portrait of Russia that wrongfully situates Putin outside of the Russian tradition.

And the few accounts in existence that actually do incorporate Russian society into their analyses of Putin the president and Russia the country are just as delusory. As insightful as writers and dissidents such as Ben Judah, Vladimir Kara-Murza, Richard Lourie, and Lilia Shevtsova are, their recent works—not without a certain indulgence in wishful thinking—assume that the tiny percentage of Russians bothered by rampant corruption will eventually destroy him, or at least his style of rule. They thus argue that Putin's system must be unstable and decaying[3]; however, they fail to ascertain the ideological aspect of Putin's rule or the historical depths of authoritarianism, nationalism, and imperialism that have culminated in Putin's reign over a largely submissive population of almost 144 million for nearly two decades.

The aforementioned perspectives, with their primary focus on Putin as an individual, either directly or indirectly refer to Putin's success and control over Russia as "the Putin Phenomenon." It is a phrase that focuses Putin the man as the nation's steering force.[4] To comprehend its meaning and usefulness as a framework, though, one must consider its predecessor, the term from which it is essentially adapted: "the Gorbachev

Phenomenon." This concept has been famously wrangled by the late scholar of Soviet and Russian history Moshe Lewin in his book *The Gorbachev Phenomenon: A Historical Interpretation* (1988).

The Gorbachev Phenomenon explored the potential reasons for the Soviet government's announcements of drastic policy and attitude shifts in the 1980s (namely, perestroika and glasnost). It subverted the basic impression of "the Gorbachev Phenomenon" by asking: could the final Soviet General Secretary Mikhail Gorbachev's personality as a leader really be *the* catalyst for change, as many onlookers at the time believed, or were ailments such as an untenable economic situation, a newly emerging civil society soon to burst on the scene under the weight of seven decades of repression, a wasteful bureaucracy, and others responsible? Moreover, were these changes genuine, and would they last?

Lewin's book was crucial in 1988—and is still crucial now—because it approached a society's functioning as a study of change from the few elites above versus change from the many civilians below. Ultimately, it contended that societal trends heavily influenced change in the Soviet system, and that Gorbachev himself should not be given all the credit.[5] The same sentiment needs to be applied to Vladimir Putin as well, if we are going to understand how he could be so popular for so long, and to understand why the Russian population (in addition to a growing number of illiberal, antidemocratic groups across the globe) clings to the Putinist style.

The "Putin Phenomenon," then, usually points to Putin's alleged personal strengths to explain the otherwise baffling nature of Vladimir Vladimirovich Putin's rise to power. Since the little-known ex-KGB (*Komitet Gosudarstvennoy Bezopasnosti*, or Committee for State Security) agent and otherwise ordinary man was first drafted by oligarchs onto Russia's national stage in 1999 as acting prime minister with popularity ratings of 2 percent, he has been elected (albeit with varying degrees of fraud) to the Presidential Office of the Russian Federation four times and enjoys approval rates typically upward of 70 percent and even 80 percent.[6] This phenomenon does, indeed, beg analysis. It has enabled Putin to dominate the Russian political scene for nearly two decades and capture international attention to the point where news anchors and journalists across the globe spend hours each day debating his motivations and intentions.

But examinations of Putin's advantageously amorphous and deliberately elusive personality alone cannot fully explain the "Putin Phenomenon" or his profoundly effective role as head of state. As insightful as these excellent texts are, they fail to explain the cultural and ideological reasons culminating in the cult of personality built around Vladimir Putin and in the imperial myth that has swollen around the idea of Russia for centuries. As of 2019, our task is not to ask the single question of "How has Putin clung to power for so long?" We must now consider two related questions: why have the masses clung to Putin for so long, and how does ideology factor into Russia's current society? Simply put: why do Russians support Putin?

Debunking the "Putin Phenomenon" and Recentering Putinism

Our book diverges from the old mold and the old question. It considers Putin himself as an ideological vessel shaped by a set of cultural beliefs that belong to a deeply rooted Russian milieu, evincing the reality that Russia's problems are not limited to Putin's leadership. We disagree with the typical approach associated with the "Putin Phenomenon" and generally prefer to utilize the term "Putinism" in our work. Rather than focus on Putin the man and his rise from obscurity, we decenter him, remove him from the central place on the historical stage, and instead focus on public reaction, societal mobilization, and historical trends to which Putin himself succumbs. We make this decision because, over time, Putinism has become most remarkable for how Russian citizens consistently offer their approval of Putin even while he restricts their freedoms, stagnates their economy, and sends their friends and loved ones in the military to potentially sacrifice their lives for unnecessary international aggressions. In other words, we find the cultural and societal elements surrounding Putin's success to be more intriguing than his actual achievements or personality.

Contrary to the Russian dissident Vladimir Kara-Murza's optimistic opinion that "Putin is not Russia,"[7] we firmly state that Putin is, in fact, representative of Russia. This is partly due to Putin's status as a product of Russian history and society, and partly due to his status as someone who has tapped into a widespread, populist desire for nationalist glory over humility. Crucially, this revelation signifies that simply removing Putin from office will not be enough to guarantee Russia's freedom. Russians do not believe in Putin alone: they believe in a wider ideology that he happens to share and embody himself. Putin's rule is conditional and will end with his death (or removal from all seats of power, although such a scenario is hard to envision); the criminal and/or aggressive actions conducted by the Russian state at Putin's request, on the other hand, are something the

Russian population will most likely continue to favor, whether they live under Putin or the next leader of whom they can approve.

Likewise, we disagree with Russian political scientist Lilia Shevtsova's conviction that Putin heads a "half-baked despotic regime" that runs off of a fear-inducing personalized power system but cannot possibly rule Russia forever.[8] While Shevtsova is correct in her assertions that Putin will not always be in power (we can, after all, say with a fair degree of confidence that Putin himself will not find the Fountain of Youth, and that the year 2100 will not see him as Russia's ruler) and that fear plays a key role in silencing alternative modes of thought, she misses the meaning of Putinism. It is not just the work of a "half-baked" leader or, for that matter, group of leaders. The despotic regime to which Shevtsova refers is rooted in a cultural trend that (1) will succeed as long as society lets it, and (2) begins before Putin and will last beyond Putin.

This is not to disparage the majority of previous research conducted on Putin's Russia or all the other products of outspoken critics like Kara-Murza and Shevtsova. Putin's advent to power and his desires are, of course, crucial to understanding today's Russian society. Yet, without comprehension of the cultural practices behind Putin, those studies could never properly analyze Russian society or determine how best to liberate it. Take the issue of Putin's enormous wealth, for example. Despite Russia's rough economic situation, Putin is speculated to be one of the richest people in the world, if not *the* richest. His financial worth is valued somewhere between $40 billion and $200 billion,[9] but while some Americans condemn Donald Trump solely on the basis that he did not release his tax returns, the Russian media and the Russian population hardly ever mention Putin's exorbitant and likely ill-gotten riches as an issue.

Examinations into powerful ideological regimes like those of Josef Stalin, Adolf Hitler, Nicolae Ceaușescu, Juan Perón, and Fidel Castro reveal that a leader's individual greed and their commitment to a nation's collective ideology are not incompatible, regardless of the theoretical, political, and moral paradox this presents. It does not matter whether the leader in question rules a Communist country or today's Russia, a country with one of the highest income inequality rates in the world.[10] For some reason, the Russian population does not find Putin's selfishness and vast accumulation of money to be suspicious or treasonous, whereas the riches of elites have often been cause enough to incite popular distrust of them in the eyes of voters and subjects, particularly in Western communities.[11]

As our book will go on to explain in greater detail in Chap. 6, the rationale behind this is ideological.

This is a pivotal point to understand, for it reveals the deeper connection between society's approval of Putin and the lengths to which he can go in his affairs, be they national or private. Putin's wealth is just one example out of many regarding the immensely contradictory situation between the Russian people's expectations and reality. And while the Russian example could never be repeated in the exact same manner elsewhere in the world, the general trends and themes which we emphasize could teach the world valuable lessons on what it means to struggle for—or against—liberty, democracy, and human rights.

To do so, we introduce the constituting features of the culture that gives way to Putin and the ideology of Putinism. They include historical trends, popular desires for authoritarianism, kleptocratic structures, and various other isms—most notably nationalism, imperialism, militarism, racism, and chauvinism. Our book explores the methods by which the Kremlin takes advantage of these features in order to mobilize the Russian population in support of Putin. In the process of highlighting these ideological and cultural practices, our research intends to challenge the dominant assumptions about Russia held more generally throughout Western society, assumptions that obscure the meanings and dangers of Putin's success.

For example, take former U.S. Secretary of Defense Leon Panetta's assertion at the Global Security Forum 2016 that "Putin's main interest is to try to restore the old Soviet Union."[12] This is a dangerously uninformed opinion (to be fully explained and debunked in later chapters of our book), for it fails to consider the motivations or to prepare for the plans of a nation-state that seeks a mission much more alarming than a return to the Soviet Union. Panetta's is a presumption that wrongfully portrays Putin as a simple caudillo hack, rather than as an influential leader of an ideological mass movement directed against liberalism and democracy.

Furthermore, a different yet similarly flawed assumption informed the U.S. Congress' decision to pass a law in August 2017 that would sanction more sectors of Russian society. Proponents of the document argued that Western sanctions would force Putin to back down in Ukraine and "to reduce serious human rights abuses."[13] However, sanctions themselves cannot transform an ideological country that already does not respect universal human rights or democratic freedoms, as Russia's continued violations of international law demonstrate (and, in further proof, as we will confirm in our book). This is not to say that sanctions imposed upon Russia are unfair; on the contrary, they are very much necessary. But national governments and international organizations should realize that they cannot stake change in Russia upon sanctions alone. Sanctions and other comfortable, easy simplifications give the impression of action but only culminate in virtual appeasement, inaction, and, when it comes to victims, extra terror.

These are just two out of many myths that cloud judgments of foreign policymakers or those interested in learning about Russia (or about the dangerous intents of their own domestic political representatives who might believe, in the words of U.S. President Donald Trump, that it would "be a great thing if we get along with Russia" and its leader, a guy who "could not have been nicer"[14]). To be sure, those wary of Putin's Russia are allies to our research. However, if they reject Putin for erroneous reasons—as Panetta did—then they only accelerate a vicious cycle of misinterpretation and incorrect policymaking. On a general level, those who fail to truly understand Putin's regime could never hope to resolve Russia's illiberalism or accurately perceive Russia's national goals. Overall, they only give Putin an opportunity to deny their incorrect assumptions and thus reinforce his image as a leader strong enough to defend Russia against ignorant attacks from the West.[15]

That being said, our book insists that the vantage point of democratic and human rights[16] is not a sufficient enough context in which to analyze or combat Putinism and its supporters. Those who believe that Putin is *the* obstacle preventing Russia from attaining liberal democracy and hence target only Putin and the Kremlin think too narrowly. Putin could not be in the position to block liberal democracy from Russia if the population did not elect him as their chosen representative, and on multiple occasions, at that. How democratic—or perhaps the better word is liberated—could a population be if it votes for a leader who restricts their rights and other freedoms?

While our research would never dream to absolve Putin of any guilt, it does stress that Putin is not the only impediment to a free civil society in Russia: there is a key ideological component involved in Putinism, one of which Putin is both propagator *and product*. With this language, we wish to acknowledge and thank the late Karen Dawisha, a highly distinguished scholar on the Soviet Union and Russia, and the damning analysis of Putin's Russia offered in her book *Putin's Kleptocracy: Who Owns Russia?* (2014). In it, she writes that Putin is a "product and producer of this pervasive system of corruption"[17]; her phrasing helped to inspire our book and its new level of analysis of Russian society as a whole, an analysis that extends beyond the system of corruption that Dawisha so carefully explored.

We are indebted to Dawisha and hope to evolve her ideas across different sectors of Putin's Russia. In that vein, we strive to demonstrate why it is that for every crime Putin commits, the vast majority of Russians who support him are also guilty of that crime (as are Trumpists who support Trump, Chavistas who support Maduro, Nazis who supported Hitler, Leninists who supported Lenin, etc.). We accordingly call for an examination of the often-overlooked forces of historical trends, desires of the people, and impacts of nationalist ideology on the majority of the Russian population's mindsets in order to present a more accurate depiction of the challenges engrossing Russian society today. More specifically, we demand an analysis of the masses and of cultural behaviors as both effects *and roots* of Putinism, things that could easily outlive Putin the man.

To further complicate this issue, the uninformed people (such as Panetta circa 2016) who center Putin as the problem and fail to take into account the cultural legacies of Russia or the power of ideology are not the only ones who hold distorted opinions. Putin's followers, too, can argue nonsensical points. Our research exposes the pitfalls found within the Putinist viewpoint, a stance located at the opposite end of the spectrum from the aforementioned detractors of the current Russian president. Consider typical Russian citizens in St. Petersburg and Moscow who frequently admit (be it in personal conversations, to journalists, or to one of the authors of this book [KL] while she was living in Petersburg in the fall of 2015) that Putin could be "a little harsh," yet still defend his decisions. For many of these supporters, it is as Arendt once wrote: "The sad truth is that most evil is done by people who never make up their minds to be good or evil."[18]

Or even consider famous Russians like Soviet-era dissident Aleksandr Solzhenitsyn. On multiple occasions, he refused to accept prizes from Mikhail Gorbachev and Boris Yeltsin for his work in asserting the totalitarian nature of Soviet governance. He rejected their prizes as a matter of principle because, directly or indirectly, they represented the continuation of totalitarian Soviet practices. Somehow, though, Solzhenitsyn died in 2008 as a vocal supporter of Putin's regime—a regime that rehabilitates the very system which Solzhenitsyn dedicated his life to denouncing. When asked why he approved of Putin, Solzhenitsyn insisted that Putin deserved praise because he is responsible for the gradual restoration of the

Russian nation.[19] Whether speaking about Solzhenitsyn or an average Russian citizen, the common denominator of their pro-Putinist stances seems to be that, in their understandings, Putin is fulfilling his presidential role as a pragmatic, successful leader who aims to ensure the prosperity and security of the Russian state in a competitive international order. By this standard, who cares that he invades other countries, so long as it benefits Russia?

And this benefit need not be material or tangible; it suffices if an action or policy undertaken by the Kremlin simply strokes the ego of Russian national glory. It is an alarming scenario when a group of people celebrate their country's actions without considering how those actions affect others or even their own personal situations. How does an average Russian citizen see their own lot in life improved as a result of the illegal annexation of Crimea, after all? Perhaps this is the wrong question to ask, however. Perhaps they do not primarily care about their own individual benefit; instead, they might place the nation's pride above all else, so if the Russian government claims it can take satisfaction in some international event, then the ordinary citizen feels fulfilled. Unfortunately, this kind of collective cooperation is not to be admired because it is based on racist, exclusive grounds. It only succeeds because it relies upon the hatred of certain non-Russians (e.g. those who identify themselves as Ukrainians) and on the militaristic chauvinism of one nation. Russian support for Putin, then, is fundamentally at odds with the goals of liberal democracy and liberty for all.

Plenty of non-Russians—including U.S. House of Representatives member Dana Rohrabacher (R-CA),[20] U.S. Senator Rand Paul (R-KY),[21] American filmmaker Oliver Stone,[22] American scholar Stephen Cohen,[23] former prime minister of France and failed presidential candidate François Fillon,[24] and more—openly admire Putin as a strong leader as well. They and other Putinists often "answer" the question of "Isn't it egregious that Russia's media are not independent?" with another question, a favorite being "Well, can you trust the American media?"[25] U.S. President Donald Trump himself sidestepped questions from American television host Bill O'Reilly about Putin's criminality as an individual, countering with, "Do you think our country is so innocent? Do you think our country is so innocent?"[26] This kind of reaction deflects criticism of the Kremlin and sweeps ideological issues under the rug by pointing charges laid against Russia right back at other national governments. Some of those charges might be warranted, but in these scenarios they are used as useless, antagonizing tactics that aim to aid and abet the Russian government's criminality.

Like Cohen, such Putinists (or Putinophiles) might even write articles entitled "Stop the Pointless Demonization of Putin," in which they chide the American media for malpractice in "Putin-bashing," yet make no mention of Russia's systematic takeover of news outlets across the nation.[27] Or they might think like American author and lawyer Dan Kovalik. Kovalik, a self-described liberal peace activist and human rights lawyer with a law degree from Columbia University, who wrote a book entitled *The Plot to Scapegoat Russia: How the CIA and the Deep State Have Conspired to Vilify Russia* (2017). In it, he defends Putin's Russia against an apparently vengeful American media and corrupt foreign policy. He spends most of the book detailing the United States' habit of "running wild on all sorts of military adventures," rather than considering the egregious behavior of Putin's regime. When he does mention Russia, his negligent conclusions protest that the country could not possibly have the political will nor the military might to terrorize the rest of the world.[28] This statement that would be laughable if it were not so appalling that Kovalik had forgotten the struggles Ukraine has experienced since the 2014 invasion, and subsequent seizure, of Crimea. And the Ukrainian example is just one among many.

Worse still, Kovalik's book embodies the distorted world vision that might surface if one never considers ideology and its forces. He writes, "I wring my hands over my own country"[29]; we authors appreciate this statement, but ask why can't Americans and global audiences also do this over Russia? And why can't Russians do this over their own country, too? If people only focus on themselves according to their nationality, then they shut the rest of the world out. This is how the international community let Syria drop into the abyss. Caring about our own countries alone does not result in a better world for everyone: it only reduces the number of people living with dignity, or living at all, as regimes murder *en masse* and degrade humanity. Unlike Kovalik's perspective, we [KL and VT] insist that there is a way to think about the globe and care for all people without being imperialist—and that we are obligated to do so.

In voicing their uninformed yet heavily biased opinions, Kovalik, Cohen, and those who hold similar worldviews acquiesce to the notion that diplomats and citizens should no longer condemn nor challenge anyone, no matter how heinous or ongoing their crimes against others. People like them are misguided. They think the world can live in peace, when it is this mentality—embodied by a figure like former U.S. President Barack Obama—that perpetuates death and opens space for people like Putin to make their boldest moves yet and, say, decide to violate international law by invading another sovereign country. To recommend how the forces of good should approach and counter opponents, our book can only do so if it first establishes its loyalty to human rights. If, like Cohen and Kovalik, someone cannot find human rights worth the fuss, then our text will fall on deaf ears.

Through our book, we hope to highlight how irrelevant and dangerous such apologists' responses are and how dangerous it is to ignore ideology and the forces of culture in explaining the Kremlin's behaviors. According to the aforementioned example about national news, it must be articulated that the American media's moral sins have no direct impact on Russian media, nor do they factor into the Kremlin's decision-making or attempts to expand material power. The actions of the United States, or other Western countries for that matter, cannot be the analytical point of departure from which to judge Putin's regime. The issue at hand is Russia, and it cannot continue to evade blame for its wrongdoing. Russian media are censored because the Kremlin wishes them to be so, convincing media figures that it is morally "right" to spew the state government's line. Thus, apologists give frustrating retorts that reproduce inimical tensions between Putin protestors and Putin supporters without advancing the discourse.

To avoid the aforementioned, misguided approaches to Putinism, our research centers around ideology, culture, and the masses, rather than on Putin. We assert that there is a certain kind of *exclusionary, nationalist idea driving the Kremlin's policy*, one designed to foster feelings of nationalist superiority among the population. In turn, this sustains Putin's legitimacy. It allows him to act as the most powerful man in Russia and as the executor responsible for securing the best interests of the Russian state. While it is difficult (not to mention unnecessary) to pinpoint exactly what Putin's goals are, it must be kept in mind that *there is an intense social construction at play, and it is an end goal in its own right*. Putin enjoys plenty of room for creative maneuvering, but it is crucial to recognize that he can only act within the confines of utopian authoritarianism that the Russian people helped to set for him.

Putin and his Kremlinologists know how to manipulate historical traditions and the citizenry's perceptions in contradictory yet effective manners, which are far more complex than the average person (Russian or otherwise) might detect. Our book is, in part, dedicated to uncovering these incongruities and explaining how they ironically strengthen Putinism. After all, what revolution has ever appeared logical to the observer, whether during the actual event or long beyond its conclusion, even to influential thinkers such as Edmund Burke or Rosa Luxemburg, Alexis de Tocqueville or Leon Trotsky? Yet those revolutions are generally found to be satisfactory (or, if anything, not to be radical and chaotic enough) for the revolutionaries and their supporters. Only after understanding how entire populations can become swept up in the frantic search for Utopia against a terrifyingly sinister yet imaginary enemy can anyone comprehend the magnitude of seemingly illogical ideologies, ones that might seem like madness to outsiders but salvation and liberation to those who believe.

When it comes to Russia, many outsiders fail to understand that what they see as chaos typically appears coherent in the eyes of the indoctrinated Russian population. Consider U.S. lawmakers who believe Russia will crumble under economic strain caused by sanctions: they overlook the crucial point that Putin's staying power is remarkably strong because it is founded on a flexible and robust imperial repertoire. The repertoire provides his regime plenty of space to politically maneuver, depending on the day, the newest national enemy, the latest economic challenge, and so on—all the while never losing its legitimacy, or at least not to irrecoverable levels.

Despite all the tension between them, a wide swath of both Putin's condemners and Putin's apologists implicitly agree on the concept that Russia is inherently antithetical to the West. Here, their arguments might be on to something in theme, yet misguided in detail: Putin himself has engaged in the classically Western (or, even more specifically, European) processes of imperialism in spaces like Crimea and eastern Ukraine—and this was no first for Russia. An entire century prior to 1648's Treaty of Westphalia, which paved the way for a world order constituted by nation-states and social contracts between citizens and their governments, Russia had forged a tsarist empire that vowed to guarantee the security of those within its boundaries. To further convolute the already erroneous assumption of Russia as the West's antipode, Putin apologists will say the West is Russia's enemy within the same breath as they argue Russia cannot be judged on its repressive media censorship precisely because the situation is similar in the West. This sort of illogicality contributes a great deal of incoherence to the conception of Russia both within its own state and internationally, for it implies that the West is, in fact, equal to Russia, or at least that commonalities exist between them.

And then there are still others who act under the façade of Westernism and might, for instance, go so far as to organize a Russia-United States Summit, as President Trump did in Helsinki, Finland on 16 July 2018. The summit was billed on either side as a friendly attempt to continue dialogue between two civilized, democratic countries. Of course, that is nonsense, considering Putin's repression of civil society in Russia, the Kremlin's longtime slandering of democratic freedoms in the United States and overall vilifications of the West as a decadent den of liberal heathendom, and Trump's racism in the United States. And there is also the issue of how President Trump failed at the event to confront Putin about Russia's interference in U.S. elections; actually, he sided with Russia over U.S. intelligence agencies on that count.[30]

This is all to say that neither presidential representative stands for anything compatible with Western culture, democracy, or pluralism, regardless of how they advertised the Putin-Trump Summit. Trump undermined American and world democracy in Helsinki, while Putin tried to capitalize off of such capitulation. In such a manner, Russia remains the vanguard of global counter-revolution, using modern means to pursue—and possibly achieve—its despotic view of the world. The summit can only, then, be deemed as further proof of a complex and odd relationship with Westernism on the part of Putinism (and, although it is admittedly beyond the scope of our book, on the part of the Trumpist movement in both American society and government administration).

The questionability of the totalizing "Russia versus the West" divide deepens the muck through which one must trudge in order to understand the complicated actuality: Russia itself exhibits fundamentally Western tendencies and attends Western-styled meetings with world leaders, but fluidly pretends this is not the case. This should beg the question in readers' minds of "But why, then, is Russia so intent on staking its existence and global position as an opponent to the West?" A potential answer will be found in Chap. 3 and will add yet another element of understanding when it comes to Putinism.

Just as a Western parallel is omitted from international discourse on Putin's legitimacy, so is an entire set of social practices and cultural dynamics necessary to comprehend Putinism. It is not that Putin is so powerful that he alone seized all of Russia and transformed it into an obedient regime, but that Russians voluntarily signed themselves up for autocracy (yet again) and actively helped in creating such a regime. Nor is Putin an inexplicable aberration within Russian history. In fact, there is a pattern of representation throughout Russia's authoritarian history that is unwittingly omitted from critical interventions on the matter.

This portrayal connects Putin with a whole host of other Russian tsars and Soviet heads of government, making it clear that Putin's style of leadership does *not* mark a historical rupture. Continued popular faith—not just concretely measured via elections, polls, or actions, but mainly in the personal opinion of private citizens—shows that Putin and authoritarianism, in general, was not a one-time deal for the Russian population. Even though some may now find themselves held hostage or regretting their choice for Putin and authoritarianism, it was still a willing decision for many, most of whom continue to stand by it.

Our book, then, owes much to the late American political scientist Robert C. Tucker. A specialist in Soviet and Russian politics, Tucker and his book *Political Culture and Leadership in Soviet Russia: From Lenin to Gorbachev* (1987) played a key role in inspiring our work on Putinism. In his volume, Tucker asserts that culture and politics are inseparable in places like the Soviet Union because "a culture is a society's customary way of life, comprising both accepted modes of thought and belief and accepted patterns of conduct. Political culture is everything in a culture that pertains to government and politics. In Soviet Russia, very little does not so pertain." We find this statement to have lost very little truth in 2019, even if the nation is no longer Soviet.[31]

And just as Tucker saw the need to examine the successes and choices of Soviet leadership in the context of the general beliefs and interests of the Soviet population, so do we argue that there can be no accurate comprehension of Putinism in today's Russia without an in-depth analysis of Russian society and culture, for they feed the nation's politics and leadership. They do not operate in isolated vacuums: culture helps to shape a state's system of governance on the one hand, while it simultaneously defines society's interactions with that said system, on the other.[32] Tucker's contributions are so valuable to our work that Chap. 5, entitled "Putinism as a Culture in the Making," is named as a fitting nod to Tucker's chapter in *Political Culture and Leadership in Soviet Russia*, entitled "Lenin's Bolshevism as a Culture in the Making."

For similar reasons, we dedicate our book in part to the late historian and critical intellectual Walter Laqueur (1921–2018). We are especially indebted to his work *Putinism: Russia and Its Future with the West* (2015), in which Laqueur explores the concept of Putinism as an ideology based on nationalism, anti-Westernism, sham democracy, and a highly interventionist state (in a political sense, rather than in the typical economic one). Our book was written as a kind of continuation and expansion of Laqueur's themes outlined in *Putinism*.

Keeping the approaches of Tucker and Laqueur in mind, we argue there is a popular cultural expectation that calls for a particular kind of authoritarian sovereign in Russia. This leader is (supposedly) the only actor who can guarantee the protection of Russia—its physical territory, human population, natural resources, economics, history, culture, and international reputation—at all costs. Such a desire is shaped by an autocratic legacy from tsarist times, a security imaginary from the Soviet era, and Putin's own influential rhetoric; most importantly, the desire is so popular among the Russian citizenry that it acts as a script by which Putin is expected to follow.

Again, this evinces the notion that Putin's personality is not the only factor in his popularity. The opinions of the masses matter, and he is wont to appeal to them through the same authoritarian promises that have been used throughout Russian history. Provided that a leader vows to bring about a better, more powerful society, followers might come to accept otherwise barbarian means supposedly destined to bring about that future, assuming it is tempting enough.[33] Only a low standard of morality is required. There is nothing exceptional about this: that the Right in America has nothing to say on Trump, and the Left nothing on Assad or on Nicaraguan President Daniel Ortega, shows that low morality is widespread and not just limited to Russia. An understanding of Russia's societal ills could prove beneficial for the globe.

Sure, the popular demand (or yearning) for authoritarianism has transformed since the sixteenth century, but one must not ignore the continuities. Some liberals, namely Francis Fukuyama, have forgotten the importance of this historical authoritarian tendency. Instead, they were seduced by the Gorbachev moment: they thought that once Mikhail Gorbachev introduced policies of *glasnost* [political openness] and *perestroika* [economic rebuilding or restructuring], once the Berlin Wall fell in November 1989, once the Soviet Union crumbled, and once Russians elected Boris Yeltsin as their first democratic leader in 1991, then they could embrace liberal triumphalism in Russia.[34] However, these were only potentially liberal openings that never came to fruition. They were foreclosed by the inertia of historical authoritarianism (in addition to other factors at that moment, such as the appearance of powerful oligarchs). No radical break from authoritarianism, nor turn to liberalism, ever occurred in modern Russia at the national level.

Reality, especially regarding what the majority of average citizens want, rarely deserves such optimism. Few stories in history do: even the much-beloved Gorbachev hoped not for democracy, liberty, and justice, but for merely benign totalitarianism, a one-party state with minimal executions (not to mention his genocidal imperialism in Afghanistan). Popular desires, voting outcomes, and poll numbers showing, for instance, that Russians want better relations with the United States, do not mean much in the sense that they cannot demonstrate that the people behind these wants and results actually know what they are talking about or that they actually care about human dignity. Respect for human dignity is a rare and minority value, one upheld by far fewer than many think. Acknowledging this reality is imperative in order to assist those who suffer outside the view of self-rewarding visions and comfortable optimisms.

Here we recognize Timothy Snyder, an American historian specializing in Eastern Europe, Central Europe, World War II, and related intellectual histories, for his work on the power of narratives to promote authoritarianism in politics and society. His seminal book, entitled *The Road to Unfreedom: Russia, Europe, America* (2018), investigates both Western and Russian perspectives through a framework composed of two concepts plaguing the globe today: the politics of inevitability and the politics of eternity.

The former term, the politics of inevitability, refers to "a sense that the future is just more of the present, that the laws of progress are known, that there are no alternatives, and therefore nothing really to be done."[35] It is very much reminiscent of Fukuyama's formulation of the "end of history." In the United States, for example, the politics of inevitability formulates itself as a belief that capitalism and democracy will succeed by virtue of their creation; however, the Trumpist movement and its racism, among other negative -isms, should prove that democracy can only survive if it is intentionally practiced throughout society. In the Russian account, the term essentially means that authoritarianism is better than democracy and that the Russian nation-state will be the most superior in the world once democracy falls out of fashion. The politics of inevitability, then, is dangerous in any society: it signals a taking-for-granted of politics and human nature and wrongfully suggests the good times are here to stay without people or politicians having to lift a finger or to take responsibility for current problems.

The latter term Snyder employs, the politics of eternity, "places one nation at the center of a cyclical story of victimhood," where "time is no longer a line into the future, but a circle that endlessly returns the same threats from the past" as "politicians manufacture crisis and manipulate the resultant emotion."[36] In other words, the politics of eternity are at play in states where the national authority asserts that their county's current direction and way of life is *the* direction, *the* way of life. There are no alternatives, and what is now will remain forever, without thematic change. Everything is as it will be.

In a country like Russia, where culture and society echo these conservative sentiments so much that they are coming to believe their meanings at the individual level, the politics of eternity is especially advanced, deceptive, and dangerous. We [KL and VT] find this concept to be the more alarming one at play in Putin's Russia now, for it builds upon the baseline (set by the politics of inevitability) that democracy and truth are shams in order to convince Russians—and the world—of an isolating vision of existence, one in which authoritarianism and Russian nationalism should be the state's highest goals. Isolation and atomization are perhaps some of the darkest forces that can be at play in any population, as Hannah Arendt illuminated in *The Origins of Totalitarianism* (1951). Under such circumstances, human dignity and respect for human rights can be lost in the din of nationalism, xenophobia, and fascism. Our book highlights the uncomfortable truth that Russia is already deep along this atomizing path to totalitarianism.

Of course, the Russian political culture that we explore in our book cannot be understood without the sort of community psychology approach taken in *The Road to Unfreedom*. The themes of the politics of both inevitability and eternity will prove helpful in our thorough dissection of Putinism, its relations with the masses, and the continuation of authoritarianism in Russia.

CHALLENGES TO PUTINISM AND THE SURVIVAL OF HISTORICAL TRENDS

This is not to say that Russians are inherently incapable of democratic practices. For example, on 26 March 2017, opposition leader Alexei Navalny encouraged mass protests of over 60,000 citizens across Russia to protest the Kremlin's corruption, declare "Putin is a thief," and shout for his impeachment. This kind of rally has been unheard of since the Russian government cracked down on public demonstrations following the anti-Putin protests of 2011 and 2012.[37] While Navalny is certainly not the incarnation of democracy (indeed, he might be more comparable to Poland's Law and Justice, Austria's far-rightist former Chancellor Sebastian Kurz, or other exclusionary nationalists), and national election results prove that Russians have voted rather consistently according to the dominant narrative of Putinism over the past 19 years, the events of the spring of 2017 nevertheless demonstrate that there is a budding minority of Russians who might be cognizant and brave enough to fight for change in their authoritarian society. On the one hand, imperfect change—that is, faith in Gorbachevism—is part of what led Russians to their current fate; on the other hand, it could be the first step on the journey to a belief in liberalism, rather than the updating of old authoritarian views. So, one must not rule out the possibility that their actions could open up spaces to discuss the liberal democratic opportunities that might arise within Russian society.

Nevertheless, the political opposition's numbers are still too miniscule to take down Putin's regime or to chip away at the narrative of Putinism, for the overwhelming majority of Russians handily drown out such political dissent. This should tell readers that Putinism is caused by much more than just the consistent, popular election of Vladimir Putin: without the tendency of the masses to desire an authoritarian sovereign, a leader like Putin could only claim power through illegitimate, violent means. This would only result in a chaotic series of coups, which, in turn, would destroy whatever authority he had attempted to seize.

What, then, explains Putinism and society's willingness to submit to—or actively campaign for—Putin's leadership? How does Putin ensure the consent of the population, given the potential for liberal openings? It must be admitted that there is much more political space with which to maneuver in Putin's Russia than in Stalin's Russia—so why do so few Russians venture to utilize this space? Is the common conception that Putin alone built today's Russia and rules over it without limitation an accurate portrayal?

These questions guide our thinking and our book's layout. They are especially pressing at the present time, considering how Russia is not exactly thriving when it comes to economics, international opinion, or internal cohesion. Russia's economy has struggled over the last several years.[38] Its government has been repeatedly charged with human rights violations by international organizations (including the United Nations,

Human Rights Watch, Amnesty International, etc.).[39] Its identity has been scrambled by centuries of imperialist, Orthodox tsarism, which were schizophrenically followed by decades of culturally repressive, atheist Communism.

As Russian scholar Natalia Zubarevich hypothesizes, "we are not dealing with one Russia" at the present day, nor has Russia ever truly been singular: there are deep-seated centrifugal forces remaining from the days of forced tsarist resettlement and Soviet collectivization.[40] Accordingly, Putin's state has struggled to uncover a unifying factor with which to establish a base of support.[41] Ordinarily, these displeasing factors would attribute to the administrative state a lack of credibility and respect amongst the citizenry—not generate popular unity or support for the government. Only ideology explains how this has been done so successfully.

Furthermore, Russia simultaneously faces a whole other set of challenges to legitimacy, a set that all nation-states now face: the twenty-first century has borne witness to new forms of confrontation, from terrorism to cyber-hacking, to which the nation-state structure fundamentally cannot adapt. Since the Peace of Westphalia in 1648, the nation-state had been considered to be the ultimate form of sovereign political community. However, the ever-shrinking process of globalization demonstrates that nation-states are not as sovereign as they have been assumed to be. Revolutions in technology, transportation, and intelligence means that capital, humans, goods, and services are free (for the most part, at least in comparison to the seventeenth century) to travel across borders as they please, thereby lessening the dependency individuals circa 1648—or 1948, for that matter—had on their state for access to the means of sustaining life and personal leisure. Globalization has ushered in an era of non-territorial, unbounded, and plural identities for individuals, which threaten the united and life-giving role of the nation-state. Leaders across the globe, then, are left to scramble to retain their authority. Putin's dilemma should be even more precarious, thanks to added internal economic, cultural, and political woes.

And yet, somehow, Vladimir Putin was commonly referred to in 2017, 2018, and 2019 by the American media as "the most powerful leader in the world."[42] Yes, since 2013 *Forbes* magazine has named Putin the world's most powerful person, or the world's second-most powerful person; we not trying to say that Putin was *literally* given this title only in 2019. Rather, we are trying to alert readers to recognize why the situation now is different and of so much more significance: it is the first time where the mainstream consensus is that Putin is the world's most powerful person *who also happens to influence the American president*, who is viewed as Putin's pawn, wittingly or unwittingly.

Under Trump, the idea that the United States is a bastion of human rights and *the* world power has been discredited beyond timely repair. Without America's symbolic status as "Leader of the Free World" lingering around the international order, the fact that Putin is widely recognized as the most powerful person should cause readers of all nationalities to question the directions in which our societies are headed. Take a moment to digest how bizarre this reality is. It is particularly significant for two reasons: (1) this marks the first time that the person internationally thought to be the "most powerful leader in the world" has not been the President of the United States[43]; and (2) the slew of obstacles to Putin's legitimacy presented in the preceding paragraphs are incredibly daunting.

What optimistic Western political theorists and politicians, obsessed with the United States' exceptionalism on the world stage, have denied could ever happen is currently happening. This marks a rupture in the international status quo that should encourage us to consider the unpredictable consequences of a world caught up in isolating, charismatic, and extreme political movements of both the far Right and the far Left. What better way to (begin to) evaluate the precarious times of the world, and how we got here, than to understand how the epitome of populism, Vladimir Putin, has been so successful?

It is a question that bears global weight in an age where extreme populist politics are on the rise. It urges us to ask: how does Putin's Kremlin not just survive these hindrances but continue to promote its claims to superiority and authority to such an extent where even the international community feels impacted by Putin's awing position? Why does Russian society continue to support him even in the face of those aforementioned challenges?

To combat this array of challenges to his legitimacy, Putin invokes the patrimonialism of Russia's past.[44] He has turned to the fabrication of ideological narratives designed to make citizens cling to the Russian Federation on the assumption that only it is capable of protecting their lives, rights, and property from a duplicitous, immoral, and dangerous "outside." To support these fabrications, Putin's Kremlin relies on the precedents of Russian autocracy, nostalgia for tsarist paternalism and Soviet stability, nationalist state propaganda, and manufactured fears of terrorism and global aggression to secure such a narrative and validate his legitimacy as the sovereign.

The fact that Putin utilizes so many psychological strategies in order to retain his power is key: it means he can only reproduce such a powerful sovereign authority by capturing the support of the masses, for his personality alone cannot legitimize his jurisdiction in contemporary Russian society. His strategy of achieving this internal ambition for power through external reasoning is even more telling, in that the establishment of an "us versus them" mentality among the Russian masses is what allows Putin to portray Russia as the most superior state in the world.

Russians empower Putin; Putin does not control Russians. Thus, Putin himself is not Russia's only problem, as many political pundits seem to believe. Merely replacing Putin as president will not change the state's nature or solve the political phenomenon of autocracy in Russia. Putin is, in a basic sense, a continuation of tradition himself: autocratic tsars were replaced by Soviet dictators like Lenin and Stalin, and those dictators were replaced by "democratic" presidents like Putin.

On 18 March 2018, Putin won his latest presidential election and will likely stay in power until 2024,[45] when some other protégé of his will nominally take his place (unless Putin feels bold in projecting and modeling imperial utopianism and sticks around in high places, which is a stark possibility). Assuming no moral revolution takes place, Putin will run the government, even if from behind the scenes, until he dies, at which point his trained successor will continue the ideological authoritarian trend—presuming, of course, that Russian voters deem his choice acceptable (read ideologically appealing). This vision will come to fruition because there is a desire within the Russian citizenry for such a leader to foster the growth of a superior Russian state.

It would be disastrous to assign responsibility for the current state of Russia to Putin alone; his supporters, as well, are guilty—some more than others, and perhaps not equally to Putin, but guilty nonetheless. The people's preferences, distastes, and impressions of their world matter, as historian George L. Mosse, the émigré from 1930s Germany made famous for his insights on fascism, observed.[46] To overlook the complicity of average citizens would be to cut off the head of the hydra, only to be baffled by the regenerated heads that, in this metaphor, might pop up in the same place *and* elsewhere in the world, with greater intensity. Likewise, to think that ordinary people's dissent cannot make a positive difference on a government is to deny the very idea of politics. Accountability is one of the most vital aspects of good, human rights-respecting governance. The world must not only examine Putin's will to power, lest it forget that tens of millions of average humans have the will to follow him.

Brief Chapter Outline

Our book explores the lesser-mentioned origins of Putinism. It is meant to highlight the origins, dynamics, and effects of Putinism as the legitimizing ideological construct behind a kleptocratic, corrupting political culture. In order to achieve this goal, we have looked into various concepts, methods, authors, personal conversations and experiences, and nationalized versions of history. Ultimately, our examination is based upon (a) historical legacies; (b) intellectual syncretism, sources, and resources; and (c) political culture, particularly relations between the masses and government. Our demarche exposes why Vladimir Putin resorts to external threats as a method of securing internal unity and state power, in addition to why the public largely accepts his methods. This chapter has already made the case that Putin is not some simple caudillo hack: he is the leader of an ideological mass movement, and so it is necessary to approach Putinism as an ideology. This introductory chapter also expressed the need to examine cultural behaviors and the masses in Russia as both effects and roots of Putinism.

Chapter 2 traces the origins of the present Putinism through a chronological but brief discussion of Russian history. It emphasizes how Russia's historical understanding of the sovereign and fears of external invasion culminated in a legacy of autocracy that has lasted for centuries. This autocratic trend awards the nation's rulers a great deal of power and is crucial to comprehending Putin's existence.

Chapter 3 then situates Putin's origins, formative experiences, and rise to power within Russian history and culture. With the previous chapter in mind, this specific discussion of Putin the man demonstrates that his leadership is not all that shocking; rather, it is a continuing—not to mention darkly sinister—progression of historical illiberalism. Though it is masterfully innovative in the uncharted politics of this new century of information, Putinism is nevertheless nothing surprising. Vladimir Putin capitalized off of this legacy: when the Russian people felt insecure under their government's weak authority in the wake of the Soviet Union's collapse and the subsequent, incompetent presidency of Boris Yeltsin, Putin portrayed himself as their powerful, commanding solution. Thus, Putin rose to power in a way that does not deviate from Russian history, mostly propelled by the popular desire for an autocrat.

Chapter 4 shifts the focus from Putin to Putinism. It begins by defining the meaning of ideology and goes on to establish Putinism as an ideology in itself, in opposition to what a fair number of political scientists and theorists have argued. This section situates Putinism within the category of ideology by discussing its operative aspects and themes. In order to comprehend the contradictory yet successful nature of Putinism, though, the chapter first finds it necessary to trace Putinism's origins back through Russian philosophical history to figures such as Ivan Ilyin and Aleksandr Dugin and concepts such as Eurasianism. We are careful to explain that these Russian philosophers and concepts do not define Putinism or its parameters; still, they offer crucial seeds and themes that Putinism has incorporated into its basic outlook and that a vast majority of the Russian population accepts.

Building off of the previous chapter, Chap. 5 breaks Putinism down by the thematic messages it broadcasts to the population and claims to base itself in. It elucidates how Vladimir Putin has retained popularity and power throughout his many years in office via an ideological program designed to institutionalize an animating nostalgia for both tsarist and Soviet paternalism. Said nostalgia unites the citizenry. It interpellates them into a repurposed Soviet imaginary, which calls each person to support their superior nation-state in its mission for global greatness. It also feeds the dangerous nationalist discourse that Russia is fundamentally antithetical to the arrogant, immoral West. This chapter will unearth the contrived, inaccurate nature of such a distinction and attempts to explain that Russia goes to such lengths of conjuring rigid difference in order to artificially bolster its own otherwise weak claim to unity. Most importantly, this section will emphasize the unique narrative production of national identity that characterizes Putin's Russia—a crucial yet overlooked pillar of Putinism. It means that Russians have real ideas about what is happening across the globe: they truly believe in their visions of the world, and, likewise, in the actions of their regime. This section will highlight some of the core elements of Putinism, namely ultranationalism, Russian exceptionalism, historical revisionism, anti-Westernism, imperialism, militarism, racism, chauvinism, corruption, and kleptocracy.

Chapter 6 delineates just how the Kremlin's propagandizing efforts have successfully embedded themselves within its citizenry, making nationalism and Putinist ideology an inescapable daily influence in the lives of all Russian citizens. Decades of one-sided narratives enforced by ideological state apparatuses such as the education system, the media, and the Russian Orthodox Church have squelched divergent thought among the Russian population; as a result, they themselves continue the Kremlin's mission of interpellation, reproducing nationalist tropes that serve Putin's state and foreclose avenues of friendly encounter with much of the world.[47] These pages set the stage for understanding why the Russian citizenry continuously provides Putin with a mandate for power, even if he uses this authority to engage in actions contrary to their best interests (both as individuals and as a prosperous nation, on the whole). After all, indoctrination, as Hannah Arendt explored, can be completely pervasive and totally successful.

With this established, Chap. 7 elaborates upon Putin's aggressive foreign policy decisions, specifically regarding Ukraine and Syria. The investigation will present the conclusion that President Putin manages to maintain his domestic popularity ratings through the totalitarian practice of espousing states of exception that artificially unite the country against foreign threats. As such, foreign policy is not an end in itself, but rather a tool used to further legitimize President Putin's domestic popularity (and his own power) by distracting the public from internal economic woes and instead presenting the celebratory image of a Russian state powerful enough to violate international laws with near impunity. Furthermore, this conclusion will highlight how the Russian citizenry plays a major role as an accomplice in their state's rise to totalitarianism and its violations of international law—a concept often neglected by both scholarly studies and media outlets. When genocide increases a perpetrator's approval ratings, the world should be especially troubled. In general, this chapter recognizes the reality that ideology is the essence of all that has been forgotten in the twenty-first century but is, in itself, nothing new.

Chapter 8 concludes our book. While Putinism might seem to be in its doldrums since Vladimir Putin's reelection in March 2018, this time of "quiet" or "stagnation" should not be taken as evidence that Putinism or authoritarianism in Russia are slowing down. The masses still believe in Putin and the nationalist project. They are not protesting. Perhaps this is evidence of normalizing the abnormal. The system, then, is still strong and even represents a neo-authoritarian wave that is increasingly making its effects known across the globe. It is at this point that our book will arrive full circle to the concept expressed its own title, *Putin's Totalitarian Democracy*. In a world where far-right (and far-left) political parties are winning elections at frightening paces—and mostly in European countries that were, until now, considered to be the most democratic and Western, at that—it is crucial to understand how Putinism is not limited to just one eponymous subject. In fact, it is spreading to other nation-states, as well, because political success is not guaranteed by personality alone: it requires the consent of the masses, plus some sort of imposed ideology. The unprecedented election of U.S. President Trump—someone with no political experience whatsoever, and who has rallied steadfast support for incoherent policies based on sheer verbal belligerence—demonstrates the power a populace can exercise. Here, the book will make its most controversial assertion after much careful thought: that Putin's Russia is a fascist, totalitarian regime. Through this non-traditional analysis, perhaps readers may learn how to spot the makings of totalitarianism before it is too late.

If the world hopes to reverse the rising trend of racist, ultranationalist movements, then it must learn to listen to the voters who support such illiberalism. This does not require agreement or sympathy with these voters, but it does mandate an understanding of how they interpret the world. In viewing the world through their vantages, it becomes more feasible to devise effective methods of combating those illiberal and totalitarian political practices both in Russia and elsewhere. Considering how President Vladimir Putin has been referred to as the de facto leader of this global movement of illiberalism and autocracy, a case study on the complexities of Putinism as it relates to the masses, historical trends, and ideology—and not just of the sovereign himself—is warranted.

Notes

1. Hannah Arendt, *Men in Dark Times* (New York: Harcourt Brace and Company, 1968), p. ix.
2. Consider well-researched texts such as Peter Baker and Susan Glasser's *Kremlin Rising: Vladimir Putin's Russian and the End of Revolution* (2005); Masha Gessen's *The Man Without a Face: The Unlikely Rise of Vladimir Putin* (2012); Fiona Hill and Clifford G. Gaddy's *Mr. Putin: Operative in the Kremlin* (2013). They reveal Putin to be a leader of various faces, from a statist to a thug, from an impotent KGB officer to a CEO. Both make it clear that Putin is an expert when it comes to reinventing his personas—but there is much more to be understood about this process and why the public comes to believe in Putin. Just what is going on in the minds and cultural perspectives of the Russian citizens who consistently vote for him? See also Walter Laqueur, *Putinism: Russia and Its Future with the West* (New York: Thomas Dunne Books, 2015) as a complementary take on the institutions that have set the stage for Putinism.
3. To grasp the influence of this viewpoint that dangerously portrays Putin as a tyrant on thin ice in the eyes of an active citizenry, see Ben Judah, *Fragile*

Empire: How Russia Fell In and Out of Love with Vladimir Putin (New Haven: Yale University Press, 2013); Vladimir Kara-Murza, "If Putin is so popular, why is he so afraid of competition?" *The Washington Post*, 12 January 2018; and Richard Lourie, *Putin: His Downfall and Russia's Coming Crash* (New York: Thomas Dunne Books, 2017).

4. See works by Stephen White, Ian McAllister, and Richard Sakwa for more on the early development of the term, particularly the former two authors' co-edited work, "The Putin Phenomenon," *Journal of Communist Studies and Transition Politics*, Vol. 24, No. 4 (December 2008), pp. 604–628.
5. Moshe Lewin, *The Gorbachev Phenomenon: A Historical Interpretation* (Berkeley and Los Angeles: University of California Press, 1988).
6. Levada Center, "Odobrenie dejatel'nosti Vladimira Putina," Levada Center: Yuri Levada Analytical Center, May 2018.
7. Vladimir Kara-Murza, "Putin is Not Russia," *Journal of Democracy*, Vol. 28, No. 4 (October 2017), pp. 110–116.
8. Lilia Shevtsova, "Vladimir Putin," *Foreign Policy*, No. 164 (January–February 2008), pp. 32–36, 38, and 40; Lilia Shevtsova, "Implosion, Atrophy, or Revolution?" *Journal of Democracy*, Vol. 23, No. 3 (July 2012), p. 27.
9. Voice of America, "'Terrible Crimes' Made Putin World's Richest Person, Financier Testifies," Voice of America, 27 July 2017.
10. Organization for Economic Cooperation and Development, "Income Inequality (indicator)," Organization for Economic Cooperation and Development, 2018; Timothy Snyder, *The Road to Unfreedom: Russia, Europe, America* (New York: Tim Duggan Books, 2018), p. 258.
11. Jan-Willem van Prooijen and Paul A. M. van Lange, "Power, Politics, and Paranoia: An Introduction," in *Power, Politics, and Paranoia: Why People are Suspicious of Their Leaders*, eds. Jan-Willem van Prooijen and Paul A. M. van Lange (Cambridge: Cambridge University Press, 2014), pp. 1–14.
12. Leon Panetta, "Welcoming Remarks and Plenary I—Navigating 21st Century Security Challenges" (speech, Global Security Forum 2016, Washington, DC, 1 December 2016).
13. United States Congress, *Countering America's Adversaries Through Sanctions Act*, H.R. 3364, 115th Congress (Washington, DC: United States Government Publishing Office, 2 August 2017).
14. Andrew Kaczynski, Chris Massie, and Nathan McDermott, "80 times Trump talked about Putin," *CNN*, February 2017.
15. Mikhail Gorbachev, *The New Russia* (Cambridge: Polity Press, 2016), p. 408. For the purposes of our research, the Kremlin's standard pattern of representation regarding the West will be employed throughout our book. This entails an interpretation of the West as a fundamental political ideol-

ogy promoting liberal democracy, human rights, the rule of law, and capitalist values. As will be explored later in our research, however, Russia might not be as non-Western as the Kremlin presents it to be.
16. To represent this group—people who judge Putin to be the core problem in Russia without comprehending the extent of the public's responsibility, as well—we offer the example of Vladimir Kara-Murza, a Russian opposition politician (who has likely been poisoned twice for his anti-Putinist views). At Forum 2000's conference in 2017, he argued that Russians have been fighting for democracy for over a century, and with Putin out of the way, democracy could triumph in Russia. Vladimir Kara-Murza, "Democracy Challenged" (panel, 21st Annual Forum 2000: Strengthening Democracy in Uncertain Times, Prague, 9 October 2017).
17. Karen Dawisha, *Putin's Kleptocracy: Who Owns Russia?* (New York: Simon & Schuster Paperbacks, 2014), p. 12.
18. Hannah Arendt, *The Life of the Mind* (New York: Harcourt Brace Jovanovich, 1978), p. 180.
19. Peter Eltsov, "What Putin's Favorite Guru Tells Us About His Next Target," *Politico*, 10 February 2015.
20. Isaac Arnsdorf and Benjamin Oreskes, "Putin's Favorite Congressman," *Politico*, 23 November 2016; Lisa Hagan, "Rohrabacher under fire over Russia ties," *The Hill, 8* March 2018.
21. Rebecca Morin, "After Rand Paul meeting, Russian lawmakers agree to Washington visit," *Politico*, 6 August 2018.
22. For more on Oliver Stone's pandering to Putin, watch his four-part docuseries, *The Putin Interviews* (2017), or read Emily Tamkin, "Oliver Stone's 'Putin Interviews' Will Teach You Little About Putin, and Even Less About Russia," *Foreign Policy*, 7 June 2017.
23. Stephen Cohen, "Stop the Pointless Demonization of Putin," *The Nation*, 7 May 2012.
24. Pierre Briançon, "Billionaire paid Fillon $50,000 for meeting with Putin: report," POLITICO Europe, 21 March 2017.
25. To exactly quote an exchange that transpired between audience members and guest lecturer Nicolai Petro at Vassar College in February 2017. The conversation was precipitated by the lecturer's remarks about what he saw to be an apparently thriving state of press freedoms in Russia. Later, he would ignore questions about the exorbitant number of journalists murdered for their work on Russia (a valid question, as in 2009 the Committee to Protect Journalists listed Russia as "the third deadliest country in the world for journalists"). Nicolai Petro, "Are We Reading Russia Correctly?" (lecture, Vassar College, Poughkeepsie, NY, 16 February 2017); Committee to Protect Journalists, "CPJ testimony focuses on Russian impunity," Committee to Protect Journalists, 25 June 2009.

26. Kaczynski, Massie, and McDermott, "80 times Trump talked about Putin."
27. Cohen, "Stop the Pointless Demonization of Putin."
28. Dan Kovalik, *The Plot to Scapegoat Russia: How the CIA and the Deep State Have Conspired to Vilify Russia* (New York: Skyhorse Publishing, 2017), pp. 23–24. It should come as no surprise that a person like Kovalik, a defender of Putin's Russia, also defends the murderous regime of Venezuelan dictator Nicolás Maduro. To fail to understand human rights in one country is to fail to understand them everywhere.
29. Kovalik, *The Plot to Scapegoat Russia*, p. 27. The authors admit that there is one insightful point of Kovalik's book: he insists that we should be lambasting President Barack Obama for his terrible foreign policy performance, rather than happily remembering him as a feat of the Democratic Party. He was the one who opened up the floodgates of violence in Syria because, whether readers like it or not, U.S. influence is strong in the world, strong enough to signal to Assad and Putin that they can attack if the United States will let them get away with it. And Obama did just this when he did not live up to his commitments about the infamous "red line" of chemical weaponry. Of course, Kovalik seems to admonish Obama only for his use of drones, not for his ultimate reprehensible failure to act in Syria and let millions of civilians down. But to say that the mistakes of our U.S. leader, whether those mistakes deal with Syria or drones, preclude us from discussing those of another leader, Vladimir Putin, is outrageous.
30. Steven Pifer, "U.S.-Russia relations and a second Trump-Putin summit," the Brookings Institution, 27 July 2018.
31. Robert C. Tucker, *Political Culture and Leadership in Soviet Russia: From Lenin to Gorbachev* (New York: W.W. Norton & Company, Inc., 1987), p. vii.
32. Tucker, *Political Culture*, pp. 3 and 6.
33. Vladimir Tismaneanu, *The Devil in History: Communism, Fascism, and Some Lessons of the Twentieth Century* (Berkeley and Los Angeles: University of California Press, 2012), p. 68; Jacob L. Talmon, *The Origins of Totalitarian Democracy* (London: Secker and Warburg, 1952), pp. 134.
34. Yes, in Francis Fukuyama's famous essay, *The End of History*, he explicitly states that he does not have high hopes that the Soviet Union would give way to a successful liberal society. However, he still misreads what Gorbachev's policies of political and economic relaxation meant; he assumes that they would bring an end to "ideological pretensions of representing different and higher forms of human society." As we will explore, particularly in Chaps. 2 and 3, Russia never lost such an ideological pretension; it still bases itself on the notion that it is a superior world civilization. Francis Fukuyama, "The End of History?" *The National Interest*, No. 16 (Summer 1989), p. 13.
35. Snyder, *The Road to Unfreedom*, p. 7.

36. Snyder, *The Road to Unfreedom*, p. 8.
37. Yevgenia Albats, "Russia's protests show that a new generation is finding its voice," *The Washington Post*, 28 March 2017.
38. Federal State Statistics Service of the Russian Federation, "Informacija o Social'no-Jekonomicheskom Polozhenii Rossii: Janvar' 2016 Goda," Federal State Statistics Service of the Russian Federation, January 2016; the World Bank, "Russia: GDP growth (annual %)," the World Bank, 2018. Economic statistics for Russia show a decline in the country's financial health. Its gross domestic product was nearly cut in half from $2.23 trillion in 2013 to $1.33 trillion in 2015. The annual gross domestic product (GDP) growth rate has fallen by about four percent in the last five years, dipping by over seven percentage points into the negative values in 2015. The poverty rate has increased by 3 percent in the last three years. Average personal income has fallen by a third since 2013, dropping by 52.2 percent between December 2015 and January 2016. The ruble's value has fallen by 127 percent in 2016; the list goes on. Of course, such data becomes "old" as time passes, so we authors encourage readers to look up the most recent statistics for themselves.
39. The United Nations, "Third Committee Takes Up 7 Draft Resolutions on Situations in Syria, Iran, Crimea as It Concludes Discussion of Human Rights Council's Report," the United Nations, 8 November 2016; Human Rights Watch, "Russia—World Report 2016," Human Rights Watch, 2016; Amnesty International, "Annual Report: Russian Federation 2015/2016," Amnesty International, 2016.
40. Natalia Zubarevich, "Perspektiva: Chetyre Rossii: chto dal'she," *Vedimosti*, 24 September 2013. Soviet collectivization refers to the state-mandated process which unsuccessfully tried to mix and unite 21 non-Russian ethnic republics with various economic, political, cultural, and linguistic interests that account for more than one-sixth of the world's landmass.
41. Anna Arutunyan, *The Putin Mystique: Inside Russia's Power Cult* (Northampton: Olive Branch Press, 2015), p. 305.
42. Fareed Zakaria, "Why Putin is the world's most powerful man," *CNN*, 14 March 2017.
43. *Forbes*, "Profile: Vladimir Putin," *Forbes*, 2017.
44. Arutunyan, *The Putin Mystique*, p. 5; Fiona Hill and Clifford G. Gaddy. *Mr. Putin: Operative in the Kremlin* (Washington, DC: The Brookings Institution, 2013), p. 32.
45. The Russian Constitution allows for two consecutive terms as president only, so Putin will not be able to run in 2024 (although it is important to note that during the presidency of Dmitry Medvedev—the puppet whom Putin groomed to replace him as president from 2008 to 2012 under the agreement that Putin would run the show as Medvedev's prime minister—

the Constitution was altered to extend presidential terms from four to six years each. Conveniently, the change only took affect beginning with the term following Medvedev's, when Putin ran for a third time and won). Political tweaks are always possible and, more likely than not, will favor Putin's career.
46. George L. Mosse, *The Fascist Revolution: Toward a General Theory of Fascism* (New York: Howard Fertig, 1999), p. 39.
47. These statements do not mean to gloss over the existence or efforts of Kremlin oppositionists. The contributions of Russians like Boris Berezovsky, Alexander Litvinenko, Boris Nemtsov, Anna Politkovskaya, Galina Starovoitova, Vladimir Kara-Murza, Alexei Navalny, and so on, should not be forgotten. (Note how the first five people mentioned died under suspicious circumstances, the sixth was forced to leave Russia to seek rehabilitative treatment for a suspicious poisoning attack, and the seventh has been jailed for political dissent against Putin. For a poignant collection of stories regarding the Kremlin's individual victims, see Amy Knight, *Orders to Kill: the Putin Regime and Political Murder* (New York: Thomas Dunne Books, 2017).) Unfortunately, Russian media and political discourse encourage the fading and slandering of these characters to the point where it is permissible, by the nature of reality, to claim that the overwhelming majority of the Russian population acts in accordance with their state's policies. Readers are implored to keep in mind that we will use phrasings that may seem like trite blanket assumptions for the sake of the bigger picture.

References

Albats, Yevgenia. 2017. Russia's Protests Show That a New Generation Is Finding Its Voice. *The Washington Post*, March 28. Accessed 28 March 2017 at https://www.washingtonpost.com/news/democracy-post/wp/2017/03/28/russias-protests-show-that-a-new-generation-is-finding-its-voice/?utm_term=.ec5ef9268e90

Amnesty International. 2016. *Annual Report: Russian Federation 2015/2016*. Amnesty International. Accessed 18 January 2017 at https://www.amnesty.org/en/countries/europe-and-central-asia/russian-federation/report-russian-federation/

Arendt, Hannah. 1968. *Men in Dark Times*. New York: Harcourt Brace and Company.

———. 1978. *The Life of the Mind*. New York: Harcourt Brace Jovanovich.

Arnsdorf, Isaac, and Benjamin Oreskes. 2016. Putin's Favorite Congressman. *Politico*, November 23. Accessed 4 June 2018 at https://www.politico.com/story/2016/11/putin-congress-rohrabacher-trump-231775

Arutunyan, Anna. 2015. *The Putin Mystique: Inside Russia's Power Cult*. Northampton: Olive Branch Press.
Baker, Peter, and Susan Glasser. 2005. *Kremlin Rising: Vladimir Putin's Russian and the End of Revolution*. New York: Scribner.
Briançon, Pierre. 2017. Billionaire Paid Fillon $50,000 for Meeting with Putin: Report. *POLITICO Europe*, March 21. Accessed 4 June 2018 at https://www.politico.eu/article/billionaire-paid-fillon-50000-for-meeting-with-putin-report/
Cohen, Stephen. 2017. Stop the Pointless Demonization of Putin. *The Nation*, May 7. Accessed 20 April 2016 at https://www.thenation.com/article/stop-pointless-demonization-putin/
Committee to Protect Journalists. 2009. *CPJ Testimony Focuses on Russian Impunity*. Committee to Protect Journalists, June 25. Accessed 2 February 2018 at https://cpj.org/blog/2009/06/cpj-testimony-focuses-on-russian-impunity.php
Dawisha, Karen. 2014. *Putin's Kleptocracy: Who Owns Russia?* New York: Simon & Schuster Paperbacks.
Eltsov, Peter. 2015. What Putin's Favorite Guru Tells Us About His Next Target. *Politico*, February 10. Accessed 20 September 2018 at https://www.politico.com/magazine/story/2015/02/vladimir-putin-guru-solzhenitsyn-115088
Federal State Statistics Service of the Russian Federation. 2016. *Informacija o Social'no- Jekonomicheskom Polozhenii Rossii: Janvar' 2016 Goda* [Information on the Socio-Economic Position of Russia: January 2016]. Federal State Statistics Service of the Russian Federation, January. Accessed 18 January 2017 at http://www.gks.ru/free_doc/doc_2016/info/oper-01-2016.pdf
Forbes. Profile: Vladimir Putin. *Forbes*, 2017. Accessed 30 March 2017 at https://www.forbes.com/profile/vladimir-putin/
Fukuyama, Francis. 1989. The End of History? *The National Interest* 16 (Summer): 3–18.
Gessen, Masha. 2012. *The Man Without a Face: The Unlikely Rise of Vladimir Putin*. New York: Riverhead Books.
Gorbachev, Mikhail. 2016. *The New Russia*. Cambridge: Polity Press.
Hagan, Lisa. 2018. Rohrabacher Under Fire over Russia Ties. *The Hill*, March 8. Accessed 4 June 2018 at http://thehill.com/homenews/campaign/377302-rohrabacher-under-fire-over-russia-ties
Hill, Fiona, and Clifford G. Gaddy. 2013. *Mr. Putin: Operative in the Kremlin*. Washington, DC: The Brookings Institution.
Human Rights Watch. 2016. Russia—World Report 2016. *Human Rights Watch*. Accessed 18 January 2017 at https://www.hrw.org/world-report/2016/country-chapters/russia
Judah, Ben. 2013. *Fragile Empire: How Russia Fell In and Out of Love with Vladimir Putin*. New Haven: Yale University Press.

Kaczynski, Andrew, Chris Massie, and Nathan McDermott. 2017. 80 Times Trump Talked About Putin. *CNN*, February. Accessed 22 June 2018 at https://www.cnn.com/interactive/2017/03/politics/trump-putin-russia-timeline/
Kara-Murza, Vladimir. 2017a. Democracy Challenged. In *Panel at 21st Annual Forum 2000: Strengthening Democracy in Uncertain Times*, Prague, October 9.
———. 2017b. Putin Is Not Russia. *Journal of Democracy* 28 (4): 110–116.
———. 2018. If Putin Is So Popular, Why Is He So Afraid of Competition? *The Washington Post*, January 12. Accessed 2 July 2018 at https://www.washingtonpost.com/news/democracy-post/wp/2018/01/12/if-putin-is-so-popular-why-is-he-so-afraid-of-competition/?noredirect=onandutm_term=.35aeb230f098
Knight, Amy. 2017. *Orders to Kill: The Putin Regime and Political Murder*. New York: Thomas Dunne Books.
Kovalik, Dan. 2017. *The Plot to Scapegoat Russia: How the CIA and the Deep State Have Conspired to Vilify Russia*. New York: Skyhorse Publishing.
Laqueur, Walter. 2015. *Putinism: Russia and Its Future with the West*. New York: Thomas Dunne Books.
Levada Center. 2018. *Odobrenie dejatel'nosti Vladimira Putina* [Vladimir Putin's Approval Ratings]. Levada Center: Yuri Levada Analytical Center, May. Accessed 4 June 2018 at https://www.levada.ru/indikatory/odobrenie-organov-vlasti/
Lewin, Moshe. 1988. *The Gorbachev Phenomenon: A Historical Interpretation*. Berkeley/Los Angeles: University of California Press.
Lourie, Richard. 2017. *Putin: His Downfall and Russia's Coming Crash*. New York: Thomas Dunne Books.
Morin, Rebecca. 2018. After Rand Paul Meeting, Russian Lawmakers Agree to Washington Visit. *Politico*, August 6. Accessed 6 August 2018 at https://www.politico.com/story/2018/08/06/rand-paul-russia-meeting-764589
Mosse, George L. 1999. *The Fascist Revolution: Toward a General Theory of Fascism*. New York: Howard Fertig.
Organization for Economic Cooperation and Development. 2018. *Income Inequality (Indicator)*. Organization for Economic Cooperation and Development. Accessed 2 July 2018 at https://data.oecd.org/inequality/income-inequality.htm
Panetta, Leon. 2016. *Welcoming Remarks and Plenary I – Navigating 21st Century Security Challenges*. Speech at Global Security Forum 2016, Washington, DC, December 1. Transcript available at https://www.csis.org/analysis/global-security-forum-2016-welcoming-remarks-and-plenary-i-navigating-21st-century-security
Petro, Nicolai. 2017. *Are We Reading Russia Correctly?* Lecture at Vassar College, Poughkeepsie, February 16.

Pifer, Steven. 2018. *U.S.-Russia Relations and a Second Trump-Putin Summit*. The Brookings Institution, July 27. Accessed 27 July 2018 at https://www.brookings.edu/blog/order-from-chaos/2018/07/27/u-s-russia-relations-and-a-second-trump-putin-summit/

Shevtsova, Lilia. 2008. Vladimir Putin. *Foreign Policy* 164 (January–February): 32–40.

———. 2012. Implosion, Atrophy, or Revolution? *Journal of Democracy* 23 (3): 19–31.

Snyder, Timothy. 2018. *The Road to Unfreedom: Russia, Europe, America*. New York: Tim Duggan Books.

Stone, Oliver, dir. 2017. *The Putin Interviews*. Docuseries. Moscow and Sochi: Ixtlan Productions.

Talmon, Jacob L. 1952. *The Origins of Totalitarian Democracy*. London: Secker and Warburg.

Tamkin, Emily. 2017. Oliver Stone's 'Putin Interviews' Will Teach You Little About Putin, and Even Less About Russia. *Foreign Policy*, June 7. Accessed 4 June 2018 at https://foreignpolicy.com/2017/06/07/oliver-stones-putin-interviews-will-teach-you-little-about-putin-and-even-less-about-russia/

The United Nations. 2016. Third Committee Takes Up 7 Draft Resolutions on Situations in Syria, Iran, Crimea as It Concludes Discussion of Human Rights Council's Report. The United Nations, November 8. Accessed 18 January 2017 at http://www.un.org/press/en/2016/gashc4186.doc.htm

The United States Congress. 2017. *Countering America's Adversaries Through Sanctions Act*, H.R. 3364. 115th Congress. Washington, DC: United States Government Publishing Office, August 2. Accessed 9 January 2018 at https://www.congress.gov/bill/115th-congress/house-bill/3364/text?q=%7B%22search%22%3A%5B%22sanctions%22%5D%7D&r=2

The World Bank. 2018. *Russia: GDP Growth (Annual %)*. The World Bank. Accessed 5 January 2019 at https://data.worldbank.org/indicator/NY.GDP.MKTP.KD.ZG?locations=RU

Tismaneanu, Vladimir. 2012. *The Devil in History: Communism, Fascism, and Some Lessons of the Twentieth Century*. Berkeley/Los Angeles: University of California Press.

Tucker, Robert C. 1987. *Political Culture and Leadership in Soviet Russia: From Lenin to Gorbachev*. New York: W.W. Norton & Company, Inc.

van Prooijen, Jan-Willem, and Paul A.M. van Lange. 2014. Power, Politics, and Paranoia: An Introduction. In *Power, Politics, and Paranoia: Why People Are Suspicious of Their Leaders*, ed. Jan-Willem van Prooijen and Paul A.M. van Lange, 1–14. Cambridge: Cambridge University Press.

Voice of America. 2017. 'Terrible Crimes' Made Putin World's Richest Person, Financier Testifies. *Voice of America*, July 27. Accessed 2 July 2018 at https://www.voanews.com/a/terrible-crimes-made-putin-world-richest-person-financier-tells-senators/3961955.html

White, Stephen, and Ian McAllister. 2008. The Putin Phenomenon. *Journal of Communist Studies and Transition Politics* 24 (4): 604–628.

Zakaria, Fareed. 2017. Why Putin Is the World's Most Powerful Man. *CNN*, March 14. Accessed 30 March 2017 at http://www.cnn.com/2017/03/13/opinions/putin-most-powerful-man-world-zakaria/

Zubarevich, Natalia. 2013. Perspektiva: Chetyre Rossii: chto dal'she [Perspective: Four Russias: What's Next]. *Vedimosti*, September 24. Accessed 5 September 2016 at http://www.vedomosti.ru/newspaper/articles/2013/09/24/chetyre-rossii-chto-dalshe

CHAPTER 2

The Inheritance of an Autocratic Legend

> *Do you still think the world is vast? That if there is a conflagration in one place it does not have a bearing on another, and that you can sit it out in peace on your veranda admiring your absurd petunias?*
> —Anna Politkovskaya

To understand how the "Putin Phenomenon" is a misnomer for what has actually been a recurring theme in Russian history and culture, it is necessary to briefly examine the Russian nation's past to see why it is prone to personality cults, fears of insecurity, and ideological influence. This chapter provides a brief overview of the history of Russia because, after all, "to do any good in the new century we must start by telling the truth about the old," as late British historian Tony Judt once wrote.[1] Without proposing any kind of ironclad determinism, it demonstrates that autocracy is rooted in the country's geography as much as it is in Russia's cultural past: Russia has always spanned huge territories that otherwise could not be protected without autocratic discipline. Kyivan Rus', the first eastern Slavic state that was founded in the ninth century and is considered to be Russia's earliest predecessor, spanned just over half a million square miles. Twelve centuries later, Russia's territory has grown to encompass 6.6 million square miles that extend almost halfway around the globe, making it the largest country in the world by area.

This basic fact emphasizes the Russian population's obsession with security, sovereignty, and a strong ruler. In turn, it sets the stage for understanding the rise and fall of tsarist rule, of the Bolshevik Revolution, of Russia's first democratically elected leader President Boris Yeltsin, and of Vladimir Putin himself. This chapter's selective historical summary provides more than just a context in which to situate Putin and the cultural milieu of Russia. It also lays a foundation for Chap. 4, the crux of our book, which will discuss the intellectual origins of Putinism, without which the Putin era likely would have lasted no longer, nor have been more successful, than that of Boris Yeltsin's. The philosophical and ideological ideas mentioned in this chapter never disappear from Russian history or culture.

The Basis of Tsarist Rule: Absolute Power in Exchange for Border Protection

Historically, the frontier meant insecurity and oppression: the years 1223–1240 saw the Mongols invade and destroy a weakly defended Kyivan Rus', a disaster which was nearly repeated in 1812, when Napoleon Bonaparte's French military invaded imperial Russia (albeit with ruinous consequences for France).[2] With few natural borders and sporadic rural settlements, Russia was historically characterized by an anarchic landscape upon which no group's security could be guaranteed.[3] Even today, these two foreign incursions continue to serve as a constant reminder to the Russian population of the dangers of weak borders.

An enduring concern with security developed following the Mongol raids, according to historian G. Patrick March. The Mongols' brutality instilled within the Russian population a tolerance for tyranny in an effort to assuage their fear of possible invasions. It paved the way for autocracy, for the emergence of the Hobbesian Leviathan under the title of *Tsar*. This political system was an attractive option for Russia because its territory had always been notoriously vast and diverse, making it difficult to uniformly secure itself from external hostilities. The amalgamation of dense pockets of diverse ethnic groups encompassed by that territory also instigated fears of internal hostilities, prompting suspicion even over its own inhabitants' political loyalties.[4] Placing power in a single decision-maker's hands would be, in theory, the ultimate guarantor of unity and security both inside and outside of the frontiers.

Hence, the Russian people of the sixteenth century came to "naturally"[5] desire autocracy, a concept inextricable from that of repression.

They were willing to give up some of their own freedoms in order to achieve the priority of public security, something they believed was directly associated with personal security.[6] In 1547, a prince of Muscovy created the Tsardom of Russia, a system in which one leader, known as the tsar (or tsarina), would safeguard Russian lands from external forces—but only in exchange for absolute power over the empire and obedience from all those living within it. Formed one century before the Treaty of Westphalia, Russia's tsarist government was undoubtedly one of the prototypical case studies for Thomas Hobbes' exploration of sovereign power in *Leviathan*, as well as for later theories on the social contract and state formation.

The tsar assumed the role of supreme ruler and commanded obedience from all state institutions. Such extreme political sovereignty was tied to theology: the very word *tsar* means "dear father" in Russian, implying that God himself had granted each tsar power over the territory. Essentially, the tsar was viewed as the earthly vision of God. Accordingly, the Russian Orthodox Church, a key state institution which itself demanded obedience from the Russian population, acted to reinforce the tsar's supremacy. The religious population followed suit.[7] Their obedience allowed for the foundation of a patrimonial state in which the tsar could convince the population of a great many things because, as political theorist Hannah Arendt described, it was commonly believed that the tsar spoke for both the people's best interests *and* for God. Thus, the people could not question the tsar, and the social contract—if it existed at all—held that people would serve the sovereign on the sovereign's terms.[8]

Besides the Church, the military served as another indispensable state apparatus and was primarily relied upon as a deterrent to domestic uprisings. The *Okhrana* [Guard] (1881–1917), the secret police organization created by Tsar Alexander II, was tasked with identifying and hunting down political subversives in Russian society by means of extra-legal violence and other covert methods. In tsarist times, autocracy was the norm, and dissent was criminal. Even more insightful, however, is the name of this clandestine policing unit, simply known as the Guard: it signifies that the central government relied upon secrecy and the politics of knowledge to guarantee its security and sovereignty. A public monitoring system was not enough; the regime desired to know of whatever dissonance was brewing within society against the empire's leader—a theme which, as Chap. 3 will reveal, pervades Russian history throughout the Soviet era and to the present day.

Yet another state apparatus, the education system, served as a tool for social control in promoting the imperial state. It is significant that most peasants of the Russian Empire did not receive an education. Many were treated as nothing more than serfs living in economically and morally unjust conditions under their aristocratic landlords. They had few-to-no choices, carried out orders of their landowning masters (or at least abided by their rules), and were tied to the earth upon which they worked. Mass education was not favorable to the tsars, who feared knowledge would risk the "simple and loyal" character of the peasantry.[9] Until 1714, when Tsar Peter the Great established a mandatory system in which males either attended school or were sent to military duty, only those who could afford education had the opportunity to learn. This schooling, supervised by state authorities for content, interpellated students further into imperial Russian autocracy by reinforcing the myth of the tsar as the Savior. Education in the classical style precluded Russians from learning of modern developments, such as the radicalism that culminated in revolution in France in 1789; instead, the people lived in a confined world, limited by the traditionalist beliefs of the reactionary, nationalist, xenophobic, anti-Semitic Old Russia.[10]

Even with Peter the Great's modernizing (and often destructive) efforts and subsequent education reforms, by 1897 just 20 percent of subjects living in the Russian Empire could sign their own name; in the countryside, between 14 percent and 41 percent of the population could read or write. As of 1917, over 60 percent of the entire Russian Empire remained illiterate.[11] With most of its subjects being uneducated, and even those who happened to be educated being oblivious to other political possibilities, the majority of the empire's population simply accepted the autocratic system. Some even desired this kind of authority, particularly if they had been indoctrinated by the Russian Orthodox Church. Of course, it would be a disservice to claim that all inhabitants of the Russian Empire felt fondly of the tsars—serfdom was, after all, a dehumanizing, egregious system, and ill-prepared conscripts were sent off to their deaths by the tsars, to name a few grievances. Unfortunately, few were in a position to seriously rebel against the autocratic system with success, and so it dragged onward.

The most visible exception came from universities and the intelligentsia,[12] which turned into sources of dissent following the death of the particularly despotic Tsar Nicholas I in 1855. Despite his hallowed status as tsar, he garnered much scorn from his subjects because his policies wrecked the economy, prevented modernization, and resulted in a humiliating military defeat during the Crimean War (1853–1856). These factors meant he had failed as the sovereign to protect imperial Russia economically, physically, and culturally. Controlled by intellectuals, higher education helped to spread the populist, anarchist, and other anti-monarchist revolutionary ideas arising from Nicholas I's dismal performance.[13]

His successor, Tsar Alexander II, had little choice but to win back the trust of the grumbling populace. He enacted various reforms, the most influential of which was his "emancipation" of the serfs in 1861. In reality, his plan was a disaster: he had provided no mechanism for the integration of millions of serfs into the state's economy, and they were still required to buy the land they had so arduously worked for generations. "Freed" serfs were left to drown in society without support.

Alexander II's reform had been half-baked in more than just content, though: its motivations were disingenuous, as well. As political scientist and historian Robert C. Tucker noted in *Political Culture and Leadership in Soviet Russia: From Lenin to Gorbachev* (1987), it was only after Alexander II read Russian novelist Ivan Turgenev's *Sportsman's Sketches* (1852)—a short story collection with abolitionist overtones—that he informed the nobles of Moscow, "It is better to abolish serfdom from above than to await the time when it will begin to abolish itself from below" via "revolutionary upheaval." Alexander II did not embark on reform out of the goodness of his heart or his concern for human dignity; rather, he acted to nip future unrest in the bud, hoping that emancipation would be a small cost in the big scheme of control. Hence the Emancipation Decree of 1861 that technically abolished serfdom, but kept the "autocratic, centralized, and bureaucratic system of government" intact and failed to improve the lot of the lower classes.[14]

In this case, reform was not as it seemed. What appeared on the surface to be a radical reconstruction of the tsarist empire—admittedly one that went so far as to tamper with its socioeconomic foundations—was really an attempt to preserve the ruling order. Historian Alfred J. Rieber, in his article in the edited volume *Perestroika at the Crossroads* (1991), generalizes this idea of duplicitous reform as a part of autocratic and authoritarian Russian culture. He highlights that impulses to reform only came as "a response to a systemic crisis that threatened the stability and even the survival of the body politic"; thus, change only occurred when Russia's status as a great power was at stake.[15] Russia's position relative to the rest of the world mattered so much because, for Russia to be a great power, this would mean that it enjoyed control, security, and stability. These are aspects that, as discussed already in our book and many other sources, plagued the formation of the Russian identity and empire since their inceptions. Rieber captured this psychological need when he wrote,

> There was always the danger that loss of power at the center would intensify the centrifugal forces on the periphery. The vulnerable frontiers, the restlessness of nationalities massed in territorial blocs along the frontiers, the suspicion mixed with contempt of rival powers could easily combine to threaten the leadership with the prospect of the disintegration of the state. Such at least were the fears of the past. To state the dilemma boldly: Russia had to be a great power in order to remain a power at all.[16]

Knowing this, it becomes increasingly evident that autocracy, conservatism, and resistance to change have long characterized the Russian political tradition and leadership style as smaller pieces of the bigger picture. This bigger picture ultimately comprised an intense desire for stability.

Again, we remind readers that politics, leadership, and culture are not autonomous: it is important to note that Russian society, too, exhibited the aforementioned traits. In the example of the emancipation of the serfs, neither the leadership nor the overwhelming majority of society genuinely favored the idea of reform. Despite the poor treatment of these millions of people, some subjects of the Russian Empire continued to justify tsarism by arguing that Russia required a strong ruler and strict order if it wanted to survive; in their opinion, if laws had been tighter and the serfs had not been freed, the country would be in better shape.

Leninism Continues the Autocratic Legacy

Essentially, imperial Russia could not be compatible with notions of liberty, freedom, progress, or prosperity. With the onset of World War I, high food prices, fuel shortages, and the incompetency of Tsar Nicholas II's military policy caused Russians to rebel against him.[17] This toppled the entire tsarist regime in 1917. But it was no revolution, in the sense that tsars were simply replaced as the ruling autocrats by Communist Party leaders. Citizens of revolutionary Russia partly accepted the continuation of autocratic trends because these Bolsheviks presented their new government as a necessary measure to rectify historical misdeeds (even though many of these injustices were worsened, in fact, by Soviet rule).[18] The tradition of the tsars' Okhrana, too, was continued by Soviet secret police, in the forms of the Cheka, GPU (*Gosudarstvennoe Politicheskoe Upravlenie*, or State Political

Administration), NKVD (*Narodni Komissariat Vnutrennikh Del*, or People's Commissariat for Internal Affairs), MVD (*Ministerstvo Vnutrennikh Del*, or Ministry of Internal Affairs), KGB (*Komitet Gosudarstvennoy Bezopasnosti*, or Committee for State Security), and others. These security forces of the Communist Party did not accept any political competition: dissenters were jailed, exiled, or executed, and the entire population was policed even in their own homes. Privacy became increasingly scarce as surveillance practices proliferated. Soviet citizens were simultaneously transformed in the eyes of the state into both potential criminals and potential informants or law enforcers.[19]

Despite this tenuous relationship in which one citizen might report a fellow citizen for their less-than-revolutionary flair at any point, Vladimir Lenin managed to unite (read "force") the people under the banner (read "fantasy") of Marxism-Leninism. Lenin himself wrote that "it is devilishly important to *conquer* the trust of the natives," which is exactly what he set out to do by telling all those living in the Soviet Union (or in the peripheral lands that Lenin saw as future opportunities for expansion) that they were working toward a utopia in which everyone would be equal.[20] This dream could only be achieved through autocracy, through a strong leader who supposedly knew what was best for the nation as a whole. Combined with the facts that, under Lenin, the people had access to free and universal education from the ages of 3 through 16, the country industrialized, and its economy grew with remarkable rapidity, autocratic rule was overwhelmingly accepted. The people who believed in the Marxist dream saw this as reason to be happy with their relatively better quality of life. They felt as though they were recognized as equals by the state, each being called to accept Communist laws and subordinate individual freedoms for the betterment of the entire society. Those who disagreed were silenced in inhumane ways, but Marxist-Leninists rationalized this repression as a necessary cleansing that need not merit attention or questions directed against Soviet authority.

Of course, Lenin's narrative failed to consider the full extent of the sacrifices those living in the Soviet Union had to make, nor did it mention how lifestyles and even lives would be crushed irrevocably, for the purpose of attaining utopia. State repression, forced collectivization, family disruptions, famines, the threats presented by the secret police, and so on were all major features of the totalitarian, ultra-autocratic empire-state which Lenin built in order to achieve the conquest of difference and the indigenization of Soviet control over neighboring, yet non-Russian, lands. People living within Soviet borders were all referred to as the *narod* [the people] regardless of their differing ethno-nationalities—a sign that the

Soviet state desired to violently impose, upon as large of a group as possible, a civic identity based on common citizenship that promised to escort each community member to the ultimate terminus of History.[21] (Ironically, such founding violence and erasure of difference is damning evidence of the Soviet Union's inherent imperialist nature, despite Lenin's persuasive façade that imperialism was a Western evil and, as his eponymous manuscript from 1917 claimed, "the highest stage of capitalism."[22])

Lenin never allowed the people a chance to dissent against autocracy or to promote individualism. He and his movement convinced the citizenry not to value individual freedoms. State propaganda attacked the West for its "hedonistic," "selfish" celebration of freedoms and individualism. As a contrary position to the Western account, the Communist Party proclaimed that equality for the masses should be the state's true pursuit. The Party compelled citizens to act according to ideological imperatives in the belief that their country was ineluctably moving in the direction of historical progress. This omission of the personal sacrifices, not to mention the preclusion of both individual freedoms and differences, forced upon each Soviet citizen by the Bolshevik dogma reveals the importance of autocratic rule in the peoples' acceptance of the totalitarianism that was to fully come to fruition as the Soviet period marched onward.

A few years after his death on 21 January 1924, Lenin was succeeded as ruler of the Soviet Union by Josef Stalin. Though both of them belong to the same category of mass-murdering dictators, Lenin's deeds have been particularly emphasized in our book because: (1) Lenin was the founding leader of the Soviet utopian project, and (2) for whatever mystery, Lenin's memory is rarely viewed in the general public's eye through as critical a lens as Stalin's memory. The latter understanding of popular misconceptions surrounding Lenin and the horrible destiny of the Soviet project that he began is particularly elaborated upon in historian Robert Gellately's *Lenin, Stalin and Hitler: The Age of Social Catastrophe* (2011). In it, Gellately explains that Stalin fundamentally "wanted people to have complete happiness and earthly salvation, necessary through violence and terrorism"; that Stalin's policies embodied the Soviet project; and that this project, in turn, embodied the desires of its original leader, Lenin.[23] Because Stalin is already more widely understood to be a genocidal dictator across the globe (except maybe in antidemocratic regimes like Russia, China, North Korea, etc.), our book will not say much about him besides this: Stalin was a perfect Leninist who continued to carry out totalitarianism where Lenin left off.[24]

Again, this chapter does not intend to digress into the horrors of Soviet history or its different phases of terror. For in-depth research on the subject, we refer readers both familiar and unfamiliar with the course of Soviet leadership to comprehensive works such as political scientist Archie Brown's *The Rise and Fall of Communism* (2009), historian Orlando Figes' *Revolutionary Russia, 1891–1991* (2014), and historian Martin Malia's *The Soviet Tragedy: A History of Socialism in Russia, 1917–1991* (1994). Otherwise, we will continue to set the scene for Putinism by making fleeting mention of the longer-lasting Soviet rulers for the sake of exemplifying the continuity of autocracy and authoritarianism throughout Russian history.

Repressive governance held strong long after Stalin's death on 5 March 1953. After a short power struggle, Nikita Khrushchev served as the head of the Soviet Union until October 1964. Erroneously believed to be a reformer due to the "Secret Speech" in which he denounced Stalin at a closed Communist Party Congress and then set about removing Stalin statues from the Soviet Union without much public discussion, Khrushchev also was a thoroughly authoritarian, Soviet subject. His successor, Leonid Brezhnev, oversaw a period of stagnation between 1964 and 1982, from which began to emanate the odor of an ulcerating bureaucracy; while in no sense did Soviet authorities loosen their repressive grip on the population, ideological adherence to Communist dogma among Soviets began to decay.

By the time Mikhail Gorbachev came to power in March 1985, popular belief in Lenin's utopian myth had noticeably waned. Due to the corrosive effects of preceding leaders' Communist rule, among other reasons discussed in books such as Brown's *The Gorbachev Factor* (1996), historian Stephen Kotkin's *Armageddon Averted: the Soviet Collapse, 1970–2000* (2001), and political scientist William Taubman's *Gorbachev: His Life and Times* (2017), Soviets began to lose faith in the general Communist project. They also perceived Gorbachev's administration as weak, especially under his (in some respects) radically divergent policies of glasnost and perestroika.[25] This is not to say that Gorbachev represented a break from the despotic legend begun in Imperial Russia centuries before. Do not forget that Gorbachev, like any Soviet leader, was no good reformer: he may have amnestied some political prisoners during his time in power, but the Gulag camps were still operational.[26] Even the motivations behind those releases are suspect: Gorbachev only called for the infamous 1987 amnesty after the international community expressed outrage over the death of Anatoly Marchenko, the popular Soviet prisoner of conscience who had helped to expose the Soviets' continued usage of the Gulag and its terrible conditions and later embarked on a hunger strike to protest for the release of all political prisoners, in the Chistopol prison hospital in December 1986.

Yet, even then, deeply scarred Soviet people saw vulnerabilities in a comparatively less totalitarian regime, which eventually gave way in December 1991. What appeared to be Gorbachev's lack of autocratic and authoritarian aptitude, combined with his willingness to compromise Soviet ideals, left the new Russian national population feeling uncertain and anxious about the future.

THE GHOST OF AUTOCRACY HAUNTS MODERN RUSSIA

Stalin's biographer Robert C. Tucker relayed a colloquial saying in his book *Political Culture and Leadership in Soviet Russia*: "the old doesn't surrender without a fight."[27] He wrote this in connection to the Stalinist legacy, which includes nationalists, chauvinists, conservatives, and so on, and it still holds true today. This history of autocratic rule in both tsarist and Soviet periods resulted in a predisposition for the modern Russian Federation. A history of despotic, then totalitarian, rule left Russian society without any tradition of democracy or civil society to turn back the tide of history and change their new state's autocratic course. Even though Communism had collapsed by the end of 1991, it did not take the ashes of authoritarianism with it; yes, many people had lost all faith in Communism itself, but they still believed in the need for a strong leader because no other ideological system was put in place to contest the old framework. Habits regarding culture, politics, and the promises of politics (namely the long-held millenarian fantasy of achieving a utopian society) have not undergone serious transformation or realignment, so Putin's Russia continues as an amalgam of the old and the new. Local-level election administration official Anton Dugin expressed this continuity of authoritarian rule and societal expectations when he remarked to a journalist on 4 March 2012 (a presidential election day), "Russia has always had autocracy. It has always had a Tsar. And that has always been good for some people and bad for others."[28]

Even on the peripherals of the political realm, cultural productions in today's Russia point to the embeddedness of the country's history in everyday life. In many different ways, Russians can move "forward" and distance themselves from their country's past extreme ideology, but they can never actually escape the ghosts of Lenin or Communism, or the autocratic malaise of Russia. These cannot be erased from history and will always linger.

Once the Soviet Union crumbled by 1991, the Russian nation-state was left with no distinctively Russian script to unify itself in the newly liminal territory it occupied. Just under 150 million people suddenly "ceased to be a nation," as philosopher Aleksandr Zinovyev put it.[29] What did it even mean to be Russian now, anyway? The population referred to this post-1991 period as *bespredel* [without limit]. It proved to be a quite apt label, for it encapsulated the encouraging plethora of opportunities available for the reinvention of Russia while also ominously reminding everyone of the lack of rules and traditions with which to carry out this transitional phase.[30]

Anarchical infighting among oil giants and business tycoons prevented the first democratically elected leader in Russian history, President Boris Yeltsin (1991–1999), from establishing anything but a weak central government.[31] The introduction of liberal capitalism to Russia did not translate into popular democracy or negate autocratic tendencies (although it should be noted that "liberal capitalism" was never truly extended to all members of society and was instead spearheaded by the government in an attempt to build a corrupt oligarchy), as scholars such as Francis Fukuyama assumed it would.[32] Instead, it brought fears of instability and economic disaster. The national GDP declined by 34 percent between 1991 and 1995, a larger diminution than the United States experienced during the Great Depression; Russia defaulted on its debts in August 1998; economic and social inequality skyrocketed to levels the Russian people had never known before; and government officials and business men engaged in blatant corruption. The Russian state was in anarchy. The fledgling legal system struggled to establish itself, never mind enforce its laws throughout society.[33]

A small group of lucrative oligarchs rose to prominence by exploiting the Yeltsin administration's economic ineptitude and legal loopholes, claiming they could fill in the gaps left by his government's weak authority. Their corrupt deals and capturing of major financial and energy businesses meant the average Russian citizen had little opportunity to participate in liberal capitalism; essentially, the market-devouring oligarchs were another form of autocratic control precluding the Russian state from more robust democratic opportunities. This vying for power between businessmen, oil giants, and the Russian mafia exacerbated the biggest fear among ordinary Russian citizens: the instability they associated with the lack of a strong ruler. Citizens feared their state was not progressing, even though the fall of Communism had been widely celebrated as the way toward prosperity and stability. By 1999, Yeltsin's popularity rating had fallen to single digits. Meanwhile, the country's population count had plummeted since the collapse of the Soviet Union: a decline in births, a drop in life expectancy (a result of lowered quality of life), and increased emigration rates meant the population numbers fell by one million Russians per year.[34] Altogether, the country was experiencing excruciating anxieties, bitter disappointments, and political despair. As in the last years of Weimar Germany, there was rampant yearning for a magical savior.

The Russian population had placed its faith in their first-ever democratically elected president (who, coincidentally, had been interested in improving relations with the West) but received in exchange economic, political, and ideological turmoil. The transitioning nation was plagued by impoverishment and criminalization. The 1990s was a period of turmoil, embarrassment, and nostalgia for the days of Soviet glory. This decade wracked the nation's psyche, eating away at the hope for a unified community that spurred on many dissenting Russians in the 1980s and early 1990s.[35] Writing at the end of Yeltsin's presidential stretch, political scientist Ilya Prizel captured this sense of chaos in an essay published within Sorin Antohi and Vladimir Tismaneanu's co-edited volume, *Between Past and Future: The Revolutions of 1989 and Their Aftermath* (2000). Prizel noted that in 1995, 64.5 percent of the Russian population was ashamed of the country and that 82 percent reported a desire for Russia to attain great power status on the world stage.[36] Summing up the dissatisfaction and volatility in post-Soviet Russia, he commented,

> It is symptomatic of the psychological disorientation befalling Russia that eight years after the breakup of the Soviet Union, Russians have yet to agree on the proper name for the country, much less its borders, flag, seal, or national anthem. Russia at the end of the twentieth century has yet to find its "usable past"—its historic heroes and villains or, for that matter, a universal definition of what a Russian is.[37]

Centuries of tsarist reign, decades of Soviet rule, and less than one decade of the weak, democratically elected Yeltsin government culminated in an existential, desperate search for answers to the following grand questions: what is the Russian state's identity? Is it based on language, race, civic tradition, or some other conception? What unites its people? How will the Russian state survive? How does it relate to the rest of the world?[38]

Notes

1. Tony Judt, *Reappraisals: Reflections on the Forgotten Twentieth Century* (New York: Penguin Books, 2008), p. 9.
2. Hugh Seton-Watson, *The Russian Empire, 1801–1917* (Oxford: Oxford University Press, 1967), p. 13; Richard Lourie, *Putin: His Downfall and Russia's Coming Crash* (New York: Thomas Dunne Books, 2017), pp. 84–85.
3. Robert D. Kaplan, *The Revenge of Geography: What the Map Tells Us About Coming Conflicts and the Battle Against Fate* (New York: Random House Trade Paperbacks, 2012), p. 159; Serhii Plokhy, *Lost Kingdom: A History of Russian Nationalism from Ivan the Great to Vladimir Putin* (London: Allen Lane, 2017), pp. vii–xii and 3–19.
4. Alfred J. Rieber, "The Reforming Tradition in Russian History," in *Perestroika at the Crossroads*, eds. Alfred J. Rieber and Alvin Z. Rubinstein (Armonk: M.E. Sharpe, Inc., 1991), p. 6.
5. "Naturally" only because their perceptions of the world, in addition to police and religious authorities, made autocracy seem as though it were the only viable possibility. Autocracy is a primordial myth, not a natural desire of its own accord.
6. Hannah Arendt, *Origins of Totalitarianism* (New York: Meridian Books, 1958), p. 141.
7. Anna Arutunyan, *The Putin Mystique: Inside Russia's Power Cult* (Northampton: Olive Branch Press, 2015), pp. 226 and 289.
8. Arendt, *Origins of Totalitarianism*, p. 106; Nikita Mikhalkov, "Pravo i Pravda. Manifest Prosveshchennogo konservatizma," *Polit.ru*, 26 October 2010.
9. Richard Pipes, *Russia Under the Old Regime* (London: Weidenfeld and Nicolson, 1974), pp. 153 and 162.
10. Yves Ternon, "Russian Terrorism, 1878–1906," in *The History of Terrorism: From Antiquity to Al Qaeda*, eds. Gerard Chaliand and Arnaud Blin (Berkeley: University of California Press, 2007), pp. 136 and 142.
11. Ben Eklof, "Russian Literacy Campaigns 1861–1939" in *National Literacy Campaigns and Movements: Historical and Comparative Perspectives*, eds. Robert F. Arnove and Harvey J. Graff (New Brunswick, NJ: Transaction Publishers, 2008), pp. 128–29.
12. The term "intelligentsia" refers to those elite intellectuals who influenced society, culture, and politics out of concerns for morality and desires for social justice. It is a Russian word that arose in the early nineteenth century in conjunction with the appearance of European revolutionary movements. Members of the intelligentsia were meant to be free of class loyalties or organized religions and instead committed to achieving radical social

change. James H. Billington, *Fire in the Minds of Men: Origins of the Revolutionary Faith* (New York: Basic Books, Inc., 1980), pp. 208–231; Isaiah Berlin, *Russian Thinkers* (New York: Viking Press, 1978), p. 117. For more on the intelligentsia, see Leszek Kołakowski, "The Intelligentsia," in *Poland: Genesis of a Revolution*, ed. Abraham Brumberg (New York: Random House, 1983) and Andrzej Walicki, "Milestones and Russian Intellectual History," *Studies in East European Thought*, Vol. 62, No. 1 (March 2010), pp. 101–107.

13. Ternon, "Russian Terrorism," p. 147; Samuel D. Kassow, *Students, Professors, and the State in Tsarist Russia* (Berkeley: University of California Press, 1989), p. 3; for more on the different strains of revolutionary turbulence that (albeit belatedly) came to consume Tsarist Russia, see Billington's *Fire in the Minds of Men*, particularly Chapter 14, "The Bomb: Russian Violence."
14. Robert C. Tucker, *Political Culture and Leadership in Soviet Russia: From Lenin to Gorbachev* (New York: W.W. Norton & Company, Inc., 1987), p. 21. Readers should keep in mind this kind of duplicitous behavior on the behalf of Russian leaders; it will resurface in discussions about Putinism and among the beliefs of those who support the Kremlin's policies (such as in Putin's 2018 announcement and subsequent "revision" of pension age hikes, or in Russia's supposedly benevolent bombings of Syria that only help Putin to cement a friendly relationship in the Middle East with dictator Bashar al-Assad and repress freedom fighters beyond Russia's own borders).
15. Rieber, "The Reforming Tradition in Russian History," p. 4. By the later chapters of our book, readers will recognize this trend as one that endures through imperial Russia, Soviet Russia, and even Putin's Russia.
16. Rieber, "The Reforming Tradition in Russian History," p. 13.
17. Marci Shore, *The Taste of Ashes: The Afterlife of Totalitarianism in Eastern Europe* (New York: Crown Publishers, 2013), p. 7.
18. Joseph Frank, *Through the Russian Prism: Essays on Literature and Culture* (Princeton: Princeton University Press, 1990), p. 87; Tucker, *Political Culture*, p. 57.
19. Michel Foucault, *Discipline and Punish: The Birth of the Prison* (New York: Vintage Books, 1977), pp. 195–228.
20. Vladimir I. Lenin, *Polnoe sobranie sochinenij*, 5th ed. (Moscow: Institute of Marxism-Leninism, 1965), p. 190.
21. Vladimir Tismaneanu, *Fantasies of Salvation: Democracy, Nationalism, and Myth in Post-Communist Europe* (Princeton: Princeton University Press, 1998); Adeeb Khalid, "The Soviet Union as an Imperial Formation: A View from Central Asia," in *Imperial Formations*, eds. Anna Laura Stoler, Carole McGranahan, and Peter C. Perdue (Santa Fe: School for Advanced Research Press, 2007), pp. 120, 124, and 135.

22. Vladimir I. Lenin, *Imperialism, the Highest Stage of Capitalism* (New York, 1939), p. 102. Vladimir Ilyich Lenin's tendency toward Janus-like behavior should be kept in mind when considering the figure of Vladimir Vladimirovich Putin. Similarities in both leaders indicate that Putin is a product of the Soviet Union and continues to use its imaginary imperial repertoire to illiberally legitimize his own authority in today's Russia; these continuities will resurface for discussion in Chap. 5.
23. Robert Gellately, *Lenin, Stalin and Hitler: The Age of Social Catastrophe* (London: Vintage Publishing, 2011), pp. 134–140.
24. For thorough research on Stalin, his dictatorial personality, and his enduring legacy on Soviet and post-Soviet culture, see especially Robert C. Tucker, *Stalin as Revolutionary, 1879–1929: A Study in History and Personality* (New York: Norton, 1973) and American historian Stephen Kotkin's series *Stalin*, two of three volumes of which have already been published under the names *Paradoxes of Power, 1878–1928* (2014) and *Waiting for Hitler, 1929–1941* (2017).
25. Leon Aron, *Roads to the Temple: Truth, Memory, Ideas, and Ideals in the Making of the Russian Revolution, 1987–1991* (New Haven and London: Yale University Press, 2012), p. 23.
26. Alvin Z. Rubinstein, "Gorbachev's Third-World Policy: Tendencies," in *Perestroika at the Crossroads*, eds. Alfred J. Rieber and Alvin Z. Rubinstein (Armonk: M.E. Sharpe, Inc., 1991), p. 322. Stephen Kotkin, *Armageddon Averted: the Soviet Collapse, 1970–2000* (Oxford: Oxford University Press, 2001).
27. Tucker, *Political Culture*, p. 182.
28. Arutunyan, *The Putin Mystique*, p. 278.
29. Vittorio Strada, "Posle imperii: staraya i novaya Rossia" in *Vtoraya Navigatsiya*, ed. Lidia Starodubtseva (Kharkiv: Prava Liudiny, 2010), p. 8; Aleksandr Zinovyev, *Russkaja tragedija: gibel' utopii* (Moscow: Algoritm, 2002). Once a critic of Brezhnev's cult of personality, Zinovyev (born in 1922) was exiled from the USSR. Incidentally, Zinovyev would die in 2006 as a steadfast supporter of Stalin with a wistfulness for Soviet life. In this way, he is a prime example of the cultural rupture that occurred upon the Soviet Union's fall: many lived through the collapse but refused to adapt to the successor "democratic" country. The rest, for the most part, replaced their collective Communist dogmas with unifying nationalist ones. If not a nation, the Russian Federation is a cult of community, negatively held together by geopolitical isolation and other exclusionary bonds.
30. Serguei A. Oushakine, *The Patriotism of Despair: Nation, War, and Loss in Russia* (Ithaca: Cornell University Press, 2009), p. 1.
31. Michael McFaul, *From Cold War to Hot Peace: An American Ambassador in Putin's Russia* (New York: Houghton Mifflin Harcourt Publishing

Company, 2018), pp. 47–51. Though Yeltsin was democratically elected, the process was by no means fair or free. McFaul reminds us that Yeltsin had deployed state resources in his campaign, and that there had been complaints of election fraud, to name just a few issues surrounding his presidential candidacy; these details are in keeping with the themes of our book, further demonstrating that the problems of Putin's Russia are embedded in Russia's cultural and political past.

32. Francis Fukuyama, *The End of History and the Last Man* (New York: Avon Books, 1992), p. 43.
33. Anne Garrels, *Putin Country: A Journey into the Real Russia* (New York: Farrar, Straus and Giroux, 2016), p. 8; Masha Gessen, *The Man Without a Face: The Unlikely Rise of Vladimir Putin* (New York: Riverhead Books, 2012), p. 13; Archie Brown, *Seven Years that Changed the World: Perestroika in Perspective* (New York: Oxford University Press, 2007), p. 328.
34. Gessen, *The Man Without a Face*, p. 11; Garrels, *Putin Country*, p. 58.
35. David Satter, *The Less You Know, the Better You Sleep: Russia's Road to Terror and Dictatorship Under Yeltsin and Putin* (New Haven and London: Yale University Press, 2016), p. 24; Gessen, *The Man Without a Face*, p. 13.
36. Ilya Prizel, "Nationalism in Postcommunist Russia: From Resignation to Anger," in *Between Past and Future: The Revolutions of 1989 and Their Aftermath*, eds. Sorin Antohi and Vladimir Tismaneanu (Budapest and New York: Central European University Press, 2000), p. 343; Nataliia Tikhonova, "Mirovozzrecheskie tsennosti i politicheskii protsess v Rossii," *Obshchestvennye Nauki i Sovremmenost'*, No. 4 (1996), pp. 15–27.
37. Prizel, "Nationalism in Postcommunist Russia," p. 337.
38. Garrels, *Putin Country*, p. 12; Aron, *Roads to the Temple*, p. 23.

References

Arendt, Hannah. 1958. *Origins of Totalitarianism*. New York: Meridian Books.
Aron, Leon. 2012. *Roads to the Temple: Truth, Memory, Ideas, and Ideals in the Making of the Russian Revolution, 1987–1991*. New Haven/London: Yale University Press.
Arutunyan, Anna. 2015. *The Putin Mystique: Inside Russia's Power Cult*. Northampton: Olive Branch Press.
Berlin, Isaiah. 1978. *Russian Thinkers*. New York: Viking Press.
Billington, James H. 1980. *Fire in the Minds of Men: Origins of the Revolutionary Faith*. New York: Basic Books, Inc.
Brown, Archie. 1996. *The Gorbachev Factor*. Oxford: Oxford University Press.
———. 2007. *Seven Years that Changed the World: Perestroika in Perspective*. New York: Oxford University Press.

———. 2009. *The Rise and Fall of Communism*. New York: HarperCollins Publishers.
Eklof, Ben. 2008. Russian Literacy Campaigns 1861–1939. In *National Literacy Campaigns and Movements: Historical and Comparative Perspectives*, ed. Robert F. Arnove and Harvey J. Graff, 123–146. New Brunswick: Transaction Publishers.
Figes, Orlando. 2014. *Revolutionary Russia, 1891–1991*. New York: Metropolitan Books.
Foucault, Michel. 1977. *Discipline and Punish: The Birth of the Prison*. New York: Vintage Books.
Frank, Joseph. 1990. *Through the Russian Prism: Essays on Literature and Culture*. Princeton: Princeton University Press.
Fukuyama, Francis. 1992. *The End of History and the Last Man*. New York: Avon Books.
Garrels, Anne. 2016. *Putin Country: A Journey into the Real Russia*. New York: Farrar, Straus and Giroux.
Gellately, Robert. 2011. *Lenin, Stalin and Hitler: The Age of Social Catastrophe*. London: Vintage Publishing.
Gessen, Masha. 2012. *The Man Without a Face: The Unlikely Rise of Vladimir Putin*. New York: Riverhead Books.
Judt, Tony. 2008. *Reappraisals: Reflections on the Forgotten Twentieth Century*. New York: Penguin Books.
Kaplan, Robert D. 2012. *The Revenge of Geography: What the Map Tells Us About Coming Conflicts and the Battle Against Fate*. New York: Random House Trade Paperbacks.
Kassow, Samuel D. 1989. *Students, Professors, and the State in Tsarist Russia*. Berkeley: University of California Press.
Khalid, Adeeb. 2007. The Soviet Union as an Imperial Formation: A View from Central Asia. In *Imperial Formations*, ed. Anna Laura Stoler, Carole McGranahan, and Peter C. Perdue, 123–152. Santa Fe: School for Advanced Research Press.
Kołakowski, Leszek. 1983. The Intelligentsia. In *Poland: Genesis of a Revolution*, ed. Abraham Brumberg, 54–67. New York: Random House.
Kotkin, Stephen. 2001. *Armageddon Averted: The Soviet Collapse, 1970–2000*. Oxford: Oxford University Press.
Lenin, Vladimir I. 1939. *Imperialism, the Highest Stage of Capitalism*. New York: International Publishers.
———. 1965. *Polnoe sobranie sochinenij* [Complete Public Writings]. Vol. 53, 5th ed. Moscow: Institute of Marxism-Leninism.
Lourie, Richard. 2017. *Putin: His Downfall and Russia's Coming Crash*. New York: Thomas Dunne Books.

Malia, Martin. 1994. *The Soviet Tragedy: A History of Socialism in Russia, 1917–1991.* New York: Simon & Schuster.
McFaul, Michael. 2018. *From Cold War to Hot Peace: An American Ambassador in Putin's Russia.* New York: Houghton Mifflin Harcourt Publishing Company.
Mikhalkov, Nikita. 2010. Pravo i Pravda. Manifest Prosveshchennogo konservatizma [Right and Truth: Manifest of Enlightened Conservatism]. *Polit.ru*, October 26. Accessed 12 July 2018 at http://polit.ru/article/2010/10/26/manifest
Oushakine, Serguei A. 2009. *The Patriotism of Despair: Nation, War, and Loss in Russia.* Ithaca: Cornell University Press.
Pipes, Richard. 1974. *Russia Under the Old Regime.* London: Weidenfeld and Nicolson.
Plokhy, Serhii. 2017. *Lost Kingdom: A History of Russian Nationalism from Ivan the Great to Vladimir Putin.* London: Allen Lane.
Prizel, Ilya. 2000. Nationalism in Postcommunist Russia: From Resignation to Anger. In *Between Past and Future: The Revolutions of 1989 and Their Aftermath*, ed. Sorin Antohi and Vladimir Tismaneanu, 332–356. Budapest/New York: Central European University Press.
Rieber, Alfred J. 1991. The Reforming Tradition in Russian History. In *Perestroika at the Crossroads*, ed. Alfred J. Rieber and Alvin Z. Rubinstein, 3–30. Armonk: M.E. Sharpe, Inc.
Rubinstein, Alvin Z. 1991. Gorbachev's Third-World Policy: Tendencies. In *Perestroika at the Crossroads*, ed. Alfred J. Rieber and Alvin Z. Rubinstein, 303–325. Armonk: M.E. Sharpe, Inc.
Satter, David. 2016. *The Less You Know, the Better You Sleep: Russia's Road to Terror and Dictatorship Under Yeltsin and Putin.* New Haven/London: Yale University Press.
Seton-Watson, Hugh. 1967. *The Russian Empire, 1801–1917.* Oxford: Oxford University Press.
Shore, Marci. 2013. *The Taste of Ashes: The Afterlife of Totalitarianism in Eastern Europe.* New York: Crown Publishers.
Strada, Vittorio. 2010. Posle imperii: staraya i novaya Rossia [After the Empire: Old and New Russia]. In *Vtoraya Navigatsiya*, ed. Lidia Starodubtseva, 6–17. Kharkiv: Prava Liudiny.
Taubman, William. 2017. *Gorbachev: His Life and Times.* New York: W.W. Norton & Company, Inc.
Ternon, Yves. 2007. Russian Terrorism, 1878–1906. In *The History of Terrorism: From Antiquity to Al Qaeda*, ed. Gerard Chaliand and Arnaud Blin, 132–174. Berkeley: University of California Press.
Tikhonova, Nataliia. 1996. Mirovozzrecheskie tsennosti i politicheskii protsess v Rossii [Worldview Values and the Political Process in Russia]. *Obshchestvennye Nauki i Sovremmenost'* 4, 15–27.

Tismaneanu, Vladimir. 1998. *Fantasies of Salvation: Democracy, Nationalism, and Myth in Post-Communist Europe.* Princeton: Princeton University Press.

Tucker, Robert C. 1987. *Political Culture and Leadership in Soviet Russia: From Lenin to Gorbachev.* New York: W.W. Norton & Company, Inc.

Walicki, Andrzej. 2010. Milestones and Russian Intellectual History. *Studies in East European Thought* 62 (1): 101–107.

Zinovyev, Aleksandr. 2002. *Russkaja tragedija: gibel' utopii* [The Russian Tragedy: The Death of Utopia]. Moscow: Algoritm.

CHAPTER 3

Enter "the Hero"

The perceived chaos of the 1990s, combined with a history of autocracy, led the Russian people to desire state-sponsored stability and order. On the verge of existential crisis, Russia conveniently found solace in the obscure name of Vladimir Vladimirovich Putin, a man who claimed he could guarantee the security of the nation. His life before entering the political realm, however, was hardly exceptional. Vladimir Putin was truly a child of Soviet political culture, particularly the version espoused by the KGB. Born in Leningrad on 7 October 1952, he was raised in a city that had seen unimaginable horrors less than a decade prior during World War II. His father, the older Vladimir Putin, had been left crippled after one of his many NKVD missions to sabotage the Germans. Somehow both the disabled Vladimir and his wife, Maria, survived the Siege of Leningrad; this period lasted from 1941 to 1944, set off by the German army's blockading of the former capital of the Russian Empire, in combination with Josef Stalin's unpreparedness for war and unwillingness to divert supplies from the Red Army troops to Leningrad's two million trapped civilians. This culminated in nearly 900 days of extreme famine, cannibalism, and German bombardments. It was the most lethal siege in world history, with 800,000 civilian casualties—roughly one-third of the entire city's population.[1]

Leningrad had seen severe destruction, and even by the time young Vladimir Putin was born to Maria and the elder Vladimir, its education system had not yet been repaired. He entered first grade at the age of eight

© The Author(s) 2020
K. C. Langdon, V. Tismaneanu, *Putin's Totalitarian Democracy*,
https://doi.org/10.1007/978-3-030-20579-9_3

and did not seem interested in schooling, preferring instead to place "a great emphasis on portraying himself as a thug" and getting into fistfights. His violent behavior earned him the rare punishment of being banned from the Young Pioneers, the youth organization for Communists; for three years, he was a visible outcast, attending school without the red kerchief around his neck that almost all the other students wore between the ages of 10 and 14. After hearing that the KGB sought new recruits in recent college graduates who were skilled in hand-to-hand combat, Putin began to train dutifully at his *sambo* (Soviet martial arts) classes. He applied himself academically, gained membership to the Young Pioneers, and was even elected as class chairman. A portrait of Yan Berzin (1889–1938), the first head of the Soviet military intelligence service (known as the GRU), who also spearheaded the development of the GRU's foreign dimension of intelligence collection and infiltration, occupied a special place on young Putin's desk.[2] Putin had begun setting himself up as a loyal Soviet agent since grade school, soaking up Sovietism and the lessons of Bolshevik partocracy.[3]

Thinking back on his adolescent years in later interviews, Putin expressed that he had developed an admiration for Max Otto von Stirlitz, a fictional book, television, and movie character. Essentially the Soviet equivalent of James Bond, Stirlitz was a spy who infiltrated Nazi Germany's security forces in order to protect the USSR from its declared fascist nemesis. Historian Richard Sakwa quoted Putin in his book, *Putin: Russia's Choice* (2008), as having said of Stirlitz, "What amazed me most of all was how one man's effort could achieve what whole armies could not."[4] Putin's interests in Stirlitz, deception, and espionage were notable forces that guided his path as a young boy.

In fact, Stirlitz still mattered to him as an adult: one week before Putin's first presidential election, popular Russian magazine *Vlast* [Power] featured Stirlitz and Putin on its cover with the headline, "Von Stirlitz: Our President."[5] The secret policeman's cult-like figure apparently resonated with Putin (and the rest of the Russian population) after nearly three decades had passed since Stirlitz's most famous appearance in the television miniseries *Semnadtsat' mgnoveniy vesny* [Seventeen Moments of Spring] in 1973. This cultural detail is crucial to keep in mind as we return to outlining the rest of Putin's rise to power, for it signals that Putin—and Russian society—has long been interested in spectacle and national security.[6]

Putin found himself on a Stirlitz-like track after entering law school at Leningrad University, one of the Soviet Union's two top institutions of higher education. Despite being a mediocre student, he was accepted (which has spawned the conspiracy theory that the KGB ensured he would be admitted) and, in his fourth year, was picked up by KGB recruiters. As for his personal life, at the late age of 31 he married a flight attendant from Kaliningrad named Lyudmila Shkrebneva in 1983. She has been quoted as saying, "At first sight, Putin seemed unremarkable and poorly dressed," adding that he communicated ineptly. Apparently, however, he had less trouble communicating to his KGB bosses his dream that "a single intelligence officer could rule over the fates of thousands of people." According to his answers in later interviews, Putin was assigned mainly to combating Soviet dissidents. (Of course, we cannot be sure if Putin has exaggerated or omitted parts of his background, which he has tried rather successfully to shield from public knowledge.) Later, in 1985, he was moved to Dresden, in the German Democratic Republic (GDR, or East Germany), where he conducted undercover yet fruitless and disappointing surveillance[7] in a land already under the paternalistic influence of the Soviet Union.

In fact, since its establishment in October 1949 as the self-proclaimed first German state of peasants and workers, the socialist leadership of the GDR had spouted the line that only unconditional solidarity with the Soviets would guarantee their country's survival, given its geographic location next to Western, capitalist aligned states. In accordance with this vow, a staggering 400,000 Soviet troops were stationed throughout East Germany—the most troops to be stationed in any of the Soviet-aligned states at one time. Ironically, these troops meant that the GDR would constantly suffer from a crisis of legitimacy: without Soviet influence, manipulation, threats of violence, and ideologically repressive nature, the socialist GDR likely would have ended in collapse. It would have had only its hollow Marxist platform to rely upon for support, which would have been little match for the challenge posed by the GDR's proximity to the West and ability to receive uncensored information through Western radio, television, and relatives. Thus, GDR and Soviet authorities tried to compensate. They pushed the narrative that East Germany was perpetually threatened by the evils of external intervention and by dissidents employed by foreign governments.[8] They militarized the country and promoted unity—both among East Germans and with the Soviet Union—as the only way to ensure the GDR's survival.

Putin, then, had been assigned to what disappointingly seemed like a territory that was already heavily occupied, a totally militaristic state that indoctrinated its people through its control of the media, education, and societal behavior. As reality would have it, though, this utopian fantasy began to crumble in front of his eyes by the late 1980s.

THE DRESDEN CONNECTION

Putin's time in Dresden proved formative. We linger here to tell a crucial piece of the puzzle of Putin's perspective on power, control, and society. Generally speaking, in Dresden Putin was finally exposed to conditions outside of Soviet Russia and was thus surrounded by a foreign lifestyle of a significantly higher quality: he and his wife spent many a weekend traveling with their own personal car (an unheard-of luxury back in the Russian Soviet Federative Socialist Republic for anyone but the top elites), looked over German fashion magazines, bought their own stereo, and played on their own Atari gaming system, according to the research of *New York Times* correspondent Steven Lee Myers.[9]

Of course, Dresden was not comparatively better than Soviet Russia simply because a wider array of consumer goods were more available and affordable. While the East German security services, the Stasi, were indeed just as terrorizing as their former Nazi counterparts, and despite three decades of Soviet influence, by the mid- to late 1980s an independent peace and human rights movement had risen in the face of militarism and ideological conformity. What had once begun as a small mound of grievances against unmet promises of socialism, rather than as genuine hatred of Communism or Marxism or genuine love of democracy and liberalism, fomented under repressive authorities into an emergent civil society capable of rebellion. At the impetus of this democratizing movement, the city of Dresden saw more civil action and more opposition against its authorities than Putin ever imagined back in Soviet Russia, which he had left before the onset of Mikhail Gorbachev's glasnost and perestroika policies.[10]

Moreover, Putin was stationed in the East German city as surrounding Bloc states—with their governments being little more than imperialist tools of the Soviet Union to enforce its militaristic practices and repressive totalitarian ideology—were also dealing with their own resistance movements, namely Charter 77 in Czechoslovakia and Solidarity in Poland. Such civil actions were met by violent repression ordered by each of their governments and condoned by their Soviet comrades. Before these movements proved successful in hastening the end of Communism, their very existence alone signaled that perhaps totalitarian rule was not so perfect and in control as had been once perceived.[11] One of the co-authors of this book [VT] lived under Communism in Romania and visited East Germany and other Soviet satellites. He highlighted the impact of these independent initiatives in his edited volume *In Search of Civil Society: Independent Peace Movements in the Soviet Bloc* (1990), writing that,

> With immense courage and unfettered inventiveness, independent groups and movements in those countries have striven to reinvent the very notion of politics. They have discovered the basic principles that make people associate and commonly aim at the improvement of the social order. Their notion of change represents the opposite of the logic of acquiescence: they speak up against injustice, defend the values of honesty, decency, and opened, and try to purify the political realm of the corruptive relics of totalitarianism. Radical de-Stalinization culminates in the reinstatement of politics in its own right.[12]

Thus, the four or so years that Putin spent in Dresden (roughly between August 1985 and December 1989) ushered in a time of monumental turmoil and change for the entire Communist region in ways that had been largely inconceivable for many living on the inside and on the outside. Those years of social revolution bore witness to themes of civil society's awakening and political power, of the forces of democratization, of rebellion against inherently violent systems, and of the weaknesses of stagnant bureaucracies—themes that Putin would become wary of for the rest of his life and realize the need to closely manage.

It was there in Dresden, in the fall of 1989, that Putin cemented within himself an utter revulsion to any sort of spontaneous initiative from civil society—be it a massive revolt or a small demonstration on a quiet street. When the Berlin Wall fell in November 1989, German protestors flooded the streets of various cities and began raiding police buildings that had denied them freedom for decades. Putin witnessed these exhilarating moments in Dresden, but he was far from appreciative of the atmosphere of liberation. The fact that these protestors only grew more radical when the GDR reacted with its traditional repressive strategies (raids, assaults, arrests, etc.) attested to the genuine power of civil society[13] and shattered the myth of the controlling utopian state under which Putin had matured. Instead of admiring those independent centers of individual initiative that were revealing themselves strong enough to break dictatorial government control, Putin found himself confronting angry German protestors outside his KGB outpost.

Without any word from the Soviet military command on how to react—word which, of course, was sacred and necessary for every step taken or not taken—to the potential crisis, and without the authorization of any additional security forces, Putin and his colleagues found themselves desperately shoving KGB documents into the furnace all night long and fearing assault. In fact, there was so much paperwork (unsurprisingly, given that this was a surveillance outpost, and a very bureaucratic, very Soviet one, at that), the furnace exploded. Putin's colleagues attempted to destroy the remaining documents with gasoline, but even this method proved insufficient. With the Soviet military command's lack of direction and supplies (namely a promised order of napalm as the next best option for destruction of papers), the Dresden office had to load the documents on twelve trucks for safekeeping in Russia.[14] Stirlitz would never have had to do this.

Putin has since lamented what he deems as the "upsetting" nature of the Dresden protests. Several years later, in a rarely insightful interview early in Putin's political career, Putin said he sympathized with the protestors but was disappointed in their behavior against state security forces because those institutions were also part of society.[15] These words confirm Putin's status as a man of KGB culture, as a man who values the state and order over the people and their rights as human beings.[16] Additionally, Putin bemoaned the tragic silence of Moscow during the event, as well as the "paralysis of power" that essentially characterized the entire rule of supposed reformer Mikhail Gorbachev, the man who (unintentionally) helped to bring about the demise of the Soviet Union.[17] Dresden, then, plagues Putin's memory in terms of the powers of civil society and of the impotency of national authorities. The events of November and December 1989 in Germany devastated Putin, for he realized that the structure, power, and integrity of the Soviet Union were crumbling.

Moreover, those events were emblematic of the idea that "small islands of autonomy can eventually torpedo the continuum of state-controlled heteronomy."[18] Putin, then, had witnessed how social causes—such as disappointment with unfulfilled government promises, discontent under ideological dogma, and curiosity for pluralism—could culminate in the rebirth of a powerful civil society under even the most unyielding of authoritarian-bureaucratic regimes. It is this action of "humanizing the social space" and confronting officialdom that scares a man like Vladimir Putin, not to mention many of his most ardent supporters.[19]

The protests in East Germany have proved to be formative memories and fears in not only Putin's mind, but in the collective culture of a stability-craving Russia, as well, which we reference throughout the following text. It should come as no shock that Putin has spent his time in power influencing the Russian population and legal system in such a way as to best guard against the creation of independent social spaces that could potentially repeat the themes of the Dresden protests and, more generally, the destruction of the Soviet order; and, as it turns out, such a task is executed with relative ease when the national population believes—and even actively supports—their government's campaigns and excuses.

AFTER THE SOVIET FALL

When Putin, his wife, and their two daughters returned from Dresden to Leningrad after the East German events of December 1989, he took a temporary KGB assignment as the assistant chancellor for foreign relations at his alma mater, Leningrad University. In many senses, his short time abroad had transformed him into an "outsider": he had dutifully left his home in the Russian Socialist Republic in order to serve the Soviet empire on its periphery, only to return to the deathbed of his government (and, accordingly, of his political identity as a subject of the Soviet empire). But as Putin's story and Chap. 5 will go on to tell, the Soviet Union's imaginary imperial repertoire—the one that blurred the boundaries between domestic and foreign and sought to sculpt its interpellated population as citizens in an ideal image of the state—did not die with its socialist government.[20]

Within three months, Putin was offered a job as the head of the Committee for External Relations by Anatoly Aleksandrovich Sobchak, a law professor-turned-mayor of St. Petersburg between 1991 and 1996. Putin's kleptocratic habits revealed themselves quickly: he was investigated and found responsible in 1992 for the disappearance of the equivalent of $92 million in natural resource exports. These resources were Petersburg's only form of currency, thanks to devastating hyperinflation. Putin had supposedly made a deal to offer $92 million worth of metals to various foreign traders in return for public food aid—but this aid never materialized, as Putin and his friends were pocketing the money from the sales of the city's precious metals.

The corrupt deal was an early indicator for the unscrupulousness that would characterize Putin's presidential administrations. Moreover, the way in which the scandal was handled also spoke volumes to entrenched societal values on the matter: the morally versatile Sobchak did not fire Putin precisely because he showed promise as a skilled negotiator and thief. Defending Putin, Sobchak praised his employee as a man with the rare ability to carry out informal regulations and to make the corrupt comply in an otherwise lawless, broken country.[21] In essence, corruption was far from unusual or unethical in the Russia of the 1990s—it was even admired and looked to as a potential method for bettering the entire society through economic gain.

True to Sobchak's "insightful" defense, Putin made a name for himself among political administrations as someone who could get things done (but do not dare to ask him *how*). When President Boris Yeltsin's health severely declined after he shelled his own Parliament building in an attempt to control the nation's legislators, and in midst of a proliferating power struggle between Yeltsin and the rising oligarchs such as Boris Berezovsky, Vladimir Gusinsky, Mikhail Khodorkovsky, and Vladimir Potanin, Putin joined the president's team in Moscow in 1996. His various titles included the Deputy Chief of the Presidential Staff; by 1998, Yeltsin had appointed Putin to be the Director of the Federal Security Service (FSB), the successor intelligence organization to the KGB. Putin acted as a loyal protector of Yeltsin and Russia from the hungry oligarchs and crusading intelligence officers who threated Yeltsin's legitimacy in addition to that of the elites he had cultivated.[22]

In just over one year, Putin was promoted to acting prime minister of Russia. Yeltsin, considering Putin to be an intelligent and loyal person, announced he wanted Putin to be his presidential successor. Later that same day, Putin confirmed he was a presidential candidate for the fast-approaching 2000 election. It is necessary to emphasize that Putin found his way into the political spotlight not by campaigning, traveling, speaking, or appealing to the Russian masses; he worked his way to the top through a series of bureaucratic standards, top-down choices of elites, and corrupt, nepotist practices.[23] Putin did not get his start as a power-thirsty individual or as a rabble-rousing demagogue by any stretch of the imagination: rather, he was a humble, quiet, fanatical servant within the state with little connection to the rest of the citizenry. Yet the Russian population more than accepted him in the years to come.

All the while, Yeltsin had been giving annual presidential addresses in which he asserted claims that Russia needed order and that "only a strong government authority which makes reasonable decisions and is capable of ensuring their effective implementation is in a condition for fulfilling its obligations" to the people. Political engineers were, at the same time, transforming Putin's identity in order to fulfill the lame President Yeltsin's wish for his successor; after announcing his candidacy, Putin clung to this statist rhetoric. He proclaimed that Russia was undergoing a "crisis of statehood" similar to the *Smytnoye Vremya* [Time of Troubles], the term usually used to refer to the years following the death of the last tsar of the Rurik Dynasty in the late sixteenth century, thrusting the Russian Tsardom into political chaos without a leader. Furthermore, Putin declared that "Russian society was crying out for order" and needed a *vertikal vlasti* [vertical of power], or a powerful centralized authority, to stabilize the nation. In adopting the apocalyptic rhetoric of the ruling political elites of the time, Putin was able to present himself as a dedicated *gosudarstvennik* [builder, or servant, of the state] who could guarantee order and safety in the life of the country and its people.[24] With this, a star (or is it tsar?) was born, one who would continue to capitalize off of a paternalistic history.

Apartment Bombings and the Need for a National Savior

Vladimir Putin was introduced to the Russian people from the shadows during Yeltsin's presidency on a simple platform: that he could provide the country with the stability and order they desired. And this was imperative for Putin to deliver on, since unrest was high. In 1999, a Levada survey found that 58 percent of respondents preferred "that things return to the way they were before 1985" and the onset of perestroika, marking a 14 percent increase since 1994.[25]

Seeing as how Putin did not exude a compelling or sociable personality with which to capture mass popularity, he resorted to exploiting the people's fears of insecurity—the same fears that have roots from the devastation caused by the Mongol invasion almost eight centuries ago—in order to gain power. Leading up to the presidential election of March 2000, a sudden spray of apartment bombings randomly terrorized the smaller Russian cities of Buynaksk and Volgodonsk, as well as the capital city of

Moscow. These mysterious attacks of September 1999 left 293 people dead and over 1000 others injured, thrusting Russia into national panic.[26] With this very literal act of founding violence (no matter who was responsible), Putin exploited his opportunity to present himself to the nation-state as the only authority capable of making the Russian population live in the midst of a supposedly exceptional era of terrorism.

Even though Russian officials did not have proof of the perpetrator's identities, the Kremlin referred to a "Chechen trail" of (unsubstantiated) evidence and insisted the bombings were committed by a Caucasian Islamic terrorist group. This was a convenient population to target, considering Russia's long history of conflict with Chechens and other "barbaric" tribes living in the southern Caucasus Mountains, not to mention the globally rampant stereotypes of "dangerous" Muslims. Accordingly, the Russian citizenry looked to the state and its police to protect them from those deemed to be harmful elements. One deputy governor sympathized and agreed, "The more alert we are, the better we can fight the evil that has taken up residence in our country." This sudden flare of security obsessions meant Russian citizens found hope and strength in then-Prime Minister Putin, who responded to the bombings with a provocative yet "endearing" statement made on national television: "We will chase terrorists everywhere. If in an airport, then in the airport. So if we find them in the toilet, excuse me, we'll rub them out in the outhouse. And that's it, case closed."[27] His decisive (and macho) words evoked the sense that he could be Russia's next sovereign, its next protector.

Days later, there was another bombing attempt in the Russian town of Ryazan that was suspiciously omitted from the national media. This attack, unlike the others, was unsuccessful: a vigilant citizen noticed the explosives and called the police, who removed them after confirming they contained the same dangerous substance—hexogen—as the other exploded bombs. At first, the FSB commended the citizen's successful catch as a prevention of another terrorist attack. Once it was leaked that the two people seen planting the materials were FSB officers, however, the secret police organization backtracked. They suddenly remembered the bombs had never been real threats, that their presence was only part of an "exercise," and that "nothing was prevented." Later the same day, journalists began to suggest all the apartment bombings had been orchestrated by the FSB all along—but suddenly their news pieces were drowned out by Putin's immediate orders for an air raid campaign on Grozny, the capital of the Chechen Republic. After this Ryazan plot, no more deadly explosions occurred. The subject, together with the question of the FSB's involvement, was replaced in headlines by a new war with Chechnya.[28]

The FSB's contradictory statements and association with the explosives, in addition to the fact that no conclusive evidence had ever been offered by the state police to implicate Chechen Muslim terrorists in the bombings, led to a common theory on the Internet and among experts on Russian media and politics. They claimed the bombings were merely a ploy meant to unify Russians by instilling both a common fear for safety and a frenzied yearning for a fresh, reliable, and even domineering leader who was not afraid to use violence or to be bashful when confronting enemies of the nation. The bombings gave the people a reason to fear, to blame an external force, and to look for the closest source of protection—even if it came in the form of an unqualified, mysterious person in his 40s.

At the same time, the bombings gave the little-known Putin an excuse to make aggressive statements and portray himself as *the* leader capable of uniting and defending Russia. Whether or not Putin himself ordered the bombings will never be known, but it is a fact that he capitalized on the ensuing hysteria.[29] He got his start by manufacturing fear—fear that involved the killing of hundreds of Russian civilians—and then leading the public to believe he was the tough-talking, tough-acting sovereign with the answers to their insecurities.[30]

This founding violence established that the world was becoming unpredictably dangerous. Accordingly, the Kremlin was justified in its assertion that new counter-tactics were needed to combat new global threats, regardless of how many old international and national laws these methods violated. Putin's rise to the presidency marks a politically significant turning point in Russian society: the new Kremlin administration obliterated the possibility that the transitioning Russian state could move beyond the limits of its security-obsessed past. Instead, it guided the population into actively maintaining old themes of Russian history, including hyper-vigilance, distrust of difference, and a cult of personality around the leader. Each of these themes has prevailed for almost two decades now under Putin.

War as a Distracting and Mobilizing Force

The second literal occurrence of founding violence that rallied the most public support for Putin dealt with the wars in Chechnya. Putin treated the apartment bombings as a pretext for the Second Chechen War. The fighting was launched on 1 October 1999 when he declared the authority of Chechen President Aslan Maskhadov to be illegitimate and announced that Russian troops would be sent to the region. Russia and Chechnya had been in conflict for years and had already gone to war from 1994 to 1996 over the Chechen Republic's claims of independence from the Russian nation-state. However, this war was not very popular among the Russian citizenry and even the Russian military. Their opposition was summed up by the resignation statement of the deputy commander of the Russian Ground Forces, General Eduard Vorobyov: "It is a crime to send the army against its own people."[31]

With one short complaint, Vorobyov unleashed (probably unintentionally) a slew of political ailments. First off, his comment suggested that the state was not fulfilling its duty to protect the lives of its population—in fact, it was actively killing those living within its borders. What good could the state be bringing to the people, then, and why should it rule them? Additionally, Vorobyov was a high-ranking military official; the Kremlin could not simply ignore him, as the military is a major institution of the Russian state (as well as most others around the world). As French philosopher Michel Foucault would argue, this dissonance between the military representative and the central government would indicate that the latter did not, in fact, enjoy sovereign power if its own institutions did not adhere to policy.[32] Although Putin was working in St. Petersburg's city government at the time of the First Chechen War, he carried with him the awareness of the kinds of dangers a person like Vorobyov presented to authority. Putin would ensure that his future actions were presented in ways (e.g. via biopolitical persuasion, to be discussed in Chap. 5) that insulated him from such criticism. This was the case with the Second Chechen War.

The second time around, Russians approached the idea of a Chechen war differently. Owing to the fear aroused by Russian government's unresolved blaming of the 1999 apartment bombings on the Chechens, a majority of the Russian population came to see the Chechen Islamists as non-human beasts eager to unleash unfathomable horrors upon the innocent. The painting of Chechens and Muslims as terrorists helped to unite Russia, giving the people a commonality and a slightly more defined national identity than the ambiguous one they had been left to piece together upon the fall of the Soviet Union. They now felt more united based upon the discovery of the exclusionary idea that Islamic Chechens were now enemies who did not fit into the Russian identity. Yugoslav writer Danilo Kiš's definition of nationalism can be seen at play here, holding that "Nationalism is first and foremost paranoia, individual and collective paranoia. As collective paranoia it is the product of envy and fear and primarily the result of a loss of individual consciousness; it is thus nothing but a set of individual paranoias raised to the degree of paroxysm."[33]

Mikhail Gorbachev, the last leader of the Soviet Union, also gave into the paranoia of the need for security when he offered a ringing endorsement of Putin's call to war, stating, "I have no doubt he took the right decision. It was essential to destroy a hotbed of terrorism in Chechnya."[34] National rhetoric began to proclaim that anyone who did not support the war in Chechnya was a traitor dishonoring both the Russian army and nation. (Anatoly Chubais, a figure famous for introducing private ownership and market economics in the 1980s and 1990s, was a major proponent of this language.)[35]

Most Russian citizens, then, came to support the Second Chechen War. More importantly, they came to support Putin himself. In August 1999, just one month before this next war began, only two percent of Russian voters favored Putin for the upcoming presidential election; by November of that same year, almost two months after the start of the second war, the percentage had vaulted to 45 percent.[36] By the time the presidential election occurred on 26 March 2000, Putin managed to win with 53 percent of the national vote.[37] His mastery of biopolitics, fear-mongering, and strong-arming had succeeded in convincing the population that they *needed* an empowered authority to protect their lives.

Recognizing the Need for the People's Approval

It is essential to recognize that Putin never just took power for himself. There was more at work in his rise to power rather than simply the dominant narrative of Putin as an all-powerful dictator. In order to gain power, he required the consent of the Russian citizenry. Similar to cases of past populist dictators like Hitler, as Hannah Arendt reminded the intellectual world, Putin knew he needed to win the approval of a majority of the people if he hoped to achieve his own interests.[38] By appealing to the security of the nation-state through the apartment bombings and gambits in Chechnya, Putin's actions implicitly admit that he could only take power if the people willed him to do so.

He had to first psychologically manipulate the people into believing he was a necessary requirement for the safety of Russian citizens. Putin (rather, the media controlled by the Kremlin) convinced people that their needs were one and the same with the nation's. Then he had to set the fear that the most pressing priority was national security, which his Kremlin wrote into the National Security Concept in January 2000 by adhering to the idea that "a number of states are stepping up efforts to weaken Russia politically."[39] Combined with the national security risks which the Kremlin and FSB generated on their own, these words and fears led the Russian population to demand that their leader be entrusted with the state's power.

Furthermore, Putin himself was not the original source of such populist, security-focused rhetoric. While his presence as the Russian president was a crucial impetus for instituting this distrustful worldview among the state's population, these ideas have been embedded within Russian history from its very beginning, as was already discussed in Chap. 2. This follows the logic of American moral philosopher Eric Hoffer, who wisely stated in his book, *The True Believer* (1951), that a leader "cannot create the conditions which make the rise of a movement possible."[40] Only once the majority aids the establishment of these conditions *might* a leader become indispensable. Putin, at the start of his political rise to power, served partly as a vessel that communicated a larger historical political script (the need for internal security and fear of the external) to the entire population.

Through increased propaganda and the preaching of this script, however, Putin has since emerged as a political actor in his own right, one with the authority to steer the already-existent Russian national narrative, to decide who the next enemy is, and to manipulate both law and public opinion, domestically and internationally, with impunity. Coincidentally, these exploitative techniques constitutive of Putin's regime are also located at the core of Leninism. No doubt these Messianic similarities, while probably not consciously recognized, eased the transition from the Soviet Union to a "democratic" Russia for those who sought security, familiarity, and continuity between their pre-1991 life and post-1991 life.[41]

Putin's "Millennium Speech," an address he delivered to the nation on 30 December 1999 as prime minister, is exemplary of his rhetorical devices and emotional manipulation. He struck fear into the Russian citizenry by cautioning them, "For the first time in the past 200 to 300 years, [Russia] is facing a real threat of sliding to the second, and possibly even third, echelon of world states." This threat would prevent Russia and its population from becoming "better, richer, stronger, and happier," Putin warned.[42] In order to carry on Russia's "preconditioned" status as a great power, Putin convinced his listeners that they needed a strong state with a strong leader (read "Putin"). What journalist Andrew Jack shared in his book, *Inside Putin's Russia: Can There Be Reform Without Democracy* (2004), should come as no surprise, then: in one of Putin's earliest meetings with the recently-elected parliament's party leaders in December 1999, the new president toasted not to democracy, but to Comrade Stalin.[43]

Barely three months later in March 2000, voters made it clear that they had heeded Putin's words about the need for strong leadership. Exit pollsters heard justifications of people who had chosen Vladimir Putin to be Russia's next president along the lines of, "We long for a strong power, power that is united. We are the kind of people who need an arbiter." Even more remarkably, this exact statement was uttered by a Chechen man who also admitted he had been discriminated against with fervor since the start of the Second Chechen War—but he still believed it was more important for Putin to guide the country to safety rather than for his own biopolitical identity to be respected.[44]

The media also portrayed Putin as the spokesperson for the entire nation. Putin's name became synonymous with Russia as a whole. Head of the Russian State Agency for Youth Vasily Yakemenko said at a seminar in December 2011 with the pro-Kremlin youth group *Nashi* [Ours], "Imagine that the government is the husband, and that all of us—the society—is the wife. In 2000, our society married Vladimir Vladimirovich Putin. Society voted for him and said: Vladimir Vladimirovich, be our husband, care for us, protect us, and give us work."[45] Yakemenko's statement expresses the Russian population's fetishization of Putin as a strongman. They fancied Putin as Russia incarnate and called on him as their sovereign.

They were so enthusiastic about him that he did not even campaign for the presidential election or show up for nationally televised presidential candidate debates. In fact, all Putin needed to do was roughly conform, without straying too far, to the idolized personality his voters imagined for him.[46] For example, Putin made a point of never appearing on national TV with alcohol, in an effort to further distance himself from associations with the economic and political chaos of the frequently drunk President Boris Yeltsin's administration. This willingness of the population to loudly call for an autocratic leader evidences how the people so desperately desired stability and found promise in Putin.

In the words of Oleg Orlov, leader of a civil rights group (known as *Memoriyal* [Memorial]) dedicated to both uncovering Soviet-era political repressions and monitoring current human rights violations in Russia, "People agreed on a pact with the devil." They had sought to give their individual freedoms up to Putin in return for his guarantees of economic stability. Some citizens responded to criticisms similar to Orlov's with disgust; after all, they reasoned, "What good is freedom of speech if my fridge is empty?"[47] Retorts like this stress that the people voted for Putin because they believed he could make them live. To them, the state's guarantee of life was a greater priority than that of individual rights.

At first, Putin made good on the population's expectations. Owing more money to the International Monetary Fund than the state possessed in its foreign currency reserves, Russia had gone bankrupt under Yeltsin before Vladimir Putin was elected to the presidency in 2000. After Putin's first eight years as president, the World Bank declared Russia had almost attained a macroeconomic revolution, largely through reforming the tax system, enacting state control of the oil and natural gas sectors, and penetrating international energy markets.[48] The Russian economy grew from the twenty-third largest in the world in 1999 to the ninth largest in 2008.[49] The state's nominal gross domestic product had increased six-fold, and some economists projected the value could reach $2 trillion before 2010.[50] In 2008, Russia was the most economically prosperous it had ever been; the average Russian got to experience some of this wealth for a change, as salaries had risen from 2200 rubles ($90) in 2000 to 12,500 rubles ($500), and the poverty rate halved to 14 percent.[51] Putin was hailed as *TIME*'s 2007 Person of the Year for saving "a country on the verge of becoming a failed state."[52]

Meanwhile, outside of these achievements, Putin was busy making political changes. He continued Yeltsin's tactic of concocting fake, docile opposition groups. He limited the voters' voice in gubernatorial elections, replacing their popular elections with Kremlin appointments. Freedom House re-ranked Russia from "partially democratic" to "not free" in 2007, citing a cornucopia of reasons, the highlights of which include the assassination of journalist Anna Politkovskaya (a brave and hugely vocal critic of the Kremlin's policies in Chechnya), the suffocation of the independent media, the explosion of government corruption, and the crackdowns on foreign-funded NGOs.[53] Still, these violations of political rights added up to a cost that most Russians were willing to pay (and be silent about) in return for stable wages, pensions, consumer goods, and so on. The spirit of the common Soviet phrase, "sausages for freedom," apparently did not die with the Union.[54]

Shaking the Unshakeable: Crises of the Economy and Legitimacy

Russia's economic success during Putin's first two presidential terms earned Putin the title of "The Most Effective Economic Reformer Russia Has Ever Had."[55] But as time went on, Russia's economic statistics told a different story. The global financial crisis that had begun in 2007 with the U.S. housing bubble collapse reached Russia just as Putin was swapping the presidential office with Dmitry Medvedev's prime ministerial one in May 2008. Although Russia's economy recovered from the ensuing Great Recession by the end of 2009, the inadequacies of Putin's policies of the previous eight years—namely the failure to diversify and a dependency on energy sales—had been exposed.[56]

When Putin was elected in 2012 as president for the third time, he understood the state's GDP growth would not boom as it had previously done during his first two terms. The state was simply too dependent on oil and gas. While these can be lucrative trade items, they are also highly sensitive to global price fluctuations, which can spell economic disaster (and did, in Russia's case, for their sales comprised over 51 percent of the nation's entire budget).[57] By 2014, this dependency, as well as the impact of sanctions imposed by Western nations over Russia's invasion of Ukraine and illegal annexation of Crimea, had brought about an economic situation worse than that of 2008–2009. Average wages fell by ten percent in 2015, the first year since 2009 to see a negative GDP growth rate (−2.828 percent, specifically).[58]

Putin had failed to deliver a stable economy. Fortunately for him, economics rarely offer the whole picture when it comes to the rise of populist, politically extreme, fascist, and totalitarian governments. It had never been merely his economic program about which the electorate cared: he had already been exploiting the most volatile of all public paranoias through an ideological program focused on national security in the face of a dangerous West. With the help of the media, education, the Russian Orthodox Church, and other avenues of public messaging, Putin has managed to increase, or at least retain, his domestic popularity ratings. For almost two decades, he has succeeded in distracting the public from economic and social woes even as national poverty levels rise, average incomes plummet, and the state continues to spend over five percent of its already weakened GDP on defense.[59]

What better way to ensure power over a citizenry than to shape their mentalities and ethics through an indoctrinating ideology? Those who are shocked that Russia is still trudging on as a nation-state despite its economic failures are searching for answers to the wrong question in the wrong places. Instead, they must understand the most significant (and most-overlooked) aspect of Putinism: ideological at its core, it has always been most preoccupied with instituting an ideological layer among society.

Some thinkers might argue here that all nation-states require some degree of ideological manipulation and promotion of a nationalist myth amidst their subjects; accordingly, they might then insist Russia is nothing special on that front. We, however, disagree with such reasoning because not all national myths imply an ideology, much less a rather totalizing ideological layer that is inherently violent, isolating, and atomizing. But this is the case in today's Russia. The nationalist forces which the Kremlin and Russian society propagate are so intense that they affect the political direction of the country enough to set Putin's Russia apart from most other nation-states and the cultures and beliefs they promote. So, yes, while the point made by political scientists like Ilya Prizel that "Every polity relies on a mythical national ideal that determines the contours of its political life and institutions" is true, the Russian case takes this to an abnormal, troubling level.[60]

For this reason, Chaps. 4 and 5 are, respectively, dedicated to investigating the origins and practices of ideology, the quintessential form of state legitimation, in Russia.

Notes

1. Anne Reid, *Leningrad: The Epic Siege of World War II, 1941–1944* (New York: Walker and Company, 2011), p. 410.
2. Masha Gessen, *The Man Without a Face: The Unlikely Rise of Vladimir Putin* (New York: Riverhead Books, 2012), pp. 48–49 and 52. Starting as a low-level Latvian Communist guerrilla, Yan Berzin made a name for himself as a talented Bolshevik for his work in organizing and executing Vladimir Lenin's Red Terror. After working for the Cheka, one of the earliest iterations of the Bolsheviks' secret police, he became the first head of an expanded military intelligence service, the *Glavnoye Razvedyvatel'noye Upravleniye* [Main Intelligence Directorate] (commonly referred to as the GRU). Berzin particularly focused on building up the GRU's command over the collection of foreign intelligence and espionage. He even personally recruited many intelligence operatives, planned infiltration attempts in

various countries, and spent time in Spain supervising the Republican Army during the Spanish Civil War. Ironically—yet, in no way shockingly, to those versed in Leninism, Stalinism, and/or Communism—Berzin was executed in 1938 as part of a Stalinist purge. While the first leader of the GRU, the one admired by young Putin, died in disgrace, the GRU continued on: it still thrives today under Putin's leadership as Russia's largest arm of foreign intelligence, and in a brand-new building complex that cost almost 10 billion rubles to construct. In 2010, the GRU underwent a slight name change to the Main Directorate of the General Staff of the Armed Forces of the Russian Federation, or the GU. Small changes aside, though, Putin still seems to admire this foreign intelligence agency just as he did as a boy; in fact, the GU was crucial to Russia's illegal annexation of Crimea in 2014. Jeffrey T. Richelson, *A Century of Spies: Intelligence in the Twentieth Century* (Oxford and New York: Oxford University Press, 1995), pp. 58–59 and 88–89; Gordon M. Hahn, *Ukraine Over the Edge: Russia, the West and the "New Cold War"* (Jefferson: McFarland & Company, Inc., Publishers, 2018), pp. 268–269.
3. Vladimir Tismaneanu, "BOOK REVIEW: The new tsar: the rise and reign of Vladimir Putin. By Steven Lee Myers," *International Affairs*, Vol. 92, Iss. 3 (1 May 2016), p. 743.
4. Richard Sakwa, *Putin: Russia's Choice* (New York: Routledge, 2008), p. 6. Furthermore, Sakwa also noted that Stirlitz's character was dedicated to the task of protecting his Soviet Motherland from foreign enemies, rather than from internal opposition to Communist rule. Whereas Sakwa erroneously takes this to mean that Putin is not ideological himself, we approach this interest of Putin's as groundwork for the besieged-fortress mentality he would strongly promote, beginning in his first presidential term. That mentality rather conveniently feeds into Putinist ideology, as Chap. 5 will discuss in greater detail.
5. Ivan Zasoursky, *Media and Power in Post-Soviet Russia* (New York: Routledge, 2016), p. 238.
6. Catharine Theimer Nepomnyashchy, "The Blockbuster Miniseries on Soviet TV: Isaev-Stierliz, the Ambiguous Hero of Seventeen Moments in Spring," *The Soviet and Post-Soviet Review*, Vol. 29, No. 3 (2002), pp. 275–276; Nina L. Khrushcheva, "Homo Sovieticus," *Los Angeles Times*, 24 September 2000. Russian society was so interested in Stirlitz that when Vyacheslav Tikhonov, the actor most famous for his role as the Soviet super-spy, died in December 2009, then-President Dmitri Medvedev and the Foreign Intelligence Service of the Russian Federation sent their condolences to the Tikhonov family. "Svoi soboleznovanija sem'e aktera Vjacheslava Tihonova vyrazil Dmitrij Medvedev" [Dmitry Medvedev expressed his condolences to the family of actor Vyacheslav Tikhonov], *Rossiyskaya gazeta*, 4 December 2014.

7. Timothy Snyder, *The Road to Unfreedom: Russia, Europe, America* (New York: Tim Duggan Books, 2018), p. 44.
8. Vladimir Tismaneanu, "Against Socialist Militarism: The Independent Peace Movement in the German Democratic Republic," in *In Search of Civil Society: Independent Peace Movements in the Soviet Bloc*, ed. Vladimir Tismaneanu (New York: Routledge, 1990), pp. 135–137.
9. Steven Lee Myers, *The New Tsar: The Rise and Reign of Vladimir Putin* (London: Simon and Schuster, 2015), p. 42.
10. Tismaneanu, "The new tsar," p. 743; Richard Lourie, *Putin: His Downfall and Russia's Coming Crash* (New York: Thomas Dunne Books, 2017), p. 39; Tismaneanu, "Against Socialist Militarism," pp. 144–146 and 169–170.
11. Vladimir Tismaneanu, "Preface," in *In Search of Civil Society: Independent Peace Movements in the Soviet Bloc*, edited by Vladimir Tismaneanu (New York: Routledge, 1990), p. vii.
12. Tismaneanu, "Preface," p. viii.
13. Tismaneanu, "Against Socialist Militarism," p. 173.
14. Karen Dawisha, *Putin's Kleptocracy: Who Owns Russia?* (New York: Simon and Schuster Paperbacks, 2014), p. 47.
15. Andrei Kolesnikov and Natalya Timakova. *Ot pervogo lica: razgovory s Vladimirom Putinym* (Moscow: Vagrius, 2000).
16. Alain Besançon, interview by Marius Stan and Vladimir Tismaneanu, "I'm for the Cold War!" *Contributors.ro*, 28 June 2015.
17. Fiona Hill and Clifford G. Gaddy, *Mr. Putin: Operative in the Kremlin* (2013) p. 19; Myers, *The New Tsar*, pp. 49–51; Michael Stuermer, *Putin and the Rise of Russia* (New York: Pegasus Books, 2009), pp. 91–93.
18. Vladimir Tismaneanu, "Epilogue," in *In Search of Civil Society: Independent Peace Movements in the Soviet Bloc*, ed. Vladimir Tismaneanu (New York: Routledge, 1990), p. 181.
19. Tismaneanu, "Against Socialist Militarism," p. 174.
20. Adeeb Khalid, "The Soviet Union as an Imperial Formation: A View from Central Asia," in *Imperial Formations*, eds. Anna Laura Stoler, Carole McGranahan, and Peter C. Perdue (Santa Fe: School for Advanced Research Press, 2007), p. 114.
21. Hill and Gaddy, *Mr. Putin*, p. 15.
22. Myers, *The New Tsar*, pp. 122–123. In a lesser-known twist of fate, Yeltsin also displayed professional appreciation for Boris Nemtsov. In 1997, Yeltsin appointed Nemtsov as first deputy prime minister, a position through which Nemtsov combatted the-then eroding influences of the oligarchs. Such a role made Nemtsov vulnerable, though, and when the national economy collapsed in 1998, his reputation was tarnished by association. Had it not have been for that economic misfortune, scholarly diplomats

like Michael McFaul theorize that Nemtsov might have been Yeltsin's pick for successor, not Putin. Where Nemtsov stalled, Putin rose. And Nemtsov forever remained an enemy of Putin not only because he was once a direct rival, but moreover because he stood with civil society and against economic and political mafias. His assassination on 27 February 2015 is a blatant indictor that Putin's Russia has ascended to criminal levels of political extremism that also engage in blunt terror of the populace. Michael McFaul, *From Cold War to Hot Peace: An American Ambassador in Putin's Russia* (New York: Houghton Mifflin Harcourt Publishing Company, 2018), pp. 58–59; Vladimir Tismaneanu and Marius Stan, "Counter-Revolution and Political Murder in Putin's Russia," *FrontPage Magazine*, 8 March 2015; and Amy Knight, "The Crime of the Century," *New York Review of Books*, 21 March 2019.

23. Masha Gessen, *The Future is History: How Totalitarianism Reclaimed Russia* (New York: Riverhead Books, 2017), p. 205.
24. Hill and Gaddy, *Mr. Putin*, pp. 37, 45, and 49; Anna Arutunyan, *The Putin Mystique: Inside Russia's Power Cult* (Northampton: Olive Branch Press, 2015), p. 4.
25. Gessen, *The Future is History*, p. 202.
26. Julie A. Cassiday and Emily D. Johnson, "Putin, Putiniana and the Question of a Post-Soviet Cult of Personality," *The Slavonic and East European Review*, Vol. 88, No. 4 (October 2010), p. 685; Edward Lucas, *The New Cold War: Putin's Russia and the Threat to the West* (New York: St. Martin's Press, 2014), p. 29.
27. Remi Camus, "'We'll Whack Them, Even in the Outhouse': On a Phrase by V.V. Putin," *Kultura* (October 2006), p. 3; Gessen, *The Man Without a Face*, p. 38; David Satter, *The Less You Know, the Better You Sleep: Russia's Road to Terror and Dictatorship Under Yeltsin and Putin* (New Haven and London: Yale University Press, 2016), p. 2.
28. Ben Judah, *Fragile Empire: How Russia Fell In and Out of Love with Vladimir Putin* (New Haven: Yale University Press, 2013), p. 32; Gessen, *The Man Without a Face*, pp. 23 and 39; Satter, *The Less You Know*, p. 11. To add to suspicions of government involvement, Gennadiy Seleznyov, a member of the Russian State Duma, announced in an official session on 13 September that a building in Volgodonsk had been blown up—three days prior to its actual destruction on 16 September. Seleznyov says he had gotten the information from an FSB officer.
29. Jordan Luber, "Putin May Have Bombed His Own Metro," *Public Seminar*, 19 April 2017; Amy Knight, *Orders to Kill: the Putin Regime and Political Murder* (New York: Thomas Dunne Books, 2017), pp. 80–99.
30. Marc Bennetts, *I'm Going to Ruin Their Lives: Inside Putin's War on Russia's Opposition* (London: Oneworld Publications, 2014), p. 15.

31. Carlotta Gall and Thomas de Waal, *Chechnya: Calamity in the Caucasus* (New York: New York University Press, 1998), p. 179.
32. Michel Foucault, *Discipline and Punish: The Birth of the Prison* (New York: Vintage Books, 1977), p. 7.
33. Danilo Kiš, "The Gingerbread Heart, or Nationalism," in *Homo Poeticus: Essays and Interviews*, ed. Susan Sontag (New York: Farrar Straus Giroux, 1995), p. 15.
34. Mikhail Gorbachev, *The New Russia* (Cambridge: Polity Press, 2016), p. 142.
35. Arkady Ostrovsky, *The Invention of Russia: From Gorbachev's Freedom to Putin's War* (New York: Viking Press, 2015), p. 261.
36. Satter, *The Less You Know*, p. 12.
37. Ostrovsky, *The Invention of Russia*, p. 258.
38. Hannah Arendt, *Origins of Totalitarianism* (New York: Meridian Books, 1958), p. 139.
39. Official Internet Resources of the President of Russia, *Koncepcija nacional'noj bezopasnosti Rossijskoj Federacii (utratila silu)*, Official Internet Resources of the President of Russia, 10 January 2000.
40. Eric Hoffer, *The True Believer: Thoughts on the Nature of Mass Movements* (New York: Harper Perennial, 1989), pp. 111 and 113.
41. Geoffrey Hosking, "The Russian National Myth Repudiated," in *Myths and Nationhood*, eds. Geoffrey Hosking and George Shöpflin (New York; Routledge, 1997), p. 209.
42. Vladimir Putin, "Rossija na rubezhe tysjacheletij," speech, 30 December 1999.
43. Andrew Jack, *Inside Putin's Russia: Can There Be Reform Without Democracy?* (New York: Oxford University Press, 2004), p. 14.
44. Gessen, *The Man Without a Face*, p. 148.
45. Anna Garbuznyak, "Zapad dolzhen uvidet' pravil'nuju kartinku," *Moskovskie Novosti*, 25 November 2011.
46. Gessen, *The Man Without a Face*, p. 31.
47. Bennetts, *I'm Going to Ruin Their Lives*, p. 6.
48. Konstantin Rozhnov, "Russia Attracts Investors Despite its image," BBC News, 30 November 2007.
49. Hill and Gaddy, *Mr. Putin*, p. 145.
50. Center for Strategic and International Studies, "Economic Change in Russia," Center for Strategic and International Studies, 2009.
51. Sputnik News, "Russia's economy under Vladimir Putin: achievements and failures," Sputnik News, 3 January 2008.
52. Richard Stengel, "Person of the Year 2007: Choosing Order Before Freedom," *TIME*, 19 December 2007; Hill and Gaddy, *Mr. Putin*, p. 145. The extent to which "Putin's policies contribute[d] to economic success

from 1999 to 2008" is questionable, as his time in office happened to coincide with a sharp increase in global oil prices. Nevertheless, Putin was still credited with reviving the nation's economy.
53. Freedom House, "Freedom in the World 2007: Russia," *Freedom House*, 2007; Bennetts, *I'm Going to Ruin Their Lives*, p. 6.
54. Daphne Skillen, *Freedom of Speech in Russia: Politics and Media from Gorbachev to Putin* (New York: Routledge, 2017), p. 26.
55. Harry G. Broadman, "Putin May Be The Most Effective Economic Reformer Russia Has Ever Had," *Forbes*, 30 September 2015.
56. Megan Davies, "Insight: No more easy pickings in Russia's banking market," *Reuters*, 22 May 2013.
57. Broadman, "Putin May Be."
58. Kathrin Hille, "Russia: Putin's balance sheet," *Financial Times*, 7 April 2016; the World Bank, "Russia: GDP growth (annual %)," the World Bank, 2018.
59. Molly K. McKew, "Putin's real long-game," *Politico*, 1 January 2017.
60. Ilya Prizel, "Nationalism in Postcommunist Russia: From Resignation to Anger," in *Between Past and Future: The Revolutions of 1989 and Their Aftermath*, eds. Sorin Antohi and Vladimir Tismaneanu (Budapest and New York: Central European University Press, 2000), p. 335.

References

Arendt, Hannah. 1958. *Origins of Totalitarianism*. New York: Meridian Books.
Arutunyan, Anna. 2015. *The Putin Mystique: Inside Russia's Power Cult*. Northampton: Olive Branch Press.
Bennetts, Marc. 2014. *I'm Going to Ruin Their Lives: Inside Putin's War on Russia's Opposition*. London: Oneworld Publications.
Besançon, Alain. 2015. "I'm for the Cold War!" Interview by Marius Stan and Vladimir Tismaneanu. *Contributors.ro*, June 28. Transcript available at http://www.contributors.ro/cultura/%E2%80%9Csunt-pentru-razboiul-rece%E2%80%9D-un-dialog-cu-alain-besanc%CC%A7on-realizat-de-marius-stan-%C8%99i-vladimir-tismaneanu-paris-28-iunie-2015/
Broadman, Harry G. 2015. Putin May Be The Most Effective Economic Reformer Russia Has Ever Had. *Forbes*, September 30. Accessed 5 January 2017 at http://www.forbes.com/sites/harrybroadman/2015/09/30/putin-may-be-the-most-effective-economic-reformer-russia-has-ever-had/#463c19995fc1
Camus, Remi. 2006. 'We'll Whack Them, Even in the Outhouse': On a Phrase by V.V. Putin. *Kultura*, October.
Cassiday, Julie A., and Emily D. Johnson. 2010. Putin, Putiniana and the Question of a Post-Soviet Cult of Personality. *The Slavonic and East European Review* 88 (4): 681–707.

Center for Strategic and International Studies. 2009. Economic Change in Russia. *Center for Strategic and International Studies*. Accessed 5 January 2017 at https://www.csis.org/programs/russia-and-eurasia-program/russia-and-eurasia-past-projects/economic-change-russia

Davies, Megan. 2013. Insight: No More Easy Pickings in Russia's Banking Market. *Reuters*, May 22. Accessed 5 January 2017 at http://www.reuters.com/article/us-russia-banks-insight-idUSBRE94L07920130522

Dawisha, Karen. 2014. *Putin's Kleptocracy: Who Owns Russia*. New York: Simon and Schuster Paperbacks.

Foucault, Michel. 1977. *Discipline and Punish: The Birth of the Prison*. New York: Vintage Books.

Freedom House. 2007. Freedom in the World 2007: Russia. *Freedom House*. Accessed 5 January 2017 at https://freedomhouse.org/report/freedomworld/2007/russia

Gall, Carlotta, and Thomas de Waal. 1998. *Chechnya: Calamity in the Caucasus*. New York: New York University Press.

Garbuznyak, Anna. 2011. Zapad dolzhen uvidet' pravil'nuju kartinku [The West Needs to See the Real Picture]. *Moskovskie Novosti*, November 25. Accessed 4 January 2017 at http://mn.ru/politics/20111125/307770840.html

Gessen, Masha. 2012. *The Man Without a Face: The Unlikely Rise of Vladimir Putin*. New York: Riverhead Books.

———. 2017. *The Future Is History: How Totalitarianism Reclaimed Russia*. New York: Riverhead Books.

Gorbachev, Mikhail. 2016. *The New Russia*. Cambridge: Polity Press.

Hahn, Gordon M. 2018. *Ukraine Over the Edge: Russia, the West and the "New Cold War"*. Jefferson: McFarland & Company, Inc.

Hill, Fiona, and Clifford G. Gaddy. 2013. *Mr. Putin: Operative in the Kremlin*. Washington, DC: The Brookings Institution.

Hille, Kathrin. 2016. Russia: Putin's Balance Sheet. *The Financial Times*, April 7. Accessed 5 January 2017 at https://www.ft.com/content/cbeae0fc-f048-11e5-9f20-c3a047354386

Hoffer, Eric. 1989. *The True Believer: Thoughts on the Nature of Mass Movements*. New York: Harper Perennial.

Hosking, Geoffrey. 1997. The Russian National Myth Repudiated. In *Myths and Nationhood*, ed. Geoffrey Hosking and George Shöpflin, 198–210. New York: Routledge.

Jack, Andrew. 2004. *Inside Putin's Russia: Can There Be Reform Without Democracy?* New York: Oxford University Press.

Judah, Ben. 2013. *Fragile Empire: How Russia Fell In and Out of Love with Vladimir Putin*. New Haven: Yale University Press.

Khalid, Adeeb. 2007. The Soviet Union as an Imperial Formation: A View from Central Asia. In *Imperial Formations*, ed. Anna Laura Stoler, Carole

McGranahan, and Peter C. Perdue, 123–152. Santa Fe: School for Advanced Research Press.

Khrushcheva, Nina L. 2000. Homo Sovieticus. *Los Angeles Times*, September 24. Accessed 28 September 2018 at http://articles.latimes.com/2000/sep/24/books/bk-25823

Kiš, Danilo. 1995. The Gingerbread Heart, or Nationalism. In *Homo Poeticus: Essays and Interviews*, ed. Susan Sontag, 15–34. New York: Farrar Straus Giroux.

Knight, Amy. 2017. *Orders to Kill: the Putin Regime and Political Murder*. New York: Thomas Dunne Books.

———. 2019. The Crime of the Century. *New York Review of Books*, March 21.

Kolesnikov, Andrei, and Natalya Timakova. 2000. *Ot pervogo lica: razgovory s Vladimirom Putinym* [From the First Person: Conversations with Vladimir Putin]. Moscow: Vagrius.

Lourie, Richard. 2017. *Putin: His Downfall and Russia's Coming Crash*. New York: Thomas Dunne Books.

Luber, Jordan. 2017. Putin May Have Bombed His Own Metro. *Public Seminar*, April 19. Accessed 19 April 2017 at http://www.publicseminar.org/2017/04/putin-may-have-bombed-his-own-metro/#.WPeBURTGxZV

Lucas, Edward. 2014. *The New Cold War: Putin's Russia and the Threat to the West*. New York: St. Martin's Press.

McFaul, Michael. 2018. *From Cold War to Hot Peace: An American Ambassador in Putin's Russia*. New York: Houghton Mifflin Harcourt Publishing Company.

McKew, Molly K. 2017. Putin's Real Long-Game. *Politico*, January 1. Accessed 2 January 2017 at http://www.politico.eu/article/putin-trump-sanctions-news-hacking-analysis/

Myers, Steven Lee. 2015. *The New Tsar: The Rise and Reign of Vladimir Putin*. London: Simon and Schuster.

Official Internet Resources of the President of Russia. 2000. *Koncepcija nacional'noj bezopasnosti Rossijskoj Federacii (utratila silu)* [The National Security Concept of the Russian Federation]. *Official Internet Resources of the President of Russia*, January 10. Accessed 20 November 2016 at http://www.mid.ru/ru/foreign_policy/official_documents/-/asset_publisher/CptICkB6BZ29/content/id/589768

Ostrovsky, Arkady. 2015. *The Invention of Russia: From Gorbachev's Freedom to Putin's War*. New York: Viking Press.

Prizel, Ilya. 2000. Nationalism in Postcommunist Russia: From Resignation to Anger. In *Between Past and Future: The Revolutions of 1989 and Their Aftermath*, ed. Sorin Antohi and Vladimir Tismaneanu, 332–256. Budapest/New York: Central European University Press.

Putin, Vladimir. 1999. Rossija na rubezhe tysjacheletij" [Russia at the Turn of the Millennium]. *Speech*, 30 December. Transcript available at http://pages.uoregon.edu/kimball/Putin.htm

Reid, Anne. 2011. *Leningrad: The Epic Siege of World War II, 1941–1944.* New York: Walker and Company.
Richelson, Jeffrey T.A. 1995. *Century of Spies: Intelligence in the Twentieth Century.* Oxford/New York: Oxford University Press.
Rozhnov, Konstantin. 2007. Russia Attracts Investors Despite Its Image. *BBC News*, November 30. Accessed 5 January 2017 at http://news.bbc.co.uk/2/hi/business/7096426.stm
Sakwa, Richard. 2008. *Putin: Russia's Choice.* New York: Routledge.
Satter, David. 2016. *The Less You Know, the Better You Sleep: Russia's Road to Terror and Dictatorship Under Yeltsin and Putin.* New Haven/London: Yale University Press.
Skillen, Daphne. 2017. *Freedom of Speech in Russia: Politics and Media from Gorbachev to Putin.* New York: Routledge.
Snyder, Timothy. 2018. *The Road to Unfreedom: Russia, Europe, America.* New York: Tim Duggan Books.
Sputnik News. 2008. Russia's Economy Under Vladimir Putin: Achievements and Failures. *Sputnik News*, January 3. Accessed 5 January 2017 at https://sputniknews.com/analysis/20080301100381963/
Stengel, Richard. 2007. Person of the Year 2007: Choosing Order Before Freedom. *TIME*, December 19. Accessed 5 January 2017 at http://content.time.com/time/specials/2007/personoftheyear/article/0,28804,1690753_1690757,00.html
Stuermer, Michael. 2009. *Putin and the Rise of Russia.* New York: Pegasus Books.
Svoi soboleznovanija sem'e aktera Vjacheslava Tihonova vyrazil Dmitrij Medvedev [Dmitry Medvedev Expressed His Condolences to the Family of Actor Vyacheslav Tikhonov]. 2014. *Rossiyskaya gazeta*, December 4. Accessed 28 September 2018 at http://www.kremlin.ru/events/president/news/6244
The World Bank. 2018. *Russia: GDP Growth (Annual %).* The World Bank. Accessed 5 January 2019 at https://data.worldbank.org/indicator/NY.GDP.MKTP.KD.ZG?locations=RU
Theimer Nepomnyashchy, Catharine. 2002. The Blockbuster Miniseries on Soviet TV: Isaev-Stierliz, the Ambiguous Hero of Seventeen Moments in Spring. *The Soviet and Post-Soviet Review* 29 (3): 257–276.
Tismaneanu, Vladimir. 1990a. Against Socialist Militarism: The Independent Peace Movement in the German Democratic Republic. In *In Search of Civil Society: Independent Peace Movements in the Soviet Bloc*, ed. Vladimir Tismaneanu, 135–180. New York: Routledge.
———. 1990b. Epilogue. In *In Search of Civil Society: Independent Peace Movements in the Soviet Bloc*, ed. Vladimir Tismaneanu, 181–185. New York: Routledge.
———. 1990c. Preface. In *In Search of Civil Society: Independent Peace Movements in the Soviet Bloc*, ed. Vladimir Tismaneanu, vii–vix. New York: Routledge.

———. 2016. Book Review: The New Tsar: The Rise and Reign of Vladimir Putin. By Steven Lee Myers. *International Affairs* 92 (3): 743–745.

Tismaneanu, Vladimir, and Marius Stan. 2015. Counter-Revolution and Political Murder in Putin's Russia. *FrontPage Magazine*, March 8. Accessed 12 March 2019 at https://www.frontpagemag.com/fpm/252738/counter-revolution-and-political-murder-putins-vladimir-tismaneanu

Zasoursky, Ivan. 2016. *Media and Power in Post-Soviet Russia*. New York: Routledge.

CHAPTER 4

The Intellectual Origins of Putinism

A plethora of people who have chosen to publish articles and books about Russia, including Russian political analyst Anton Barbashin,[1] British political scientist Archie Brown,[2] American geopolitical analyst Jacob L. Shapiro,[3] and American economist Benn Steil,[4] assert that Putin's Russia has no ideology, or at least not a genuine, magnetizing one. They instead argue that the Kremlin relies upon a vast array of tactics and themes that it cobbles together and exploits as it sees fit, and that this does not amount to ideology because it is too inconsistent, incoherent, and improvised. They also cite that in December 1999, at the outset of what was to become a very long rule, Putin overtly refused "the restoration in Russia of an official state ideology" and thus take this as proof that Putin's Russia cannot be ideological in nature.[5]

To those not under the Kremlin's spell, Putin's rhetoric and policies may be totally chaotic (and even evoke the feeling of listening to someone who suffers from an intense multiple personality disorder of some sort, as some scholars have expressed), but to assume that no ideology is at play because of these inconsistencies, because Putin publicly denied its very possibility, and because the current situation *on the surface* does not resemble the monolith of Communist dictatorship, is simply shortsighted.[6] Considering how the world is experiencing a rise in extremist movements on both the far Right and far Left, it is necessary to fathom the reasons for which masses of people are opting for racist, xenophobic, homophobic, and exclusionary societies crafted through violence. Without

© The Author(s) 2020
K. C. Langdon, V. Tismaneanu, *Putin's Totalitarian Democracy*,
https://doi.org/10.1007/978-3-030-20579-9_4

a proper understanding of people's motives, illiberal ideas can never be effectively combated; in the case of Russia, Putinism could never be explained without a proper understanding of ideology.

Those who reject the notion that the Kremlin follows a particular ideology seem to be missing a major point. An ideology need not follow the models of liberal capitalism or Marxist Communism, which each maintain a fairly rigid set of goals and guidelines on how to reach them. Putin's ideology is one that has an ultimate goal—to enhance the power of the Kremlin and its control over the population, to put it most briefly and vaguely, yet accurately—but its methods vary depending on how profitable they might be in a given situation. Ideology is not an intellectual or academic theory, but a mass phenomenon. Therefore, inconsistencies or contradictions only make the ideology more real for the populations participating in it, no matter how absurd it seems to an outsider's reasoned frame. For those who embrace it, ideology is an assuaging balm, an invitation to collective rituals of adherence, enthusiasm, and regimentation. After all, *homo sovieticus* (a term referring to the Soviet revolutionary vision of a new utopian race, which will be more deeply discussed in Chap. 5) was fundamentally an ideological man. De-Sovietization is therefore tantamount, among other components, to de-ideologization. For many, this abandoning of the ideological certainties of the Soviet era has resulted in psychological torments and mental confusion. In fact, Putinism is precisely the effort to reconstruct such ideological certitudes, a rock-solid shelter meant to create the illusion of individual and collective security.[7]

Much of it is about manipulation: Russia could condemn the United States for unjustly intervening in Iraq when it suited Russia in 2003 to smear the West, but when Putin saw an opportunity to assert Russia's own global power via military means in Syria in 2015, intervention suddenly was no longer taboo. While it may not look like other traditional ideologies, Russia's Putinism is still an ideological doctrine in its own right because it embraces an entire nation and convinces the whole population that it stands for their best interests, identities, feelings, and so on.

In the case of Russia, the ruling ideology is built on a self-centered exaltation of an alleged national destiny that prides itself on its goal of stability while questioning the merits of freedom and rejecting the West as a bastion of hypocrisy. These beliefs seem non-extraordinary, but when presented by the state as "factual" and complete knowledge, result in a unique, powerful national identity. Such an identity persuades its subjects to believe their country is a superior world power that can act with impunity on the international stage. Today, the globe is seemingly infected with this trend (marked most noticeably by resurgent nationalism but comprising much more, in addition), making it all the more important to study the creation, reproduction, and dominance of ideology in the nation-state context.

Before our book attempts to unravel these abstract mysteries of popular desire, ideology, and violence when it comes to Russia and the mass enthusiasm for Vladimir Putin (even as the economy falters and domestic human rights are restricted), we first must discuss the operational points and historical foundations of Putinism. This chapter begins by elaborating upon some of the best operational definitions of ideology. Then, it explores the intellectual origins of Putinism that allowed for a strong ideology to take hold in Russia. Readers should keep in mind that this will set the stage for Chap. 5, which will at last demonstrate how ideology works to encapsulate the majority of the Russian population and what it leads them to believe. Ultimately, the current chapter and the next combine to highlight that the Putinist ideology built itself off of historical trends and cultural desires: in other words, it was never created by Putin alone.

What Is Ideology?

The term "ideology" is a rather ubiquitous, yet ambiguous concept. It lacks criteria, eludes empirical evidence, and is interpreted differently from person to person because it is filtered by internal thoughts. However, ideology can be a valuable tool and give insight into cultural phenomena such as Putin's Russia. Hannah Arendt's definition describes ideologies as "isms which ... can explain everything and every occurrence by deducing [them] from a single premise."[8] Václav Havel's interpretation of the term further expands upon Arendt's. He writes in his essay "The Power of the Powerless" (1978),

> Ideology is a specious way of relating to the world. It offers human beings the illusion of an identity, of dignity, and of morality while making it easier to *part* with them. As the repository of something "supra-personal" and objective, it enables people to deceive their conscience and conceal their glorious *modus vivendi*, both from the world and from themselves. It is a very pragmatic, but at the same time an apparently dignified, way of legitimizing what is above, below, and on either side. ... It is an excuse that everyone can use.[9]

Arendt and Havel's descriptions tell us that, for individuals, ideologies function as a sort of moral code by which its adherents are expected to live their lives; for states, they are the mythical political doctrine that maintain the nation's social structure by fundamentally altering the thoughts, values, and assumptions of those who consider it to be the correct mode of living. The code may not be strictly uniform across believers, yet it is real, coherent, just, and binding, all the same. They make any evil possible because anything can now be justified as being righteous and good, assuming the ideology is strong enough and the population is sufficiently receptive.

And even though ideology in the twenty-first century might not be identically formulated or as unquestionable as those ideologies of Stalin's, Lenin's, or Hitler's times, it is no less of a danger. The world has not yet been inoculated against ideology. It just operates more covertly, leaves smaller body counts (in most situations, although Syrians and Venezuelans would rightly refute this), and relies on more demagogic promises, philosophical assumptions, and human naiveties than it did in the twentieth century.[10] Ideology is, indeed, alive and well. Unlike the typically shrewd Archie Brown's disappointing assessment that "nothing comparable" to Soviet ideology exists today in Russia, Putin's Kremlin thrives on its own ideology that deserves just as much attention: a fatal version known as Putinism.[11]

Cheng Chen, an academic well versed in the concept of ideology, wrote a book entitled *The Return of Ideology: The Search for Regime Identities in Postcommunist Russia and China* (2016). Chen's book spends most of its space detailing "regime ideology," or a "coherent and consistent system of ideas advanced officially by state elites to define and promote a regime identity and mission."[12] Chen also formulates that ideology is not just an excuse that provides cover for the Russian state to pursue what it wants: it is truly something that its followers actually believe. Russia's ideology is most effective because it balances the need to be coherent enough to explain what the regime is doing and why the regime is doing it with the need to be flexible enough to adjust itself while retaining legitimacy with the people. Ideology, then, is not simple. Chen's definition is immensely helpful in the pursuit of understanding Putin's Russia and the way the Kremlin operates. However, these authors depart from Chen in insisting that "regime ideology" is not all that matters in Russia because the people's perspectives are equally important. Our book takes Chen's invaluable assertions on ideology but switches the focus from the elites to the masses.

The masses must be remembered especially when dealing with the Kremlin's ideology. Non-Russian people who identify within Western philosophy often cannot understand how Russian citizens support an authoritarian leader like Putin who, for instance, limits their freedoms and breaches international law. They either admit they do not understand Russia themselves or argue that it is the West that does not understand Russia's modernization attempts. They do not allow for the possibility that Russia might simply be acting tyrannically, with no goal of democratization in mind.

For example, international relations theorist John Ikenberry (to name just one figure among many) neglected the strength of ideology in Russia and discounted its unique history when he presumed the Kremlin was willing to subordinate Russia's ideological goals in order to achieve typical Western ones, such as economic prosperity or positive relations with liberal democracies.[13] Others like Stephen Cohen advance the debate that "modernization" and "democratization" in "backward" countries like Russia will appear illiberal at first because those nations are just so far behind traditional Western ones. Aside from being a racist and imperialist way of thinking in that it tolerates and diminishes the slaughter of people simply because their nations are (supposedly) undeveloped, this perspective is also fundamentally wrong. It fails to understand that, in some places, the reality does not hold that economics drives elites to liberalize, but that politics and philosophy are driving the masses to undertake oppression for a so-called higher purpose. In the latter scenario, the masses might not be cognizant enough to know that they are actively denying themselves freedom (or they are at least somewhat aware of their self-limiting behaviors, yet choose to support oppressive forces like Putin, anyway, for what they believe to be a greater goal).

And as already mentioned in our book's introduction, material or cooperative incentives do not account for what drives Putin's Kremlin. The history of autocracy and the fear of state instability are unique to Russia, after all. They create a different politico-historical context for the state's development. It cannot be assumed that Russian citizens desire the same goals and values as the West does. In actuality, the Kremlin is pursuing its own path, characterized by a state-controlled political system, a powerful president, and a critical opinion of the rest of the world. Western audiences must be sure to open their minds to the existence of this alternative culture if they want to decipher Putin's mystique and Russian national goals.

Furthermore, should an ideology be affixed to social or political goals, as it is in Russia, then the importance and constraints of dynamic logic wither. A static logic only exists in the sense that whatever Putin says and does in the name of protecting the nation goes. It is not the exact content of the Kremlin's ideology that is most important for the world to recognize, but the processes through which this ideology becomes the societal norm and informs political (in)action.[14]

Ideology and Blurring: The Progression into Totalitarianism

Ideologies work because they interpellate a target audience, making them see themselves in a larger homogeneous community to which they belong and serve a purpose. In Russia's case, this community is the nation-state, which promises belongingness, safety, and future progress to its members, claims cultural superiority, and presents itself as an unfair victim of world enemies. The nation-state's success is the believers' success; likewise, an attack on Russia or its culture is considered an attack on all members of its community. Here we see how -isms constrain political beliefs within society. By arranging political information in a specific manner, individuals are prompted to engage in political and social actions which operate within a mass schema supporting the state's narrative.[15] At the same time, the state's narrative is built around the cravings of the people for order, power, and glory.

In this way, the Kremlin's ideology cyclically legitimizes itself because it serves to validate the truths which it purports through the enforcement of certain historical narratives upon the psyches of its subjects. To believers, these stories present a logical coherence that refocus their attention on selected topics and simplify any alternatives. By controlling the narratives, the Kremlin (typically inaccurately) illustrates the world on the ideology's terms, coaxing citizens to act and think within the boundaries it delineates. This ever-reinforcing performance helps to account for the remarkable popularity of Putin's cult of personality because the ideology instills within the Russian community a common set of values that gives it legitimacy. The state can minimize and explain away its own errors among the interpellated population, errors that non-indoctrinated people may otherwise question.

A state's ideology, as is the case of Russia, can be so strong that the public passively permits the government to declare what Italian philosopher Giorgio Agamben refers to as a "state of exception," or an incident where the sovereign act against or outside of the rule of law "in the name of the public good." Such an act stirs fear in the populace because it creates a feeling of impending danger among its citizens. Political scientist Wendy Brown warns how the government's manipulation of national security fears may ease "the way for any state measure, from undertaking invasions to suspending constitutional provisions, allied with protecting the nation," whether or not the threat is genuine and the measure is proportionate.[16] This essentially makes it possible for the state to engage in whatever policies it so wishes with impunity, free of constraints from the legal and moral processes set out in the constitution or other national foundations. Simply put: if Russians believe imperialism in Ukraine and ethnic cleansing in Chechnya is the right thing to do, they will support the regime as it carries out those tasks.

In the worst cases, Hannah Arendt warns how the inexpugnability of the state can culminate in totalitarianism, where a governing ideology organizes and informs society in such a manner that it "cut[s] the moral person off from the individualist escape"; thus, it closes their minds to all but one prefabricated decision—one which agrees with the state's power and actions.[17] One of this book's authors furthers this analysis in his book *Reinventing Politics: Eastern Europe from Stalin to Havel* (1992), demonstrating how states may use ideology for the purpose of assuaging the public's doubts and "convinc[ing] them that theirs is the only rational behavior."[18] Under totalitarianism, the state of exception becomes the rule by which an otherwise lawless dictator can take control of essentially every aspect of social life, such as economics, arts, sciences, education, morals, and private behaviors of citizens. Not only does the totalitarian ideological state totally control its population's thoughts and actions, but it also seeks to mobilize (to a controllable extent) the people in pursuit of the state's goals. Thus, news of the invasion of Ukraine meets no protests and little neutral toleration among the Russian citizenry: it is wildly endorsed in an orgy of nationalist euphoria.

This *n*th stage of ideological domination—most purely exemplified by Hitler's Germany and Stalin's Soviet Union—demonstrates the force with which the soft power of ideology can transform an individual or a nation-state into a subject or tyrannical authority, respectively. As such, it is necessary to examine the inner workings of Putin's ideology in order to comprehend what makes him so popular and what defines the threatening world in which Russians believe they live. To see through the myopic eyes of interpellated Russians reveals why an illiberal leader or dictator can amass so much authority and convince an entire nation to construct an imagined version of the world beyond Russia as a zone of evil from which the nation must be defended.

Intellectual Origins of Putinism and Beyond

To understand how Putinism works today, we must consider the past. The foundations for Putinism and its success were laid long ago. After all, ideology takes a long time to cement itself, gain enough followers, get into power, and institute its beliefs in a society. As French philosopher André Glucksmann noted, some of the most effective ideologies were first accepted and tolerated "thanks to a pre-ideological anchorage."[19] If onlookers are to comprehend the contradictory yet functioning nature of Putinism, then they must be able to trace Putinism's origins back in not only Russian political history but in the deeper intellectual history of Europe, as well.

Several of those who have written about Russia have tried to explain Putin's goals using Russian philosophy. They almost all cite the infamous event at the tail end of 2013 when Putin sent three books to his senior government officials, top members of his political party United Russia, and each regional governor as gifts for the New Year and Christmas holidays. These books included *The Justification of the Good* by Vladimir Solovyov (1853–1900), *The Philosophy of Inequality* by Nikolai Berdyaev (1874–1948), and *Our Tasks* by Ivan Ilyin (1883–1954). All three authors were Russian philosophers who focused on spirituality, nationalism, and Slavophilism. Accordingly, a fair number of writers, such as David Brooks of *The New York Times*, have touted this as evidence of Putin's "highly charged and assertive messianic ideology" and of his desire to extend this mindset to Russia's policymakers.[20]

While we do not disagree with statements like Brooks', we do believe that there is more to Putinism than the teachings of Ilyin, Solovyov, Berdyaev, and other mystical, nationalist Russian philosophers. To stop here would be to ignore many other historical comprising elements and contemporary inspiring effects of Putinism that better explain how its varied themes meld together to generate a formidable worldview staunchly opposed to Westernism, democracy, human rights, pluralism, and all other bedrocks of political liberalism. It also would not explain how such a demanding worldview can become so accessible to an entire population, either—especially if these philosophical lessons are mostly directed at elite policymakers through reading materials and then only marginally messaged to the rest of the public through brief verbal references.

Regarding his references to Russian philosophers in speeches, Putin has cited Ivan Ilyin the most. A fair number of scholars who have written on Russia, including American historian Walter Laqueur and Russian political analyst Anton Barbashin, have subsequently declared Ilyin, a well-established fascist, to be Putin's favorite and most influential philosopher.[21] They focus their attention—perhaps too much attention—on Putin's scholarly following of Ilyin, referring to the man who Putin has only publicly cited a handful of times as the Russian president's personal "guru" and "prophet." In fact, French historian Marlene Laruelle attested that, as of March 2017, Putin had publicly quoted Ilyin just five times—in 2005, 2006, 2012, 2013, and 2014, to be exact. Furthermore, these references, tucked away in long speeches as supports for their main messages, on their own are not impactful enough to convince the Russian people to adopt Putin's or Ilyin's perspectives. Neither could those references alone be sufficient enough to formulate Putinism's comprehensive ideology.

It is true that Ilyin's emphasis on Messianism, authoritarianism, nationalism, centralized power, and Russian exceptionalism are crucial ingredients of Putinism. It is also true that the very fact that Putin has cited Ilyin in his presidential speeches is undeniable and telling of his outlook. But neither of these truths prove that Ilyin is *the* ideological source of Putinism. In fact, Laruelle posits that Putin's homages to Ilyin might be more of an attempt to integrate the conservative, monarchist past of Russian Tsardom (since Ilyin's status as a White émigré heavily impacted his philosophy) into modern Russian politics and Putinism's "national master narrative" that so strives to paint an eternally fractured, ill-defined nation as a strong, united state.[22] Incorporating Ilyin's messages into Putinism is a convenient method by which to unite different phases of Russian history. By calling upon a monarchist philosopher, Putinism projects the myth that Russia has been a legitimate ethno-national political community for centuries to help mask the reality that Russia has suffered catastrophic traumas of political, economic, social, demographic, and religious nature over the last few centuries.

Additionally, it is opportune to call upon Ilyin for reasons of theoretical legitimacy. The fact that his ideas were written down almost one century ago helps to legitimize Putinism's assertions and goals. For example, Ilyin's name and writings are often connected to the idea of freedom. This does not mean his thoughts on freedom are compatible with democratic or pluralistic traditions: he espoused a very different notion of freedom, one that most adherents to the Western liberal political perspective would never accept as anything but the antithesis of freedom. Heavily influenced by his upbringing in a tsarist empire, his idea of freedom contended that freedom for Russia should be every patriot's highest goal, and that only through Russia's freedom could individuals enjoy their own freedom (which he seemed to limit to the arenas of faith, truth, creation, work, and property[23]). Again, whereas this idea of a limited, lower-priority individual freedom seems self-negating to some audiences—particularly Western-oriented ones—Ilyin's conception still manages to stand in the Russian tradition because it was written down, published, republished, and representative of a historical phase in the culture's existence.

Citing Ilyin, then, helps to legitimize Putinism by virtue of representing a thoroughly Russian viewpoint from a thoroughly Russian historical moment. As historian Timothy Snyder highlighted in his book, *The Road to Unfreedom: Russia, Europe, America* (2018), Putinism gains from its invocations of Ilyin, making its message of "the freedom of the individual to submerge himself in a collectivity that subjugates itself to a leader" seem more tolerable.[24] And since Putinism has grown so strong, a message like this becomes more than merely palatable: it becomes a highly prioritized pursuit that encompasses both the beliefs of the government and the beliefs of the national population. By invoking the Russian citizenry as crucial actors in the story of whether or not their nation achieves success, Ilyin's message-turned-Putinist mobilizes the population toward a particular goal of Russian authoritarianism and superiority on the world stage. It brings awareness to this story on a daily basis, making it difficult for citizens to live unaware and/or indifferently of their duty to the nation—a nation that has been pursuing greatness for centuries, as Putinism's choice to recall Ivan Ilyin suggests.

This is not to say that Putinism exploits Ilyin for his legitimizing value only. To be clear, Putin and Putinism genuinely do share many of Ilyin's fascist and totalitarian beliefs. Ilyin, for example, espoused a desire for the attainment of a modern Russian state through totalitarian practices such as the manipulation of law (a sentiment which later proved crucial to Nazism); in essence, he believed in the idea of subordinating legality to a greater messianic Russian mission. As Snyder pointed out in an article for *The New York Review of Books* entitled "Ivan Ilyin, Putin's Philosopher of Russian Fascism," Putin acts similarly: he invokes fantasies of a higher

Russian spirituality and geopolitics to justify the Kremlin's violations of international law (all while claiming to uphold the rule of law, as Ilyin also imagined Russia would do).[25] For both Ilyin and Putin, all (or at least most) aspects of society—morals, sexual orientation, religion, patriotism, race, individual choices, and so on—are political and should be commandeered for the supposed good of the nation and its saving virtues. This view, shared by both Putin and Ilyin, is a core feature of totalitarian regimes, according to the late political scientist Jacob Talmon (1916–1980) and his pivotal work *The Origins of Totalitarian Democracy* (1952).[26]

Despite these damning similarities, at the same time it is crucial to understand that the ideas emphasized in the Putinist narrative are rooted in a larger cultural tradition, rather than in one individual philosopher.[27] Highlighting Ilyin's presence in Putin's words and the Kremlin's actions then becomes even more powerful: no longer are citations of Ilyin mere reiterations of a single man's voice, but a reverberating echo chamber that all of Russia can hear and participate in themselves. Thus, those who identify Ivan Ilyin as the ideological role model for Putin and Putinism, and accordingly insist that deep study of Ilyin will culminate in a full understanding of Putin and Putinism, are misguided in their reasoning.

Just as the ideas behind the Ilyin-oriented approach are misleading, so are the ideas of those who submit that a fascist figure other than Ilyin is Putin's ideological role model. This alternatively oft-cited figure is Aleksandr Dugin, the Russian geopolitician, professor, and champion of neo-Eurasianism[28] and Nazism. Born in 1962, Dugin has had a rather colorful career—first as a self-declared anti-Communist (and active neo-Nazi) in the 1980s, then as an advisor to Communist Party member and then-speaker of the Duma Gennadiy Seleznyov in the mid-1990s, and later as a leading member of the National Bolshevik Party and the Eurasian Movement/Party by the early 2000s. In recent years he has garnered the nickname of "Putin's Rasputin."[29] This is because Russian media regularly connects Dugin's ideas—characterized by hatred of the West and liberalism and advocacy of conspiracy theories, Slavophilism, conservatism, Russian Orthodoxy, military offensives (e.g. attacks on Georgia and explicit genocide in Ukraine), revanchist dreams of *Novorossiya*, and other fascist lines—to Putin's imperialist messages and projects, especially the Eurasian Economic Union (to be discussed in Chap. 5) and the recent invasion of Ukraine and seizure of Crimea (to be discussed in Chap. 7). Dugin has supported Putin the man in many endeavors for years now, and Putinism for decades, telling news outlets, "There are no more opponents of Putin's course, and if there are, they are mentally ill and need to be sent for medical examination. Putin is everywhere, Putin is everything, Putin is absolute, Putin is irreplaceable."[30]

As real as the ideological connections between Putin and Dugin are, it is still nonsensical to believe that Dugin is Putin's sole ideological source or just one of a few key players behind Putinism. Take, for instance, Dugin's loud opinion that Putin did not give pro-Russian separatists in the Donbas region of eastern Ukraine nearly enough aid or weaponry, nor did he take the "necessary" step of committing genocide against Ukrainians.[31] After making such statements, Dugin was removed from his position as Head of the Sociology Department at the Moscow State University (MGU) in June 2014. In typical Russian, bureaucratic fashion, MGU reasoned that its board had revoked the appointment due to a technical error during the selection process but assured Dugin that he would still work as a professor until his contract expired in September 2014. His subsequent appeals for re-appointment as department head went unfulfilled, so he chose to resign entirely from MGU. But Dugin maintains that his removal could not have happened without the approval of President Vladimir Putin himself.[32]

The fall of Dugin should highlight that Putinism is a force of its own. It does not rely on any one intellectual, nor does it rely on even a handful of individuals. Again, those who refer to Dugin as "Putin's Rasputin" commit the same errors as those who label Ilyin as Putin's prophet: they all overplay the influence of individuals on Putin's mindset. While it is true that for over a decade now, Dugin, his ideas, and his influence on Russian political discourse have been the subjects of many research projects, citations of Dugin only began to surface in Putin's speeches following the invasion of Ukraine and the international community's (weak) criticism of the event because "Dugin's brand of Eurasianist philosophy became convenient for Putin in justifying his policies vis-à-vis Ukraine."[33]

This drives home the point that Putin still picks and chooses what he references. He calls upon whatever precedents will prove useful in promoting his Kremlin's mission to restore Russian power, a mission that itself has been formulated throughout the centuries. A viewpoint as specific, violent, and vocal as Dugin's leads to operational impracticality and could (perhaps) force the international community's hand to shut out Russia or at least block Russia's access to new sources of both political and economic capital, effectively dealing Putin's empire its death knell. It would also result in too much mass mobilization and instability, which are concepts that the conservative, stability-obsessed Russian regime does its best to avoid at all costs, as will be fully described in following chapter. It is clear that the old Bolshevik adage, first expressed by Vladimir Lenin at the second All-Russian Congress of Political Education Departments in 1921, of "*Kto kogo?*"—"Who does what to whom?" or "Who wins over whom?"—is alive and well in today's Russia and itself plays a role in the functioning of Putinism. Just as Adolf Hitler was no expert on Friedrich Nietzsche, Putin is no expert on Ilyin or Dugin, or on any other intellectual, for that matter.[34] His readings of these few philosophers mean little in the big scheme of Putinism because there is so much more both behind Putin's personal interest (perhaps feigned, in some cases) in their works and behind those philosophers' views.

Just as harmful as it is to focus on a few intellectuals like Dugin or Ilyin as the driving forces behind Putinism, so is it to zero in on narrow ideological veins like Eurasianism or neo-Eurasianism, which are also terms frequently used in articles and research about Putin's Russia. To understand why these concepts are often cited and why they are not the most useful approaches to understanding Putinism, we will first briefly define what these two concepts are and how they originated.

In a sort of cosmic irony, Russian Eurasianism was arguably most shaped by the dissident poet Anna Akhmatova's son, Soviet ethnologist and historian Lev Gumilyov (1912–1992). He expanded upon the Eurasianist ideas first outlined by nineteenth-century figures like Slavophile Konstantin Leontiev (1831–1891) and early twentieth-century figures like historian Nikolai Trubetzkoy (1890–1938), treating genetics, biology, and physics as evidence that Russia was more closely related to Asian history and culture than it was to that of Europe. Ultimately, Gumilyov's Eurasianism sought to "prove" that Russia enjoyed ethnic superiority in the geographic region encompassing both Europe and Asia.

Over the past few decades, Aleksandr Dugin has revived Eurasianism under the more fascist banner of neo-Eurasianism. Both Gumilyov's original version and Dugin's revised version refer to Moscow as "the Third Rome," asserting the highly arrogant fantasy that Moscow is the center of a civilization unto itself and capable of dominating a decadent, liberal (and, as Eurasianists are quick to insist, Jewish-controlled) Europe and a backward, weaker Asia. Both are also defined by inherently racist, messianic, and millenarian outlooks.[35] Neo-Eurasianism, however, adds a more modern form of fascism to Gumilyov's original conception. Snyder captured Dugin's contributing themes best when he wrote, "In 1997, Dugin called for a 'fascism, borderless and red.' Dugin exhibited standard fascist views: democracy was hollow; the middle class was evil; Russians must be ruled by a 'Man of Destiny'; America was malevolent; Russia was innocent."[36] Thus, neo-Eurasianism represents an ideology that turns out to be much more fascist and messianic than its basic definition made it appear.

Neo-Eurasianism is all about deciphering Russia's role in the world as a country maintaining a unique position both geographically and historically. Its believers, then, insist that Russia is destined to be its own force in international politics, one that can break the traditional dichotomy of Western versus developing countries. According to Laruelle, it is "a political doctrine in the strict sense of the word, a theory of nation and ethnos, an alter-globalist philosophy of history, a new pragmatic formulation of 'Sovietism,' a substitute for the global explanatory schemes of Marxism-Leninism, a set of expansionist geopolitical principles for Russia, and much else."[37]

Having established the defining features and themes behind Eurasianism and neo-Eurasianism, we choose not to elaborate upon them for two reasons: (1) there have already been several books published that are more narrowly dedicated in scope to this concept,[38] and (2) we do not want to perpetuate the notion that Russian culture is imperialist and nationalist *because* it adheres to Eurasianist or neo-Eurasianist thought—in truth, Russian culture is imperialist and nationalist because it is fundamentally imperialist and nationalist on its own. Eurasianism and neo-Eurasianism just happen to be useful to Putinism. Thinking along the lines of Hannah Arendt, we argue that ideology is accompanied by a series of smaller, self-legitimizing lies—and that Eurasianism and neo-Eurasianism happen to be two of those smaller elements that support a larger dominant ideology while also obscuring the extent of that ideology's violent nature.

While we do not deny that these two concepts are important to understanding Russian culture, we have decided to approach their constituent elements (ideas of ethnic superiority, Russian exceptionalism, imperialism, nationalism, chauvinism, disregard for borders, hatred of the West, etc.) as separate forces that originate from a wider cultural tradition. After all, German philosopher Georg Wilhelm Friedrich Hegel (1770–1831) was a pivotal influence on Karl Marx, yet no Communist government could be explained by Hegel's works, nor did any Communist in power bother to read or incorporate Hegel's ideas into the system. Hegel was superfluous when it came to analyzing what was really going on in this situation, just as Eurasianism and neo-Eurasianism are when it comes to analyzing what is really going on in Putin's Russia. The same goes for Lev Gumilyov, Aleksandr Dugin, Ivan Ilyin, and any other philosopher considered to be Putin's "main" ideological source. Again, these are useful figures and concepts to understand, but we stress the need to contextualize them within a larger Russian culture.

If one could paint the sources and trends of Putinism, Putin might comprise a good deal of the foreground, but an entire landscape will always exist behind him. Ilyin, Dugin, Eurasianism, neo-Eurasianism, and other Russian academics (e.g. Nikolai Karamzin, Nikolai Berdyaev, Vladimir Solovyov, etc.) and ideological concepts would make up a mere few trees in the full landscape behind Putin the leader. Such a painting would be full of far more than just Russian intellectuals and their ideas: previous leaders, historical events, cultural traditions, religious beliefs, and more would be present, as well. All of these features pour into Putinism and mold it into the powerful ideology it is today.

Thus, it matters not if Putin believes all that Dugin, Ilyin, and (neo-) Eurasianism have professed. In fact, it is misleading to assume that Putin and Putinism maintain any single ideological role model, as this presumption fails to understand the greater forces behind Putinism's success and popularity in society. Nor will in-depth analyses of Eurasianism and neo-Eurasianism be sufficient enough to explain Putinism, its goals, and its popularity. The next question to tackle, then, is not about how individual Russian philosophers like Ivan Ilyin and Aleksandr Dugin, or narrower ideas like (neo-)Eurasianism, inform Vladimir Putin and Putinism. Instead, it is more prudent to ask: is Vladimir Putin merely a selfish opportunist, or is he a true believer in Putinism? And what other paradigms comprise the foundation for Putinism?

Putin the Opportunist, or Putin the Believer?

To consider these new questions, first our book considers the most direct topic: the environment in which Putin himself grew up as a literal child of the Soviet Union and as a metaphorical child of post-Soviet Russia. It has already been said in Chap. 3 that Putin is a creature of Soviet and KGB culture. He was a natural: even before he committed himself to training to become a KGB agent in his adolescent years, he had been behaving like a KGB manipulator in school, where he constantly fought and bullied other children so much that he was barred from even the Young Pioneers.

His inability to join the youth Communist organization is ironic, considering that the Soviets were innately rather savage themselves. It was this kind of pathological dissonance—the one in which the Soviets' belief in their utopian goal prevented them from realizing their utter barbarity in means (and, to be honest, the very essence of their goal)—in which Putin spent his formative years. It should be no shock, then, that Putin's rhetoric and policies (especially when compared to those of the international community) can contradict one another so often, yet still amass him huge levels of support among the population, for the majority of them have also been raised under the same psychological dissonance and sociopolitical practice of normalizing the abnormal.

Despite his barring from the Young Pioneers, Putin came to comport himself as a good Soviet citizen: he dreamed of a KGB career and soon made it within that criminal organization. Though the world did not know it when the Berlin Wall fell and Putin's KGB station in Dresden was visited by angry German citizen-protestors in 1989, or when the Soviet Union itself finally crumbled in the subsequent months, Putin would carry on the Soviet and KGB mindsets for decades to come. These cultures instilled within their interpellated populations, among which Putin was situated, a mixture of ideologies and their tenets. Some were borrowed in bits and pieces from the past; some were totally imagined by misguided utopians; and all were twisted to fit the needs of the Soviet regime in a manner successful enough to culminate in about 70 years of devilish rule.

These tenets included, in whole or in part, imperialism, revanchism, Eurasianism, ethnocentrism, Slavophilism, Messianism, millenarianism, nationalism, militarism, tsarism, conservatism, authoritarianism, chauvinism, Bolshevism, anti-Westernism, and more.[39] This list is not at all exhaustive, and due to its scope our book will address only some of its items in depth in the remaining pages of this chapter and the next, but it nevertheless demonstrates the crisscrossing layers of -isms that Soviet society pushed upon Putin (and a fair number of current Russian citizens who also grew up in the same milieu) and influenced the formation of Putinism. The variety, diversity, and outright paradoxes that result from the combination of so many -isms do not dilute or negate Putinism as an ideology. Rather, they expand Putinism's base, allowing each individual interpellated Russian to focus on the elements they find important and neglect the contradictory parts.

Not only did a plagiarizing Soviet ideology set the stage for Putinism, but so did a long history of Soviet leadership personalities. I [VT] teach an upper-level undergraduate course by the name of "Russian Politics from Vladimir Lenin to Vladimir Putin" at the University of Maryland, College Park. The course title alone draws attention to the need to place Putin in the context of Russian history, for Putinism is composed of events and ideas that occurred before Putin, the man's birth. Lenin embodies revolutionary charisma and utopian voluntarism; Josef Stalin, revolutionary mass terror and ideological stultification; Nikita Khrushchev, revolutionary somersaults and harebrained improvisations; Leonid Brezhnev, quasi-Leninist stagnation and corrupt gerontocracy; Mikhail Gorbachev, a pathetic reinvention of Leninism that culminated in a grand failure to square the circle of the deleterious Communist ideology, along with an industrial sludge of lies about democracy and freedom within a one-party state; and Putin, revolutionary anomy and kleptocratic authoritarianism.

Of course, as our book has already suggested in Chap. 2, Putinism reaches farther back into Russian history than the twentieth century, for it calls upon the memories of tsarist leadership, as well. All of these styles, be they Soviet or Tsarist, appear in some way in Putin's Russia, although with minor tweaks that shift the focus away from the sacred status of the tsar or of Communist utopia to whatever Putin's Kremlin and the population desire.

French journalist Michel Eltchaninoff broaches this topic in his well-researched analysis of Putin's philosophy, first published in May 2015. Readers are encouraged to examine his book *Inside the Mind of Vladimir Putin*, translated into English in 2018, for a closer look at how Putin's very own way of viewing the world and his role in it has evolved since his childhood. Eltchaninoff's research is much more biographical in nature than *Putin's Totalitarian Democracy*, with a narrower yet more deeply explored topic specifically focusing on how Putin himself seeks to exploit different ideological bases and historical events in order to retain his power. We agree with Eltchaninoff's tone and thematic conclusion about Putinism:

> This doctrine operates on various levels: starting from a claimed Soviet heritage and a feigned liberalism, the first of those levels revolves around a conservative mind-set. The second level involves a theory of the "Russian Way," while the third consists of an imperial dream inspired by Eurasianist thinkings. Put together, the whole sits under the rubric of a philosophy with scientific pretensions. This hybrid and unstable doctrine promises all of us an unsettled future.[40]

Unlike those who have contested that Putin's world outlook and ideology are informed by particular intellectuals, Eltchaninoff shows that Putin is "never confined by the parameters of a specific ideology."[41] With this, Eltchaninoff helps to define the complex nature of Putinism as succinctly as possible while also holding fast to the assertion that Putinism is an ideology, even if its sources are great and its consistency level low. After all, Putinism's legitimacy as an ideology should be first and foremost measured by the seriousness of its believers, as any ideology would be.

Again, establishing the schizophrenia (split nature) of Soviet ideology and leadership should make it easier to accept that Putinism (1) is not something that arose out of the blue, and (2) is *not* extraordinary in its ability to successfully incorporate so many political and societal beliefs arising from multiple theories across several centuries. In fact, this is reminiscent of a classic Peronist-type ideological system. Named after Juan Domingo Perón, the Argentine dictator who managed to rule a movement that united disparate social groups—the military, the poor, and the Church—under the banner of redemptive nationalism in the 1940s, 1950s, and 1970s, Peronism combines competing visions of Communism and fascism in a seemingly illogical manner that ironically allows for energized individuals to zealously indulge in the elements they find pleasing, yet ignore those they otherwise would not appreciate.[42]

Despite the fact that Peronism combines multiple contradictory ways of thinking, it is still an ideology. Although he ruined the country in terms of both economics and politics, not to mention embarked on incongruous tactics such as pursuing union-friendly policies while simultaneously murdering left-wing activists, Perón was successful enough in censoring the Argentine media and denouncing foreigner imperialists to the point where his nativist national narrative won him reelection as the country's beloved president, as the late Venezuelan political thinker Carlos Rangel emphasized in his 1976 book, *Del buen Salvaje al Buen Revolucionario: Mitos y Realidades de América Latina* (published in English as *The Latin Americans: Their Love-Hate Relationship with the United States*).[43] And decades after Perón's death, the ideological movement he launched—with all its internal contradictions, respect for both fascism and socialism, repressive paternalism, and populist tactics—continues to thrive, with many presidents (most recently Néstor Kirchner and Cristina Fernández de Kirchner) pledging their political allegiance to it. Its longevity in the minds of the Argentine masses is particularly telling in regard to the power of ideology, regardless of its incoherence.

Perón might have been an opportunist at some points, but overall he was a rabid believer in Peronism. Additionally, he was an open admirer of Benito Mussolini's Italian fascism and of his acquaintances Francisco Franco in Spain and Nicolae Ceaușescu in Communist Romania. In other words, Peronism in power translates into an ideological dictatorship (i.e. popularly supported tyranny). In such a system as this, the Leader is a believer and means *almost* everything for the movement, for the Leader could not exist without the supportive masses. U.S. President Donald Trump's paradoxical, chaotic policies and statements fit this bill, although he is quite immature as a Leader; Putin and his Kremlin, on the other hand, are much more mature and smooth in their Peronist ways. Like Perón's infamous smuggery, "I have two hands, a left and a right. I use each one whenever convenient," Putin is well versed in choosing which political fad to employ next, how to do so, and when to execute it.[44] And just as Perón was a believer in Peronism, so is Putin a believer in Putinism (though perhaps not in obvious ways). Putinism, at the end of the day, is about power and a glorious Russia. This is what makes Putin a perfect Putinist, an ideal subject of Russian culture, and an even better Peronist than Perón himself.

But simply because we can situate Putinism alongside the Peronist tradition, however, does not mean that Putinism is not unique or undeserving of serious study. At the same time as the light of history can show that Putinism is founded on past precedents, it also must be noted that Putinism is unprecedented in another light: it is an ideological hybrid *in contemporary times, replete with access to global information sources and international opinions*, that functions successfully both internally and externally by blending not only different centuries' worldviews, but also different leaders' personalities, different governmental systems' operational mottos and goals, and more. Putinism is remarkable for its ability to continue the Soviet myths (myths that already bizarrely combine Communism, fascism, and democracy) despite the USSR's exposure as one of the most fraudulent, corrupt dreams of all time while repackaging those very myths in more than consumable manners to today's audiences.[45]

In a sense, Putinism is Peronism on steroids: it is packed with far more than just Communist and fascist political elements, and then it also must incorporate the already heavy and eclectic historical baggage that cannot be separated from an identity-confused Russia. We would also like to note another distinctive difference between Perón and Putin: whereas Perón himself was not of the Left or of the Right (as his writings and statements show that he sympathized with both Communists and Nazis at a rather equal balance), and whereas Perón engaged in a fair number of radical leftist economic policies, the same cannot be said for Putin. He differs from Perón's status of "neutrality," for lack of a better term. While Putin's policies and statements share the most in common with the goals of the far Right (i.e. conservatism and reactionism), and while Putin has never enacted radical socialist economic programs or expressed a desire to return to Soviet market practices, he still expresses more ideas common to the Left than most other fascists of history. (He also manages to gain sympathy from both groups on the Left and on the Right across the globe, from British Labour Party leader Jeremy Corbyn and American Green Party member and repeat presidential nominee Jill Stein to Italian Interior Minister Matteo Salvini and American white supremacist Richard Spencer.[46])

This likely can be explained by the history of Russia and the biography of Putin, both of which spent a good deal of time under the yoke of a Communist dictatorship that can never be extracted from their memories. Do not be fooled, however: it is much easier to write this explanation and accept it at face value than it is to truly trace its influential extent upon Putinism. The following chapter has been dedicated to precisely this topic. Before continuing, we wish to remind readers at this moment that such influence is not just limited to characteristics of the stereotypical far-left politics: in addition to the leftist connotations of Communism, the Soviet Union has been proven to hold a myriad of far-right, fascist ideals, least of all it similarities in its faith in mass murder, eschatological redemption, coercive order, and *Gleichschaltung* (a German concept crucial to Nazism that refers to the totalitarian coordination and control of all elements of society so as to impose collective uniformity and destroy individual independence). Many of these totalitarian aspects of both the extreme Left and the extreme Right are shared and manifest themselves as key parts of Putinism, as Chap. 5 will illuminate.

Notes

1. Anton Barbashin, "Ivan Ilyin: A Fashionable Fascist," *Intersection Project*, 13 April 2017. In this article, Barbashin explicitly writes, "To call Putin a politician who is pursuing any sort of ideological or philosophical concept on practice is, by and large, as valid as calling Trump a true republican-conservative: meaning it is total nonsense."
2. Archie Brown, "How did the end of the Cold War become today's dangerous tensions with Russia?" *The Washington Post*, 4 May 2018.

3. Jacob L. Shapiro, "Ideology is Dead," *Geopolitical Futures*, 8 April 2018.
4. Benn Steil, "Russia's Clash With the West is About Geography, Not Ideology," *Foreign Policy*, 12 February 2018.
5. Vladimir Putin, "Rossija na rubezhe tysjacheletij," speech, 30 December 1999.
6. Edward Lucas, *The New Cold War: Putin's Russia and the Threat to the West* (New York: St. Martin's Press, 2014), p. 23; Peter Pomerantsev, *Nothing is True and Everything is Possible: The Surreal Heart of the New Russia* (New York: PublicAffairs, 2014), p. 105; Cheng Chen, *The Return of Ideology: The Search for Regime Identities in Postcommunist Russia and China* (Ann Arbor: University of Michigan Press, 2016), pp. 22–24.
7. Lev Gudkov and Eva Hartog, "The Evolution of Homo Sovieticus to Putin's Man," *The Moscow Times*, 13 October 2017.
8. Willard A. Mullins, "On the Concept of Ideology in Political Science," *The American Political Science Review*, Vol. 66, No. 2 (June 1972), p. 498; Hannah Arendt, *Origins of Totalitarianism* (New York: Meridian Books, 1958), p. 468.
9. Václav Havel, "The Power of the Powerless," trans. Paul Wilson, *International Journal of Politics*, Vol. 15, No 3 (January 1985), pp. 28–29.
10. Vladimir Tismaneanu, *The Crisis of Marxist Ideology in Eastern Europe: The Poverty of Utopia* (New York: Routledge, 1988), p. 2.
11. Brown, "How did the end of the Cold War become today's dangerous tensions with Russia?" In this article, Brown asserts, "Nothing comparable [to the Soviet system's ideology] exists today. To the extent that Russia has an ideology, it is one of Russian nationalism and belief in a strong state. We could call it 'Russia First.'" Unfortunately, this statement gravely underestimates the ideological component of Putin's Russia. Underplaying such a fundamental aspect of an entire society will perpetuate global misunderstanding of Russian politics. To believe the false notion that Russia's ideology is nothing special is to live in ignorance and sow the seeds for future discord when it comes to relations with Russia and the promotion of human rights across the world.
12. Chen, *The Return of Ideology*, p. 24.
13. G. John Ikenberry, "The Illusion of Geopolitics: The Enduring Power of the Liberal Order," *Foreign Affairs*, Vol. 93, No. 3 (May 2014), p. 81; Francis Fukuyama, "The End of History?" *The National Interest*, No. 16 (Summer 1989), p. 13.
14. John L. Stanley, "Is Totalitarianism a New Phenomenon? Reflections on Hannah Arendt's Origins of Totalitarianism," *The Review of Politics*, Vol. 49, No. 2 (1987), pp. 184 and 196; Mullins, "On the Concept of Ideology," p. 507.

15. Phillip Converse, "The Nature of Belief Systems in Mass Publics," in *Ideology and Discontent*, ed. David E. Apter (New York: The Free Press of Glencoe, 1964), pp. 207 and 214.
16. Wendy Brown, *Walled States, Waning Sovereignty* (New York: Zone Books, 2010), p. 77.
17. Arendt, *Origins of Totalitarianism*, p. 452.
18. Vladimir Tismaneanu, *Reinventing Politics: Eastern Europe from Stalin to Havel* (New York: The Free Press, 1992), p. 137.
19. Chen, *The Return of Ideology*, pp. 38–39; André Glucksmann, *Cynisme et passion* (Paris: Grasset, 1981), p. 241.
20. David Brooks, "Putin Can't Stop," *New York Times*, 3 March 2014. Interestingly, media outlets across the globe reported in 2013 that Kim Jong-Un, the dictator of North Korea, gifted copies of Adolf Hitler's *Mein Kampf* to his top government officials for his own birthday in January. The North Korean regime denounced these reports days later and alleged they were nothing but lies disseminated by defectors. Of course, the regime subsequently vowed to murder those "human scum" liars, thereby failing to redeem its credibility in any way. Regardless of whether or not the story is true, there is either a precedent for dictatorial leaders to push their selected philosophy on people and/or track down supposed traitors to their regime. It is nevertheless a theme that ideological dictatorships have shared throughout time and space, and one that should always remind the rest of the world of the danger that might come with ideology in power. BBC News, "North Korea condemns Hitler Mein Kampf report," BBC News, 19 June 2013.
21. Barbashin, "Ivan Ilyin."
22. Marlene Laruelle, "In Search of Putin's Philosopher," *Intersection Project*, 3 March 2017; Walter Laqueur, *Putinism: Russia and Its Future with the West* (New York: Thomas Dunne Books, 2015), pp. 176–184; Ivan Ilyin, *Sil'naja vlast'. Russkaja ideja* (Moscow: Eksmo, reprint 2017).
23. Ivan Ilyin, "Rossii neobkhodima svoboda" [Freedom is indispensible to Russia], in *Our Mission*, Vol. 2, Book 1, p. 163, as quoted in Michel Eltchaninoff, *Inside the Mind of Vladimir Putin*, trans. James Ferguson (London: C. Hurst and Co. Publishers Ltd., 2018).
24. Timothy Snyder, *The Road to Unfreedom: Russia, Europe, America* (New York: Tim Duggan Books, 2018), p. 47.
25. Timothy Snyder, "Ivan Ilyin, Putin's Philosopher of Russian Fascism," *The New York Review of Books*, 16 March 2018; Anton Barbashin and Hannah Thoburn, "Putin's Philosopher: Ivan Ilyin and the Ideology of Moscow's Rule," *Foreign Affairs*, 20 September 2015.

26. Jacob L. Talmon, *The Origins of Totalitarian Democracy* (London: Secker and Warburg, 1952), pp. 45 and 79–80.
27. As further proof that Ilyin is not *the* intellectual force behind Putinism, we wish to point out that Ilyin was not entirely consistent in his writings. While Ilyin himself is a well-established fascist, it is also important to note that not everything the man wrote construes itself in an overtly fascist manner. Take a quote from his work *Our Tasks*, in which Ilyin stated, "It is not possible to build the great and powerful Russia on any hatred, not on [hatred of] class (social democrats, Communists, anarchists), nor on [hatred of] race (racists, anti-Semites), nor on [hatred of] political party membership." This excerpt cannot redeem Ilyin—after all, Nazis believed what they were doing was for the greater good and pledged plenty of supposedly warm-hearted hopes, similar to this statement by Ilyin—but it also does not reek of a particular ism. Putin has *not* utilized the aforementioned quote in his public speeches, even though such a quote would play well as part of the Russian government's façade of a "good," respectful government; his omission of such low-hanging fruit suggests that Putin is not a diehard follower of Ilyin's philosophy, especially when one considers the relatively low number of times Putin has publicly spoken about Ilyin. (Furthermore, in addition to the fact that Putin has failed to exploit the "friendly" quote, readers should also keep in mind that Putin's Russia is in large part built on hatred of certain groups, as will be discussed in Chap. 5.) Ivan Ilyin, *Nacional'naja Rossija: nashi zadachi* (Moscow: Eksmo, reprint 2011).
28. We will define neo-Eurasianism and its predecessor, Eurasianism, upon the conclusion of this discussion of Aleksandr Dugin. Until then, we will offer an on-the-surface definition of neo-Eurasianism here as a conservative ideology holding that Russia is more closely related to Asian history and culture than it is to those of Europe or the West. Charles Clover, *Black Wind, White Snow: The Rise of Russia's New Nationalism* (New Haven: Yale University Press, 2016), p. 233.
29. Tatyana Medvedeva, "*Aleksandr Dugin: 'Nuzhno borot'sja s "shestoj kolonnoj.*"'" *Gazeta Kultura*, 10 October 2014; Sergei Prostakov, "Aleksandr Dugin i prihod Putina k vlasti," *Otkrytaja Rossija*, 21 May 2017; Sean MacCormac, "Aleksandr Dugin: Putin's Rasputin?" Center for Security Policy, 4 March 2015.
30. Maksim Sokolov, "Putin absoljuten," *Izvestia*, 5 October 2007. Additionally, it might be interesting to note that Dugin expressed his support for Donald Trump in the 2016 U.S. presidential election. Furthermore, Nina Kouprianova, the woman who served as Dugin's promoter in the United States and as his English translator, is married to Richard Spencer,

the leader of the "alt-right" Neo-Nazi movement in the United States. On this point, the authors would like to emphasize that these ideological connections are real and reach far beyond the confines of Russian borders, making it all the more important to understand what drives Putinism. Masha Gessen, *The Future is History: How Totalitarianism Reclaimed Russia* (New York: Riverhead Books, 2017), p. 482.
31. Dmitrii Rusanov, "Vojna nachalas'! Prizyvat' k miru – predatel'stvo! Aleksandr Dugin," ANNA, 6 May 2014; Catherine A. Fitzpatrick, "Russia This Week: Dugin Dismissed from Moscow State University? (23–29 June)," *The Interpreter*, 27 June 2014. Dugin told interviewers from the pro-Russian separatist news outlet ANNA in Ukraine that Ukrainians "must be killed, killed, killed." Additionally, here it should be noted that Putin did commit genocide against Ukrainians—just not a complete or successful one. See Chap. 7 for more.
32. We admit that we cannot vouch for the actual reason why Dugin was fired from MGU: was it truly a technical error (unlikely), was the Kremlin disgusted by Dugin's genocidal encouragement (even more unlikely), was the Kremlin enraged by Dugin's limitless calls for violence and mass mobilization, or was something else at play? How involved was President Putin in the decision to silence Dugin? The Russian regime and Putinism are fond of the long game, after all, so actions that the international community might deem to be respectable—such as firing a bloodthirsty professor from his university—might actually have been committed for the wrong reasons, that is, agreeing with the professor's bloodthirsty views but fearing the backlash his opinions could unleash among the population and the poor reflection they might have on Vladimir Putin. To put it simply: we stand firm behind the likelihood that Dugin was fired with the Kremlin's approval because of the zealous statements he made, various ones among which called for genocidal violence against Ukrainians. He was not fired because the Kremlin disagreed with his goals. Rather, he was removed from power as an academic because the Kremlin feared his opinions were too mobilizing (and that, if enough of the Russian population heard his views, then they would find Putin to be a failure). The reasoning had nothing to do with morals or respect for humanity in any way. Readers should consider this individual Icarus story as proof that (1) Putinism is not ruled by any one individual, and (2) the Kremlin's secrecy is always lurking when it comes to information flows.
33. Mark Kramer, "Theoretical Introduction: Political Power and Political Discourse in Russia: Conceptual Issues," in *State and Political Discourse in Russia*, ed. Riccardo Mario Cucciolla (Rome: Reset-Dialogues on Civilizations, 2017), pp. 86–87.

34. Berel Lang, *Post-Holocaust: Interpretation, Misinterpretation, and the Claims of History* (Bloomington: Indiana University Press, 2005), p. 162.
35. No other nation-state—not France, not Spain, not even Italy—claims the Roman Empire as a legitimizing factor in their own existence or extent of power today. Neither do they take credit for the civilizational gifts that the Roman Empire bestowed upon all the centuries to come. Russia and its (neo-)Eurasianists, however, maintain the hubris and ideological devotion by which to promote Moscow as the heir to the lost Roman Empire. What is more, (neo-)Eurasianists cling to this bold, mystical assumption despite the fact that they warn against modern Western culture, the basics of which the Roman Empire founded. In an illegitimate way, the (neo-)Eurasianists separate Roman culture and democratic foundations from Roman imperialism, ironically choosing to admire ancient Rome for the latter theme and its mythical nature. As if this were not an absurd enough reason to invoke the Roman Empire, it is important to note that (neo-)Eurasianists call upon the fantasy of Moscow as the reincarnation of the Roman nucleus precisely because it was an empire—an empire that, coincidentally, would have no license to exist in the twenty-first century, considering its dictatorial rule, lack of social equality, practice of slavery, and imperialist conquests of surrounding territories. Belief or desire for "Moscow, the Third Rome," then, is inherently imperialist and ideological. It also insinuates a revision of global history, in that it rejects the legacies of the Roman Empire that appear in the Western world (e.g. republicanism in the United States, or democracy, in general) and asserts that Russia knows how to live by Byzantine civilization better than the rest of the world. In that sense, perhaps today's Russia *is* the heir of the Roman Empire—an imperialist dictatorship masquerading with democratic elements—not in a messianic way, to the chagrin of (neo-)Eurasianists, but in the way that Benito Mussolini's Italy claimed to be harbingers of the Third Rome. Martin Clark, *Mussolini: Profiles in Power* (London: Pearson Longman, 2005), Laqueur, *Putinism*, and Nicolas Zernov, *Moscow, the Third Rome* (New York: AMS Press, 1938).
36. Snyder, *The Road to Unfreedom*, p. 89.
37. Marlene Laruelle, *Russian Eurasianism: An Ideology of Empire* (Washington, DC: Woodrow Wilson Center Press, 2008).
38. For readers who wish to learn more specifically about Eurasianism and neo-Eurasianism in Russia, we recommend Clover, *Black Wind, White Snow*, pp. 233–248; Snyder, *The Road to Unfreedom*, pp. 84–99; and Laqueur, *Putinism*.
39. Vladimir Tismaneanu, "BOOK REVIEW: The new tsar: the rise and reign of Vladimir Putin. By Steven Lee Myers," *International Affairs*, Vol. 92, Iss. 3 (1 May 2016), p. 744; Vladimir Tismaneanu, *The Devil in History:*

Communism, Fascism, and Some Lessons of the Twentieth Century (Berkeley and Los Angeles: University of California Press, 2012); Chen, *The Return of Ideology*, p. 72.

40. Eltchaninoff, *Inside the Mind of Vladimir Putin*, p. 10.
41. Eltchaninoff, *Inside the Mind of Vladimir Putin*, p. 5.
42. Carlos Rangel, *Del buen Salvaje al Buen Revolucionario: Mitos y Realidades de América Latina*, 10th ed. (Caracas: Monte Avila Editores C.A., 2009), pp. 379–387.
43. Rangel, *Del buen Salvaje al Buen Revolucionario*, p. 129 and 365.
44. Vladimir Tismaneanu and Jordan Luber, "Perón in the White House: The Perils of Ethnocentric Solipsism," *Public Seminar*, 19 March 2017.
45. The hopes of many political theorists that the advent of the Internet would make fascism and genocide impossible to commit (with the logic being that surely citizens would not support blatantly incorrect ideas anymore when they could look up proof for themselves) have proven to be very wrong. If anything, the reverse has become true—particularly in Russia, but admittedly everywhere, notably in the United States. In Russia, citizens refuse to fairly consider reports from outlets other than their state-controlled ones; in the United States, citizens make decisions via Facebook and Twitter, whose algorithms create a loop of reinforcement and fake news.
46. Kenneth Rapoza, "U.K. Labor Leader Corbyn And Trump Have Something In Common: Russia," *Forbes*, 9 June 2017; Ben Schreckinger, "Jill Stein Isn't Sorry," *Politico*, 20 June 2017; Gabriela Galindo, "Salvini: Italy 'not afraid' to use EU veto to lift Russian sanctions," *Politico*, 16 July 2018; Alan Feuer and Andrew Higgins, "Extremists Turn to a Leader to Protect Western Values: Vladimir Putin," *New York Times*, 3 December 2016; Stefan Jajecznyk, "The British Left's affinity for Russian imperial lies," *New Eastern Europe*, 4 February 2019.

References

Arendt, Hannah. 1958. *Origins of Totalitarianism*. New York: Meridian Books.
Barbashin, Anton. 2017. Ivan Ilyin: A Fashionable Fascist. *Intersection Project*, April 13. Accessed 1 July 2018 at http://intersectionproject.eu/article/politics/ivan-ilyin-fashionable-fascist
Barbashin, Anton, and Hannah Thoburn. 2015. Putin's Philosopher: Ivan Ilyin and the Ideology of Moscow's Rule. *Foreign Affairs*, September 20. Accessed 18 March 2018 at https://www.foreignaffairs.com/articles/russian-federation/2015-09-20/putins-philosopher
BBC News. 2013. North Korea Condemns Hitler Mein Kampf Report. *BBC News*, June 19. Accessed 11 July 2018 at https://www.bbc.com/news/world-asia-22964081

Brooks, David. 2014. Putin Can't Stop. *New York Times*, March 3. Accessed 1 July 2018 at https://www.nytimes.com/2014/03/04/opinion/brooks-putin-cant-stop.html.

Brown, Wendy. 2010. *Walled States, Waning Sovereignty*. New York: Zone Books.

Brown, Archie. 2018. How Did the End of the Cold War Become Today's Dangerous Tensions with Russia? *The Washington Post*, May 4. Accessed 2 July 2018 at https://www.washingtonpost.com/outlook/how-did-the-end-of-the-cold-war-become-todays-dangerous-tensions-with-russia/2018/05/04/d54d527e-3d03-11e8-8d53-eba0ed2371cc_story.html?utm_term=.95cabe46960e

Chen, Cheng. 2016. *The Return of Ideology: The Search for Regime Identities in Postcommunist Russia and China*. Ann Arbor: University of Michigan Press.

Clover, Charles. 2016. *Black Wind, White Snow: The Rise of Russia's New Nationalism*. New Haven: Yale University Press.

Converse, Phillip. 1964. The Nature of Belief Systems in Mass Publics. In *Ideology and Discontent*, ed. David E. Apter, 206–261. New York: The Free Press of Glencoe.

Eltchaninoff, Michel. 2018. *Inside the Mind of Vladimir Putin*. Trans. J. Ferguson. London: C. Hurst and Co. (Publishers) Ltd.

Feuer, Alan, and Andrew Higgins. 2016. Extremists Turn to a Leader to Protect Western Values: Vladimir Putin. *New York Times*, December 3. Accessed 20 September 2018 at https://www.nytimes.com/2016/12/03/world/americas/alt-right-vladimir-putin.html

Fitzpatrick, Catherine A. 2014. Russia This Week: Dugin Dismissed from Moscow State University? (23–29 June). *The Interpreter*, June 27. Accessed 10 January 2017 at http://www.interpretermag.com/russia-this-week-what-will-be-twitters-fate-in-russia/

Fukuyama, Francis. 1989. The End of History? *The National Interest* 16: 3–18.

Galindo, Gabriela. 2018. Salvini: Italy 'Not Afraid' to Use EU Veto to Lift Russian Sanctions. *Politico*, July 16. Accessed 20 September 2018 at https://www.politico.eu/article/matteo-salvini-italy-not-afraid-to-use-eu-veto-to-lift-russian-sanctions-crimea-vladimir-putin/

Gessen, Masha. 2017. *The Future Is History: How Totalitarianism Reclaimed Russia*. New York: Riverhead Books.

Gevisser, Mark. 2013. Life Under Russia's 'Gay Propaganda' Ban. *New York Times*, December 27. Accessed 29 January 2017 at http://www.nytimes.com/2013/12/28/opinion/life-under-russias-gay-propaganda-ban.html?_r=0

Glucksmann, André. 1981. *Cynisme et passion*. Paris: Grasset.

Gudkov, Lev, and Eva Hartog. 2017. The Evolution of Homo Sovieticus to Putin's Man. *The Moscow Times*, October 13. Accessed 15 March 2019 at https://themoscowtimes.com/articles/the-evolution-of-homo-sovieticus-to-putins-man-59189

Havel, Václav. 1985. The Power of the Powerless. Trans. Paul Wilson. *International Journal of Politics* 15 (3): 23–96.
Human Rights Watch. 2014. Russia: Anti-LGBT Law a Tool for Discrimination. *Human Rights Watch*, June 29. Accessed 29 January 2017 at https://www.hrw.org/news/2014/06/29/russia-anti-lgbt-law-tool-discrimination
Ikenberry, G. John. 2014. The Illusion of Geopolitics: The Enduring Power of the Liberal Order. *Foreign Affairs* 93 (3): 80–90.
Ilyin, Ivan. *Nacional'naja Rossija: nashi zadachi* [National Russia: Our Tasks]. Moscow: Eksmo, reprint 2011.
———. *Sil'naja vlast'. Russkaja ideja* [Strong Power: The Russian Idea]. Moscow: Eksmo, reprint 2017.
Jajecznyk, Stefan. 2019. The British Left's Affinity for Russian Imperial Lies. *New Eastern Europe*, February 4. Accessed 4 February 2019 at http://neweasterneurope.eu/2019/02/04/the-british-lefts-affinity-for-russian-imperial-lies/
Kramer, Mark. 2017. Theoretical Introduction: Political Power and Political Discourse in Russia: Conceptual Issues. In *State and Political Discourse in Russia*, ed. Riccardo Mario Cucciolla, 25–90. Rome: Reset-Dialogues on Civilizations.
Lang, Berel. 2005. *Post-Holocaust: Interpretation, Misinterpretation, and the Claims of History*. Bloomington: Indiana University Press.
Laqueur, Walter. 2015. *Putinism: Russia and Its Future with the West*. New York: Thomas Dunne Books.
Laruelle, Marlene. 2008. *Russian Eurasianism: An Ideology of Empire*. Washington, DC: Woodrow Wilson Center Press.
———. 2017. In Search of Putin's Philosopher. *Intersection Project*, March 3. Accessed 3 March 2017 at http://intersectionproject.eu/article/politics/search-putins-philosopher
Lucas, Edward. 2014. *The New Cold War: Putin's Russia and the Threat to the West*. New York: St. Martin's Press.
MacCormac, Sean. 2015. Aleksandr Dugin: Putin's Rasputin? *Center for Security Policy*, March 4. Accessed 10 July 2018 at https://www.centerforsecuritypolicy.org/2015/03/04/aleksandr-dugin-putins-rasputin/
Medvedeva, Tatyana. 2014. *Aleksandr Dugin: 'Nuzhno borot'sja s "shestoj kolonnoj"'* [Aleksandr Dugin: "We Must Fight Against the 'Fifth Column'"]. *Gazeta Kultura*, October 10. Accessed 10 January 2017 at http://portal-kultura.ru/articles/person/64670-aleksandr-dugin-nuzhno-borotsya-s-shestoy-kolonnoy/
Mullins, Willard A. 1972. On the Concept of Ideology in Political Science. *The American Political Science Review* 66 (2): 498–510.
Pomerantsev, Peter. 2014. *Nothing Is True and Everything Is Possible: The Surreal Heart of the New Russia*. New York: PublicAffairs.

Prostakov, Sergei. 2017. Aleksandr Dugin i prihod Putina k vlasti [Aleksandr Dugin and Putin's Coming to Power]. *Otkrytaja Rossija* [Open Russia], May 21. Accessed 10 July 2018 at https://openrussia.org/notes/709677/
Putin, Vladimir. 1999. Rossija na rubezhe tysjacheletij [Russia at the Turn of the Millennium]. *Speech*, December 30. Transcript available at http://pages.uoregon.edu/kimball/Putin.htm
Rangel, Carlos. 2009. *Del buen Salvaje al Buen Revolucionario: Mitos y Realidades de América Latina* [From the Good Savage to the Good Revolutionary: Myths and Realities of Latin America]. 10th ed. Caracas: Monte Avila Editores C.A.
Rapoza, Kenneth. 2017. U.K. Labor Leader Corbyn and Trump Have Something in Common: Russia. *Forbes*, June 9. Accessed 20 September 2018 at https://www.forbes.com/sites/kenrapoza/2017/06/09/u-k-labor-leader-corbyn-and-trump-have-something-in-common-russia/#62c5791156f9
Rusanov, Dmitrii. 2014. Vojna nachalas'! Prizyvat' k miru – predatel'stvo! Aleksandr Dugin [The War Has Begun! The Call to Peace—Betrayal! Aleksandr Dugin]. *ANNA*, May 6. Accessed 10 January 2017 at http://old.anna-news.info/node/15794
Schreckinger, Ben. 2017. Jill Stein Isn't Sorry. *Politico*, June 20. Accessed 20 September 2018 at https://www.politico.com/magazine/story/2017/06/20/jill-stein-green-party-no-regrets-2016-215281
Shapiro, Jacob L. 2018. Ideology Is Dead. *Geopolitical Futures*, April 8. Accessed 2 July 2018 at https://geopoliticalfutures.com/ideology-is-dead/
Snyder, Timothy. 2018a. Ivan Ilyin, Putin's Philosopher of Russian Fascism. *The New York Review of Books*, March 16. Accessed 16 March 2018 at https://www.nybooks.com/daily/2018/03/16/ivan-ilyin-putins-philosopher-of-russian-fascism/
———. 2018b. *The Road to Unfreedom: Russia, Europe, America*. New York: Tim Duggan Books.
Sokolov, Maksim. 2007. Putin absoljuten [Putin Is Absolute]. *Izvestia*, October 5. Accessed 10 July 2018 at https://iz.ru/news/329407#ixzz4MJ1Pft7u
Stanley, John L. 1987. Is Totalitarianism a New Phenomenon? Reflections on Hannah Arendt's Origins of Totalitarianism. *The Review of Politics* 49 (2): 177–207.
Steil, Benn. 2018. Russia's Clash With the West Is About Geography, Not Ideology. *Foreign Policy*, February 12. Accessed 2 July 2018 at https://foreignpolicy.com/2018/02/12/russias-clash-with-the-west-is-about-geography-not-ideology/
Talmon, Jacob L. 1952. *The Origins of Totalitarian Democracy*. London: Secker and Warburg.
Tismaneanu, Vladimir. 1988. *The Crisis of Marxist Ideology in Eastern Europe: The Poverty of Utopia*. New York: Routledge.

———. 1992. *Reinventing Politics: Eastern Europe from Stalin to Havel.* New York: The Free Press.

———. 2012. *The Devil in History: Communism, Fascism, and Some Lessons of the Twentieth Century.* Berkeley/Los Angeles: University of California Press.

———. 2016. Book Review: The New Tsar: The Rise and Reign of Vladimir Putin. By Steven Lee Myers. *International Affairs* 92 (3): 743–745.

Tismaneanu, Vladimir, and Jordan Luber. 2017. Perón in the White House: The Perils of Ethnocentric Solipsism. *Public Seminar*, March 19. Accessed 19 March 2017 at http://www.publicseminar.org/2017/03/peron-in-the-white-house/

CHAPTER 5

Putinism as a Culture in the Making

"Putinism," "Putin's ideology," "the Kremlin's ideology," "Russia's ideology"—all of these terms are interchangeable because of the notion that the people, the nation-state, and the sovereign are all interdependent upon one another. As the leading face of Russia, Putin's success is interpreted as the national population's success. At the same time, he needs public approval to act, so the Russian leader's success is simultaneously dependent on the satisfaction of the citizenry. Furthermore, the government's influence on almost every single media outlet in Russia means that "the Russian point of view" is easily taken over by "the Kremlin point of view"; the concept of objective reporting is absent in Russia because the Kremlin exercises near-total control over the truth.[1] For both of these reasons, there is little to distinguish "the people's view" from "the Russian government's view." Talking of "the Kremlin" is misleading and incorrect, while talking of "Russia," that is, the Russian people, when referring to the regime's crimes is not only more appropriate but also more accurate.[2]

Fittingly, Putin's ideology is fluid, protean, deliberately inchoate, an endlessly shape-shifting conglomerate based on popular and often infrarational sentiments such as nationalism, historical revisionism, the Soviet security imaginary, and anti-Westernism. This emotional matrix is neither cohesive nor coherent. Still, its components more or less fall into two categories. They support the beliefs that Russia is (1) a uniquely superior civilization compared to any other community, and/or (2) constantly suffering attacks from immoral, self-centered Western bullies. These two

© The Author(s) 2020
K. C. Langdon, V. Tismaneanu, *Putin's Totalitarian Democracy*,
https://doi.org/10.1007/978-3-030-20579-9_5

main talking points of Russian ideology are backed by the autocratic legacy—specifically its obsession with security and desire for authority—and Soviet grandeur—specifically its anti-West security imaginary and its claim to be a superior community with a great destiny—described in earlier chapters.

Together, Putin can channel these factors to build a fluid national myth, which he can steer as challenges to the state arise. Such a sustaining myth, as Robert C. Tucker theorized, makes up the central motif of society and gives meaning to membership in it.[3] In the Russian case, this myth illustrates the Kremlin's ultimate goal of restoring the Russian nation to what it believes to be its rightful place in the world and in history.[4] Readers familiar with the concept of Zhdanovism will find parallels between the Soviet cultural movement and Putinism, both of which base(d) themselves on the sustaining myth that their culture was simultaneously superior to Western culture, yet also under attack from it.

Formulated by Andrei Zhdanov (1896–1948), Politburo member and secretary of the Central Committee in charge of ideology in close collaboration with Stalin, Zhdanovism was a massive cultural propaganda strategy between 1946 and 1953 that sought, as Tucker defined it in a 1956 article in *World Politics*, "to enlist and organize the creative intelligentsia of the Soviet Union as a corps of conscious instruments of state policy, as missionaries of patriotic enthusiasm among the dispirited multitude of the Russian people."[5] Instruments of state policy—that is, writers, artists, and other intellectuals—were meant to conform their works to Soviet perspectives. Primarily, this meant that works had to reflect the mobilizing view that the world was split along the lines of a power struggle between the "democratic" Soviet Union and an evil, imperialist West. In the bigger picture, Zhdanovism was another tactic by which the ruling government could ensure control of the Soviet population by coercing producers of culture within the population to promote Soviet goals. It meant to convince the people that their regime's objectives were necessary, morally just, and inevitable, and thus in need of their full support as the only viable path toward progress and fulfillment of utopia. As this chapter will explore, Putinism's sustaining myth promotes the same dream.

But Zhdanovism presents a valuable parallel with Putinism because it did not stop at manipulating the people's opinion on international relations and national politics: it also sought to manipulate the people's opinion on how they should behave as individuals. According to the analysis of Italian intellectual Pier Paolo Pasolini published in a volume of *October*, it attempted to enforce "a conception of life in which each person must occupy his proper place, perform his proper function, [and] identify himself with his proper duty."[6] Thus, Zhdanovism reflected a totalitarian regime's preoccupation with the uniformization of social forms. It helped authorities in power to strengthen a closed feedback loop in which they fed a single ideological possibility to the population and generated either active agreement or at least passive complacence with those ideas.

Putinism, too, does just this. In a sense, Zhdanovism still thrives today, under a regime that goes by a different name but pursues the same sort of authoritarianism. The following sections endeavor to demonstrate Putinism's Zhdanovist impulse to capture culture and elicit certain responses from society. They will deconstruct contemporary Russia's nationalist myth into its main pillars of the security imaginary, Soviet nostalgia, Russian exceptionalism, and biopolitics in order to understand how they inform one another. Additionally, the next pages will explain the motives of today's Russia as it produces a creative kind of arrogant, immoral global hegemony in a larger attempt to envision itself as a powerful, wise, superior state. This chapter as a whole, then, explains how Putinism acts as an ideology and how it has been so successful in influencing the masses to behave and to believe in certain pre-described ways that continuously reinforce the Kremlin's standing and authoritarian policies. We should add that Putin himself grew up in Leningrad, the city where Zhdanov was party boss after Sergey Kirov's murder on 1 December 1934. Zhdanov stayed there during the German blockade, then went to Moscow to supervise what Stalin regarded as "the cultural front." In 1946, Zhdanov followed Stalin's order to denounce, in an infamous speech in Leningrad, the great poetess Anna Akhmatova and the satirical writer Mikhail Zoshchenko. Zhdanov was the mastermind of the anti-cosmopolitan campaigns meant to demonstrate the Russian priority in all major scientific and artistic breakthroughs.[7]

THE SECURITY IMAGINARY: A DOMESTIC TOOL FOR DEFINING THE RUSSIAN NATIONAL IDENTITY

Hungarian philosophers Ferenc Fehér, Ágnes Heller, and György Markus wrote in their volume *Dictatorship Over Needs: An Analysis of Soviet Societies* (1983), "There is no creed without generalizing universal fear."[8] Putinism is no exception. One of the main fear-inducing ingredients of Putinism deals with a national security imaginary. Putin's designs are real-life examples of Hannah Arendt's theory that an ideology can achieve its goals through exercising its capacity to mobilize populations—often times through fear and the invocation of security.[9] Through the selective reproduction of certain histories—not to mention the distortion (or even fabrication) of "facts" and the propagandizing efforts of state-controlled media—the Kremlin manufactures crises that instill fear among the citizenry and interpellate them into a common security imaginary.

French philosopher Édouard Glissant defines this imaginary as "all the ways a culture has of perceiving and conceiving the world."[10] Since the state maintains a monopoly on knowledge and the means by which to disperse it (at least in the case of Russia, where internet trolls are hired by the government to slander potential threats to its credibility, media outlets are controlled by the Kremlin and facilitate its disinformation campaigns, and foreign organizations are legally raided and driven out of the country before they can disseminate non-Kremlin apperceptions of events to the Russian public), this imaginary can be manipulated to fulfill the state's ideology and goals.

It is highly important to recognize the national security imaginary as a contrived, imposing identity, which manufactures narratives of national unity and exceptionalism out of imagined dreams of a homogenous society.[11] Essentially, it is a compensating mechanism meant to artificially bestow a particular national identity upon a particular group of people whom the state aims to control socially by convincing them that they belong to the state's society and that there is a need for them to support the government in order to sustain their own physical and economic lives.

The hysteria surrounding the apartment bombings of 1999 is one of the earliest examples of Putin's contribution to the Russian security imaginary, since the chaos served to convince Russian citizens that Chechen Islamists, despite the lack of proof of their involvement, were sources of terror from which the Russian population needed to be secured. Putin portrayed Chechens as not belonging to Russia proper (even though the purpose of the Chechen Wars was to prevent Chechnya from politically separating from the Russian Federation, ironically); they were relegated to the world outside of Russia dominated by diversity and chaos, while Russia itself was advertised as a symbol of safety, homogeneity, and order.

Putin was thus able to convince his traditionally conservative voting base that the state was the sole guardian of the public good. He also insisted that this state was surrounded by enemies, pressuring citizens to believe that they needed the Kremlin (which, in turn, needed the people's support) in order to survive supposedly disparate forces.[12] Even today, as Chechnya is terrorized by Putin's handpicked loyalist warlord Ramzan Kadyrov, Russians cherish the "security" this has brought to what they see as Russia proper. Chechen pain is either denied, justified along the vein of a "civilizing" mission, or vengefully celebrated.

It is this kind of ersatz conspiracy that provides a prime ideological background for an illiberal leader like Putin to justify his claims to power and convince the Russian citizenry that he must act because their values and lives are under attack. Such an imaginary is semi-fluid and selective, always ready to identify another person, group, or idea either as "different" and something to be protected from, or as the "same" and something to be welcomed into the Russian nation-state. It is a constant tool for the consolidation of Russian subjects via the projection of threats onto alienated groups. According to this narrative, the state faces unimaginable threats from nefarious enemies; the fall of the holy nation and the good people would be such a tragedy that, logically, all terror committed by the state is automatically justified and treated as a normal action.

NOSTALGIA FOR THE SOVIET PARADISE

This current security imaginary is a baffling amalgam of history, myth, and anguish-driven fantasies of salvation. The crux of Russia's security imaginary has to do with Russian ideological identification and antagonism against the West, both at present and in history. Like the Soviet Union in the Cold War, the Russia of the (increasingly post-)Westphalian era is determined to cling to the global political structure of sovereign nation-states with no over-arching international command (despite the steady dissolution of state sovereignties in the face of a globalizing world where capital, people, and goods freely move about).[13]

As its own authority, the Russian nation-state adapts to the ever-globalizing, denationalizing trends of economics, travel, and identity politics that grind against the nation-state's hegemony by retreating inward and vilifying the globalized world led by the West.[14] Russia overcompensates for this slipping away of national allegiance by stepping up efforts to unify its population by securitizing within it a distinctive identity. Especially because Russia has experienced such an unstable history of extreme ideologies, radicalism, and autocracy, the creation of a coherent and unified body for the whole nation is easiest done by harkening back to Soviet characteristics with which a majority of the population is familiar (because they lived through it), as well as by emphasizing the split geographies of a civilized, good "us" versus a barbaric, evil "them" to build allegiance to their own nation-state (similar to the Zhdanovist line considered earlier in this chapter).

The Soviet security imaginary is a remnant of Russia's history that refuses to die, or is not allowed to do so by those currently in power. It is steeped in propaganda and historical imperative. The Soviet Union comprised far more than just Russian land; it also consisted of 14 other Soviet Socialist Republics, or the "near abroad." In this Cold War context, power was primarily measured in military might, ideological support, and, most importantly, territorial expanses, for land was thought to bestow upon its owner (and still is thought to bestow, in Westphalian understandings of authority) a visible, tangible power. The Soviet Union represented the hopes that the proletariat would claim their rightful power, socialism would triumph, and that its utopia would, in the words of Nikolai Bukharin, "light the fire of the world socialist revolution."[15]

Once the Soviet Union dissolved, however, an ideologically confused, non-Communist Russia—the space which had previously been the administrative core of the entire USSR—found itself in control of far fewer, yet even more fragmented, populations and territories. The diverse Russian-speaking subjects of the former Soviet Union have been disarticulated from Russia's hegemonic narrative since the Russian Federation, along with other post-Soviet nation-states, declared their independence and cultural histories. The ensuing individual identity crises, not to mention chaos in the democratic and market economy transitions, distanced many former Soviet subjects from feeling as if they belonged to the new Russian state. Several sought solace from these crises of the 1990s in nostalgic memories of Communist times. Most of these people do not look back fondly upon the Soviet era because they yearn for Communist ideology, but because they desire to reclaim the superpower status, solidarity, and utopian hope they believed the USSR had held for much of the twentieth century. This longing for superpower status, this belief that global power is a national right and a social justice, is characteristic of imperialism.

The flimsy relationship between subjects, ex-subjects, and the state is a sign of weakness to believers in the Westphalian system, where a nation-state is demarcated by a distinct population and bounded territory. Without a defined body politic upon which a constitutional state's legitimacy is based, and without a common national origin story, the state is not as secure.[16] Faced with the broken, deterritorialized pieces of the formerly

Soviet population and landscapes, Russia has resorted to constructing post-Soviet imaginaries that heal these ruptured social spaces, fabricating a community of shared meanings, knowledge, and outlooks that transcend territorial and political differences—all in an attempt to legitimize the Russian state's origins and present the state not as one based solely on its current territory or population, but also on abstract values, creeds, history, race, and ethnicity.[17] This basis for unity is all the more pertinent because Putin tells the population that "either we remain a sovereign nation, or we dissolve without a trace and lose our identity." With this, he increases the stakes of national cohesion by prevailing upon Russian citizens the notion that they must agree with their nation-state for the sake of its, and all its inhabitants', existence.[18]

Putin exploits the widespread nostalgia for the Soviet imaginary because history levies loyalty, and memory binds humans to a shared evaluation of the present. Together, they can connect generations and associate their existence with one Russian culture. By presenting his regime as the decent inheritor of, and himself as the heir to, the Soviet past, Putin prompts the current population to associate the unifying, glorifying memories of (supposed) Soviet homogeneity and utopia with today's Russian government.[19] As British geographer Derek Gregory points out in his book *The Colonial Present* (2004), humans have a tendency to reject ideas that do not make sense in their personal or collective understanding; in recycling elements of a twentieth-century security imaginary, the Russia of the twenty-first century is able to promulgate a national vision which most citizens would already understand and accept from their younger days spent living in the Soviet Union. By manipulating the nation's historical consciousness like so, the Kremlin can determine not only how its citizens comprehend the past and the present, but also the trajectory of the future and the means by which it should be attained.

Imperial nostalgia is also an effective way of distracting a population from its other woes. Russian political scientist Lilia Shevtsova broached this topic in her essay published in the *Journal of Democracy* in 2012. She cited reflections of Russia's deep-seated social trends of atomization and degradation in everyday life and

> the loss of old cultural ties and the spread of social ills—signaled by high rates of alcoholism, abortion, murder, suicide, family breakdown, and early male mortality—that plague Russia and hold broad segments of Russian society back from activism on behalf of civic dignity. And there is also the sheer inertial weight of the huge and change-averse state bureaucracy.[20]

Though these otherwise disparaging signals seem like they should be daunting and demoralizing, Shevtsova asserts that the Kremlin's promotion of imperial nostalgia offers citizens an enhanced image of the past and future that not only gives them a sense of direction and hope of improvement, but also distracts from today's gloom. In fact, it can imbibe the present with a feeling of importance. With the ironic aid of nostalgia for the past, each day becomes a steppingstone toward a supposedly brighter future—assuming one falls for the Kremlin's narrative.

One of the most obvious examples of Putin's reaching back to Soviet days is the Eurasian Economic Union. The Russian Soviet Socialist Republic had been the heart of trade throughout the entire Union. When the Union dissolved, so did Russia's economic influence in each former Soviet satellite. Though the majority of former Soviet Republics became members of the Commonwealth of Independent States (or CIS, created in late 1991 as a weakly supranational organization interested in coordinating trade and security across its members), the Kremlin still sought to expand Russia's sphere of influence in places where it wanted to reduce the power of other countries.

Putin, in particular, sought to restore Russia to the status of the post-Soviet space's geopolitical center. He announced in 2011 his plan to establish by 2015 the Eurasian Union (now known as the Eurasian Economic Union), a more comprehensive economic partnership which would build upon the Soviet Union's best values and mirror that of the European Union. Actually, the Eurasian Union was meant to do more than just mirror the European Union's economic partnership; it was meant to challenge it internationally and to poach the loyalties of European member states, thus marking "the beginning of a new ideology and geopolitics for the world," as American historian Timothy Snyder explained it in his book, *The Road to Unfreedom: Russia, Europe, America* (2018).[21] Although the Eurasian Union has not proven to be as fruitful as the Kremlin might have envisioned, Putin has still been accused of capitalizing off of Soviet nostalgia because the organization invokes the geopolitics of the Soviet Union in an attempt to centralize expanding economic power within Russia and sharpen Russia's image as the leading regional authority.[22]

This is not to claim that Russia is regressing to Soviet tactics because Putin wishes to resurrect the Soviet Union, which he himself referred to as the "greatest geopolitical catastrophe of the twentieth century" during his 2005 address to the nation. Instead it sheds further light on why Putin glorifies and reintroduces select elements of the familiar Soviet era in an attempt to resuscitate myths of national exceptionalism and superiority in a globalized world.[23] Since the nation is so sacred, the fight for its honor, whether under totalitarian (Communist) rule then or totalitarian (Putinist) rule now, is all part of one continuous struggle for "good."

A One-Sided State of Perpetual War

Russia's present-day security imaginary focuses the population's minds on geopolitics and ideology, as the Soviet Union's did during the Cold War. Putin himself roots his policy in geopolitical Soviet issues. He justifies his current foreign policy by telling the nation, "the Cold War left us with live ammunition," by which he meant that the relationship between the West and Russia had been irreparably damaged and that Cold War antagonisms still burn.[24] He even compared the present day with the 1930s and 1940s, arguing that the West cannot criticize Russia today because Stalin's Great Terror was no different from Franklin D. Roosevelt's dropping of the atomic bomb on Hiroshima.[25]

This is a continuity of Cold War Manichaeism between capitalism and Communism, between democracy and autocracy,[26] in that the Russian state still invokes a historical geopolitical rivalry, declaring itself as the main opponent to the West in order to unify its own identity as a nation unique in its own right. Putin benefits from telling the Russian population about the enemies, dangers, and violence that lurk outside of its borders (and especially in Western countries). After all, the sovereign's power is awarded on the assumption that it will guarantee a homogenous, secure life for domestic citizens, so the pretext of a threat to the nation provides a reason for him to exercise presidential authority.[27]

Guided by Putin's xenophobic, Cold War-era rhetoric, the Russian population imagines the West's capitalist, liberal essence as a threat to Russian society's conservatism, Orthodox religious traditions, and outright existence. Since Putin's second election in 2004, pollsters and journalists have reported how more and more citizens are coming to believe that enemies surround Russia.[28] Various polls by the Levada Center, an independent sociological research organization based in Moscow, reveal that the vast majority of Russia's population would agree that the West is innately hostile to them.[29] This enmity toward the West generates the same effects it assumes; in other words, Russian policy goads negative reactions from the West, perpetuates tensions, and only further convinces the Russian population that the West represents a threat from which the nation-state must protect itself.

Here we return to Putin's 2013/2014 assignment of philosophy books to his top government staffers and 80-odd regional governors, mentioned in Chap. 4. The main premise of Ivan Ilyin's *Our Tasks* is that Russia is destined to confront the West because one of the West's biggest desires is to ruin the Russian Motherland, further eternalizing the notion that Russia is engaged in a life-or-death battle of cultural values.[30] Thus, the Kremlin (read "Putin") has locked itself into what Hannah Arendt refers to as a condition of perpetual war: it relies on the constant extension of its authority and flexing of power in order to portray itself as *the* prepared guarantor of security, and as the truly legitimate sovereign, for the entire Russian Federation.[31]

The Kremlin's ideology cultivates within Russian society conspiracy theories which give further justification to the Russian state's actions (be it retroactively, at present, or in the future). For example, Russian economist and politician Sergei Glazyev's book entitled *Genocide: Russia and the New World Order* (1999) has been frequently cited in public discourse since Putin's rise to power. In it, Glazyev purports that the "sinister forces of the 'new world order' conspired against Russia in the 1990s to bring about economic policies that amounted to 'genocide.'" And Foreign Minister of Russia Sergey Lavrov wrote in a 2016 article that Europe has been trying to place "Russian lands under full control and to deprive Russians of their identity" for centuries (making one wonder what exactly Lavrov believes to be Russian territory).[32] And in recent media, Maxim Shevchenko, a Kremlin-approved TV journalist, has captured newspaper headlines with an article stating that "Russia and the West are at war. ... There is a growing feeling that most Western people belong to a different humanoid group from us."[33] This chillingly reminds one of Adolf Hitler's use of the word "subhuman." Rarely has such viscerally racist language been so forthright. Such instances of Russian citizens separating themselves from the rest of the world and devaluing Western cultures echo Kremlin propaganda. These accusations—often partly warranted, but no more than halfway—heighten fears and hype over Russia's need to overcome the West.[34]

The specter of geopolitics as it continues in the familiar "Russia versus West" distinction, then, continues to haunt the Russian security imaginary as it had in prior Soviet decades. When former Soviet satellites, like Estonia, Georgia, and Ukraine, to name a few, began to drift toward Western culture and institutions such as the North Atlantic Treaty Organization (NATO; the USSR's major intergovernmental enemy), Russian political leaders bristled. To them, the spread of Western ideology bled onto the physical landscape of a previously Soviet-laden Europe: once a state began to identify with Western values, Russian leaders colored that state's entire national territory, all the way up to its borders, as its worst type of "Other," as a member of the West.

Of course, this works to Putin's advantage, for he can scare the country with statements such as, "The process of NATO expansion has nothing to do with modernization of the alliance. ... We have the right to ask, 'Against whom is this expansion directed?'"[35] This manufacturing of constant, ever-encroaching threats to the Russian nation—the same ones that haunted Soviet Russia for decades—encourages interpellated subjects to grow so ideologically opposed to the West that they do not even realize, or care, how their obsession allows Putin to exercise more and more power with less and less worry about potential popular dissent.

Russia as a Victim

In the Kremlin's imaginary, Russia is the undeserving (yet morally virtuous and victorious) victim of the West. Under Putin's presidency, the notion that Western capitalists were responsible for almost devouring Russia in the 1990s has gained popularity. This comes despite the fact that, during the 1990s, Russian citizens were blaming their own corrupt businessmen and the often-drunk president, Boris Yeltsin, for almost letting the fledgling capitalist Russian state collapse upon the recent ruins of the Soviet Union. Additionally, Putin has asserted that Russia's economy stagnated in 2014–2015 because the West applied unfair sanctions on Russian trade, even though at other times he would minimize these sanctions as merely ineffective nuisances to Russian economic activity. He also failed to mention that Russia itself had violated international law by invading Ukraine and illegally annexing Crimea, thereby glossing over Russia's misdeeds and making the implication that the West's sanctions were downright unreasonable.

It is the United States that "has overstepped its national borders, and in every area," according to Putin. He told his national legislature that even if Russia had not intervened in the revolution against former Ukrainian President Viktor Yanukovych and could not, therefore, have been vilified as instigators of Ukraine's democratic crisis, the West still "would have come up with some other excuse to try to contain Russia's growing capabilities." Putin's version of events holds that the West is always out to get Russia, so its accusations cannot be taken seriously or trusted.[36] As of September 2015, polls show that 45 percent of Russians outright think "negatively" of the "Western lifestyle" and 44 percent would not consider moving to the West even if it meant better pay and job opportunities.[37]

Many go so far as to blame the West for Russia's current corruption. They say that the Western world forced its capitalist game upon a newly independent Russia in the 1990s and argue that this is why Russia today is a nest of corruption. Of course, this is an absolutely preposterous argument: the Soviet regime was one of the most corrupt regimes of world history. The West, therefore, did not introduce corruption to Russia. Even though many Russians can openly admit to the deep extent of their country's culture of corruption, they still refuse to accept the reasons for this reality. This marks a failure that might as well mean they do not truly understand the reality in which we all live, in general, because believers of such a narrative continue to reject Russia's total agency in the matter. To further perpetuate the myth of Russia's victimization, they execute their admissions of Russia's sins in a complimentary way: it was thanks to their culture's creativity and ability to adapt that post-Soviet Russia was able to survive the transition to Western capitalism.[38] With this tale, Russians view their country as an innocent yet scrappy nation whose wrongs cannot be judged too harshly.

Word play and untruthfulness are imperative to this fabrication of threats. As Soviet dissident Vladimir Voinovich observed in his book *The Anti-Soviet Soviet Union* (1985),

> Despotic regimes always excel in their rejection of crude words and expressions, and unbelievable cruelty is always accompanied by verbal hypocrisy. The Nazis called the annihilation of millions of Jews the "final solution to the Jewish question." In the USSR, mass repression is termed "collectivization" or "the struggle with the opposition" and, afterward, the "mistakes of the cult of personality." Aggression against other countries is given the high-sounding name "fraternal aid."[39]

Verbal hypocrisy of this grade thrives in Putin's Russia, too. It allows for Putin to present Russia's illegal annexation of Crimea in March 2014 as a victory of "Russian military glory and outstanding valor" based on a referendum "in full compliance with democratic procedures and international norms."[40] In reality, it was an absolutely imperial, illegal sham. But the Kremlin's rhetoric disguises this truth with a one-sided narrative and censored media coverage, always presenting itself as innocent and devoid of responsibility for any wrongdoing.

The average Russian citizen watches and hears Putin's one-sided narratives on national television on a daily basis. This medium, dominating all news sources, propagandizes the state's narrative into a visual spectacular. Citizens, due to their "Russianness," are thus called into being as outspoken members of their state's ideological battle with the West because they can recognize themselves and their familiar histories in national tales of loss, victimization, struggle, humiliation, uncertainty, and nostalgia for a socialist utopia that never existed. These commonalities tie personal accounts to the general story of the Russian nation. These people are called on as loyal subjects to their great country, mobilizing each individual to do their part in the security imaginary. Every citizen is implored to help unify their self-pride as a nation-state and feel as though they are fighting for something even bigger than the survival of their nation.

Rewriting History Around Russian Exceptionalism

Building upon the security imaginary and Soviet nostalgia, the Kremlin also relies upon the ideological pillar of blatant historical revisionism to validate its ideology and to perpetuate the notion that Russia has always been both a great cultural power and a victim of the West's marginalizing tactics. Stalin's version of World War II—or the "Great Patriotic War," as the widespread Russocentric opinion refers to it—is currently one of the most important myths in Russia's attitude toward its own history. The myth of undeserved aggression, extraordinary human sacrifice, and glorious victory that Stalin endorsed in the mid-twentieth century is being propagated once again by today's Kremlin. This particular recollection is meant to instill feelings of pride and superiority in average Russian citizens. Applying Italian historian Emilio Gentile's concept, it operates as a kind of political liturgy that guides its Russian audience, as a collective unit, to conceive of their "heroic" past as one that deserves sanctification and reflects the golden future of their own generation.[41]

Additionally, this line encourages them to absolve Russia of guilt in moral crimes, such as: the signing of the Molotov-Ribbentrop Pact in 1939, through which the USSR agreed to look away from Hitler's Holocaust in return for non-belligerence between the two countries; the installation of brutal Soviet concentration camps as the Red Army marched through Eastern Europe toward the German Reich; the well-documented pillaging, rape, and destruction of European villages, whether or not they had aligned themselves with the Nazis; and many more damning offenses.[42] And as Timothy Snyder underscored in a talk at the Carnegie Endowment for International Peace in May 2018, the Kremlin's version of events is so audacious that it goes beyond just absolving Russia of World War II-related guilt: they actively hold that today's Germans should feel guilty toward today's Russians and the entire past of the nation. This is preposterous for many reasons, ranging from the Soviet Union's complicit relations with Hitler's Germany to the fact that far more Ukrainians were killed by Nazis (and Soviets) than Russians were killed by Nazis.[43] But it is more convenient for the Kremlin to rewrite history, to distract from all its sins with Russocentric lies of heroism and sacrifice, to pretend to be exceptional, and thus to lay claim to a nation bound for greatness.

It is vital to note that in Russian textbooks, the "Great Patriotic War" began on 22 June 1941, the day Nazi Germany invaded the Soviet Union. Most other countries and historians recognize the official start date as 1 September 1939, when allies Hitler and Stalin invaded Eastern Europe. This discrepancy of almost two years (a third of the war's entire duration) reveals a Russocentrism that permeates Russia right down to its historical "facts." It is one example of how the Kremlin is refashioning historical events to portray them as mega-crises between itself and some other substantial evil. This implies that only Russia was (and still is) capable of diametrically opposing and defeating the fascist power that threatened to devour the globe. It also suggests Russia has a specific group of people in mind whom it celebrates as being worthy of protection. Moreover, in setting the start date in 1941, those who talk of the Great Patriotic War are unintentionally admitting, then, that it would have been permissible to live in a fraternal, peaceful alliance with Hitler even as he wreaked havoc across Europe.

Numerous statues and plaques dedicated to the Great Patriotic War and even the ever-fraternal Soviet Union still exist today in the public space, in museums, and on the streets, indoors and outdoors. Moscow's New Tretyakov Gallery art garden, for instance, is brimming with everyday cultural manifestations serving to define identities with certain historical memories that are privileged as the official truth of the country. In particular, one of the most massive sculptures on display there reads, "The Union of Socialist Soviet Republics is the stronghold of peace." While the garden of haunting statues might make non-indoctrinated individuals recoil, it also might make those indoctrinated by such messianic beliefs weep with pride and fond nostalgia.

The Kremlin's rewriting of Soviet history is also geared, in part, to refute the West's declaration of how Stalin was a monster. For the past decade or so, Stalin has been taught in Russian schools as a "controversial figure," or as an "effective manager" who had to make sacrifices (or, more accurately, who had to decide which of his citizens would make the hardest sacrifices) for the nation's survival.[44] A multitude of polls over the last decade demonstrate a public tolerance—even humor and enjoyment—in the memory of Stalin. In fact, approval ratings of Stalin's memory rose to a new record high of 52 percent following the invasion of Ukraine in the summer of 2014.[45] This public willingness to celebrate Stalin and Soviet culture is a sign that the Kremlin has turned imperial nostalgia into a fundamental source of the Putin regime's legitimacy.[46] It twists Russia's ideology to accept revised versions of the past, where the Soviet Union was not approaching utopia but actually *was* a utopia, and where Stalin was not a murderer of millions of innocent supporters and dissenters alike, but a strong leader whose accomplishments are to be respected.

While Stalin is still not openly rehabilitated by the Kremlin, to compliment any action of the tyrant, and then to go so far as to say those murderous deeds were necessary and just, sends a firm message: the nation, power, and glory matters, while the negative consequences on even millions of individuals that are forced to suffer under such actions are irrelevant. This kind of language and thinking has an intended, successful effect on the current Russian population that is already most concerned with the nation and its glory.

Reaching even further back in history, Russians are taught to see every "good" leader of the past as a tyrant, from Ivan the Terrible and Peter the Great to Lenin and Stalin. From this perspective, Russia appears as a country predisposed to aggressive leaders and the abuse of power. Once the public accepts its brutal history in such a light, it becomes possible to embrace these abusive leaders. It also encourages the justification of the authoritarian and totalitarian tactics used by sovereigns of the past *and* of the present. Stalin's precedents—taught in a way that excuses his crimes, thanks to his strongman military achievements that kept the USSR safe from Hitler's fascists—make it permissible for Putin to act in a similar fashion, one which does not follow orthodox legal procedures. When it comes to Putin himself, this attitude of paying homage to Stalin helps

Putin appear to be a stronger leader because of his willingness to appeal to a prior, "successful" authoritarian order.[47]

Of course, the Soviet Union was *not* successful. It collapsed in embarrassment, economic disaster, and crushed social hopes by 1991. But the security imaginary, nostalgia for the Soviet Union, historical revisions, and other performative practices allow the Russian nation-state to ignore such damning holes in logic. These inorganic cultural formations permit Putin to fragment time and space, breeding a different interpretation of reality among Russian citizens which bases itself in an incongruent history and landscape of danger, hate, and fear.

Russia as the Superior Culture

Another important component of Putinism is the belief that Russia is not just the inheritor of an inspiring Soviet past, but also a unique nation itself with superior culture and morals. In general, Russia's leaders present Russian history as a harrowing tale of an innocent, remarkable nation that has been unfairly met with external evils time and time again, precisely because Russia is a formidable challenger that other powers feel threatened by and hence want to unfairly minimize. It is a myth that blames the outside world for Russia's historical and current struggles, slyly compensating for periods of powerlessness or incompetent leadership without acknowledging flaws in Russia's behaviors.[48]

As Mikhail Gorbachev wrote in 2016, other countries could not even begin to comprehend the pain and sacrifices Russia has made through the ages. Gorbachev adds that those sacrifices continue to the present day because no other country has shouldered the burden of defense spending that Russia bears daily, in order to defend its people and territory from the attacks of NATO, Chechen terrorists, and Ukrainian fascists.[49] As such, Putin tells the citizenry they are integral pieces of the "Russian soul," which has been historically characterized by heroism and self-sacrifice and allegedly sets them apart from other peoples. The promotion of these ethnic Russian memories above the memories of others is meant to tell believers that Russia could not be anything less than an extraordinary state to have survived all of this danger.[50]

Of course, the sources deemed by the Kremlin as "threatening" have been at least halfway imagined by the Russian state, and hardly any attention is paid to the fact that millions of Estonians, Georgians, Ukrainians, and others also fought and died for the same anti-fascist cause in the 1940s. Instead, the Kremlin's ideology offers a Russocentric, nationalistic, selective version of events that produces a blinding effect among its citizenry, keeping them from even bothering to try to comprehend situations from non-citizens' perspectives.[51] For example, in Russia, the invasion of eastern Ukraine and the subsequent illegal annexation of Crimea are championed as noble fights for the rights of ethnic Russians abroad but fail to consider these actions as aggressive violations of Ukrainian sovereignty. Everything matters from Russia's selfish point of view, and no one else's is equal to its importance in questions of justice and morality. In this, one can hear the echoes of the bourgeois imperialists' calls for conquering Africa in the name of pure honor and ability. The scenario is an epitomizing example of what Voinovich warned about when he wrote in his book *The Anti-Soviet Soviet Union*, "the epithet 'sacred' is applied far too often, and sometimes to things that are not in the least holy. ... Sacred this and sacred that are drummed into our heads so often that we ourselves cannot see what nonsense we're talking."[52]

Such an asymmetry of perception allows Russians to see themselves as the superior population. Their ideology precludes consideration of other narratives because the concept of viewing a situation from another perspective contradicts the core of Russocentric thought. This derealization of other narratives pushes other modes of thought (and other human lives) into the background, giving the Kremlin's narratives center stage. This paves the way for Putin to delegitimize the cause of human rights by insisting that the West has transformed them into an excuse to violate the sacred principle of state sovereignty, and that the concept now only arises out of "pure demagogy."[53]—which, ironically, Putin verbally condemns at the same time as he himself practices. Consciously or not, the Russian population, constrained by their government's ideology, is then complicit in this devaluing of non-Russian lives and perspectives. They fail to insert a series of metaphysical questions such as, "Who counts as human?" and "What values, besides those expressed by Russian culture, politics, and history, are legitimate?" into Russia's view of the world.

Other analysts focusing on Putin's Russia, such as journalist and astute observer of Slobodan Milosevic's xenophobic militarism Roger Cohen,[54] have elaborated upon the narrative of a superior, undeservingly victimized Russia by adding the notion of "Weimar Russia syndrome" to the ideological mix. The term plays off of the ills that plagued Weimar Germany in the interwar period.[55] Those difficulties ran the gamut of the psychological, the political, the economic, and the social. They infected society and encouraged the festering of imperialist, nationalist, racist, chauvinist, and militarist beliefs that destroyed the Weimar Republic's sincere pursuit of democratization and cultural enlightenment and ultimately culminated in World War II.[56]

In an article published in the *New York Times* just after the seizure of Crimea, Cohen pointed out that the Kremlin portrays Russia similarly to how the fascists in 1920s and 1930s Germany portrayed their country, namely, as an unfairly marginalized country under attack from foreign elements. Both interwar German nationalists and current Russian nationalists were wounded by their respective country's failures on the world stage, which hurt all the more because they so fiercely believed in their own superiority. For example, Germans were humiliated by defeat in World War I and by all the baggage that came with military defeat, whereas Russians were humiliated by the breakdown of the Communist empire, by the loss of its vast territories, by the disappearance of its superpower status, by an unclear definition of what Russia is and what it means to be Russian, by rampant corruption, by economic dysfunction, and more.[57]

Rabid nationalists do not typically accept loss or a reality that does not match their expectations. They choose not to adapt to reality or to admit that their expectations were flawed, in the first place. Interwar German fascists refused to realize that they lost the war because there was no such thing as a superior German culture; post-Communist Russian nationalists (among whom fascism, too, is steadily rising) refuse to accept that Russia can no longer be an empire with superpower status and must instead play by the international community's rules. To such believers, failure can only be explained by the enemy's "unfair" tactics and by the self-serving assumption that their nation conducted itself more honorably. The Kremlin's version of reality, then, holds that the West refuses to offer Russia a seat at the international negotiating table, that the West seeks to expand and encroach upon Russia's sphere of influence, that the West has created NATO solely for their own imperialist pursuits and their desperate desire to keep Russia contained, that the West instigates revolutions in the post-Soviet space in order to violate Russia's sovereignty, and that the West sanctions Russia to further demoralize it. And all the while, Russia is portrayed to its citizens as an unfairly marginalized power that deserves better and thus needs an authoritarian leadership and a devoted following in order to live up to its potential.

BIOPOLITICS AND RACISM: SELF-OTHER DISTINCTIONS AND IDENTITY

The term "biopolitics" has been under continuous formulation since the time of ancient Greek philosophers. Most notably, French philosopher Michel Foucault defines biopolitics as the strategy by which states calculate natural life into modern politics, subjecting human processes to government authority.[58] Italian philosopher Giorgio Agamben furthers this idea by arguing that states use biopolitics to arbitrarily suggest that it is only obligated to care for people who match a certain biological profile, in effect giving "the right" to rights and protection under the law to some but excluding others that are deemed dangerous to the state for various reasons.[59] Agamben also asserts that biopolitics is an effective method of empowering the sovereign. Arguably, it provides the fundamental basis for the sovereign, in the first place. Putin seems to know this all too well.[60] Since Putin is the sovereign, he can decide which groups of people "fit" in the nation's identity and instill within them specific fears of who the enemy is and what to do about them. It is an instance where the very human body is placed under state regulations.[61] Ultimately, the fluid biopolitical dichotomy dictated by Putin allows him to unify his citizenry in support of supposedly universal, national ambitions, which, ironically, are defined by only Putin himself. Putinism plays biopolitics as a method of unifying the state's population with a common identity, citing social identification as the basis for allegiance to the nation. Collectivity gives the state a reason to be and ultimately feeds into Russia's supposed cultural superiority by aiming to portray the nation-state as Russian, through and through.

Of course, tsarist and Soviet imperialism have left Russian culture and demographics ambiguous, as discussed in Chaps. 1 and 2. While propaganda envisioning a Russia comprised of purely ethnic Russians might make for a more straightforward biopolitical campaign (in terms of theory, practicality, and in blatant sanctioned racism), the Kremlin cannot embark on this path because the demographic and cultural situation cannot accommodate this dream. It is as political scientist Ilya Prizel noted in a previously mentioned essay published in 2000: "Russia is unique in that the birth of the Russian empire preceded the birth of a distinct national polity. As a result of this reversed sequence of national development, from the sixteenth century to the present, the concept of Russianness became blurred with that of empire."[62] The idea of an ethnically pure Russia, then, is impossible, not to mention impractical. Only the most extreme political figures—such as Vladimir Zhirinovsky of the ironically named Liberal Democrats—have publicly called for one.[63]

But Zhirinovsky's vision cannot be achieved to its fullest, partly because it would require mass deportations and exterminations, and partly because the "pure ethnic Russianness" someone like him seeks does not exist after centuries of social, cultural, and demographic upheaval. As a result, it now exists more as a cultural, ideological construct than as an ethnic one. This is not to say that Russian cannot be classified as an ethnicity—ethnic Russians do exist today, of course. The point here is to demonstrate the imperialism and racism rampant in today's Russia: despite the arbitrariness of the idea of an ethnic Russian, the Kremlin continues to talk up a fantasy that would require allegiance to that singular and supposedly superior force of Russianness.

So, the biopolitical aspect of Putinist Russia is a complicated one. Putin's regime does not call explicitly for ethnic Russians to "return" to Russia's territory. At the same time, he does not call upon just any ex-Soviet subject, either, because Putinism has no desire for a truly multicultural Russia.[64] Before continuing, readers must understand that Putin's regime has been left with little choice but to expand its biopolitical reach because the Russian government has struggled for the last few decades in attracting the "return" of ethnic Russians from the post-Soviet space. Actually, between the establishment of the Russian Federation and 2008, seven million people—mostly ethnic Russians—emigrated.[65] The country, with its resource-based economy, was in desperate need of laborers willing to take low-paying, unglamorous jobs. Plenty of immigrants from the South Caucasus and Central Asia were willing to move to Russia in order to take these jobs that the ethnic Russian population could not fill. So, if it was going to survive and stave off economic disaster, Russia needed to attract large numbers of migrant laborers who were not just ethnically Russian.

Putin, being a master at playing to Russia's ingrained desires for nationalism and imperialism, even managed to adapt this necessity for non-ethnic Russian immigrants into a larger biopolitical movement. Putinism committed itself to searching for a biased demographic balance, one that perpetuates the myth of a glorious ethnic Russian history and people as well as provide the state with a healthy population size and labor force. This is not only necessary for economic reasons, but also convenient for the state to maintain a façade of liberal multiculturalism to the rest of the world when, in reality, this setup allows Putin's regime to strive for an insignificantly "multicultural" Russia that essentially operates akin to apartheid-era South Africa, where certain members of the Russian population—namely migrants from Central Asians and South Caucasus, and/or of Islamic faith—are treated as second-class citizens.

Sizeable numbers of ethnic Russian citizens negatively refer to migrants from Central Asia and the South Caucasus region as "blacks." Russian migration officials have publicly disclosed their hatred against racial "pollution" of the Russian Federation, and citizens have told journalists that such non-Slavic immigrants are no more than "unwashed heathen from central Asia who should never set foot in Holy Russia."[66] Others have attempted to change local council regulations so that female Russians would have to get married and bear at least one child before the age of 20, as a measure of increasing the ethnic Russian population. In the fall of 2015, an (ethnic Russian) professor teaching language courses at a university in St. Petersburg warned her class, of which one of this book's authors [KL] was a part, to "watch out for the Central Asians. They carry disease, you know."

Much to the chagrin of these racists, Muslims are numerous in Russia, as well. In fact, demographic studies predicting that at current migrant rates, Muslims would come to make up 20 percent of the Russian population by 2020. These numbers might read as indicators of tolerance, but numbers can be deceiving. So can official statements issued by the Kremlin, particularly ones that claim to respect Russia's four traditional religions of Orthodoxy, Buddhism, Judaism, and Islam.[67] Statements and numbers are not enough to guarantee dignified treatment, though. In the case of Russia, they obscure the actual living conditions and treatment of these migrants.

To begin with, their invitation to life in Russia is hollow and untrue: the Russian immigration authorities, the Federal Migration Service, only tacitly welcomes Muslims because it knows the country needs laborers. In reality, Russian security services are as harsh as ever on Muslim communities. Muslim organizations and religious authorities must register and be approved by the state in an effort to guard against the spread of Islamic terrorism in Russia. Those that get approved, however, often happen to be either poorly educated in the Muslim faith or not orthodoxly adherent to it. Many drink alcohol, smoke, and consume pork, making them less "noticeably different" when compared to supposedly traditional Russian citizens. As foreign correspondent for National Public Radio (NPR) Anne Garrels retells in her book *Putin Country: A Journey into the Real Russia*

(2016), some of these local Muslim leaders implore their congregations to vote for United Russia and for Vladimir Putin.[68] This is not to say that they cannot be "true" Muslims for partaking in such activities or political opinions (similar to the case of Roman Catholics who, say, engage in premarital sex or do eat meat on Fridays in Lent, against Catholic Church dogma), but it is evidence that the Russian government prefers to vet Islamic leaders who are more doctrinal to the Russian government's creed than to their Muslim faith.

Just as the Russian authorities dislike what they fear to be zealous and "too traditional" Muslims, it is also apparently possible to be "too untraditional" of a Muslim in the eyes of a Russian state that operates in fear of potential radicalism, individualism, and destabilization. Islamic community leaders who advocate for more personal spirituality have often reported cases of harassment at the hands of security services. These cases are similar to the ones experienced by Muslim leaders who are not registered with the state. Neither the more doctrinally "liberal" Muslims nor the unsanctioned Muslims curry favor with the security services. They frequently find themselves being stopped and interrogated or their homes, offices, and mosques being swept as part of investigations conducted by local Russian authorities, all because the Russian government has a very specific kind of Muslim resident in mind, one that causes little stir in the community and can be counted on to toe the Russian government's line through their complacency.[69]

The opinions and behaviors of the rest of the general Russian citizenry offer even more accurate analyses of a "multicultural" Russia. Studies show that they have been steadily transforming their longtime suspicion of the Jewish population (another group supposedly beloved by the Russian government and respected as a part of Russian society, a statement much easier to make by the government when most Jews in Russia have either been murdered or forced to emigrate en masse over the course of the nation's history) into hatred against Muslims (a trend unfortunately common throughout the world).[70] Despite already being part of the Russian state—and despite the fact that the establishment of the Muslim faith in Russia actually predates the establishment of Orthodox Christianity—Muslim Chechens are offensively commanded to "go back home" by "native" Russian citizens who have publicly vowed to "clean the streets of all the filth, all the darkies, the Muslims and their dirty money" in order for "Holy Russia" to rise once more.[71]

This treatment is not limited to just Muslims, of course. Plenty of people with "foreign" appearances are mistreated on a daily basis just for looking and dressing differently from supposedly average Russians. While Muslims, South Caucasians, and Central Asians are technically welcomed into the country, the Russian citizenry's hateful reactions to them serve as a better indicator of the Islamophobic, xenophobic, racist, and biopolitical mindsets that characterize Putin's Russia. The state, after all, does not dream of just any immigrant. It still primarily appeals to what amounts to "cultural Russians" who live in the former Soviet states, urging them to move "back home" to their "native" nation. The definition of what it means to be "culturally Russian" is artificial and comes from insincere necessity. It is a definition that can technically encompass those from once-Soviet states but also exclude them as the Kremlin and the Russian population see fit.

This way, the Russian government can issue contradictory narratives that placate, or at least confuse, the international community and present the impression of a "tolerant enough" multicultural society while also emphasizing the concept of Holy Russia, and allowing for poor treatment of those who do not fit the ideal Russian identity, to proliferate under the surface of official rhetoric. This allows for a scenario where immigrants live, as journalist Ben Judah described it, in conditions of near slavery and neglected labor codes, with poor pay, forced labor, and ramshackle tenements.[72] Individuals representative of these identity categories are not found in the Kremlin's administration or in elected offices, either, further evincing circumstances similar to apartheid.

To conclude the issue of race and ethnicity in Russia, we reference a quote mentioned in Snyder's book *The Road to Unfreedom*, in which Putin says, "The Great Russian mission is to unify and bind civilization. In such a state-civilization there are no national minorities, and the principle of recognition of 'friend or foe' is defined on the basis of a common culture." The first half of the statement sounds as though it might jive with the notion that Russia strives to be a multicultural nation-state; the second half, however, leaves the Kremlin room to negate that as a genuine possibility. In fact, if we look at this as a matter of principle, it should obliterate the idea that Russia could ever be a multicultural society: a state cannot claim to be multicultural if it openly lets everyone know that it can find enemies in anyone or refuse the idea of minority status.

As Snyder puts it, the idea that "politics begins from 'friend or foe' is the basic fascist idea, formulated by the Nazi legal theorist Carl Schmitt and endorsed and propagated by Ilyin."[73] This uncertainty, this inability of individuals to know whether or not the Russian government might be in the process of labeling them as enemies and the painful awareness this unstable feeling must present on a daily basis, is egregious but surely works in the government's favor when it comes to preserving domestic order and keeping the nation-state as "Russian" as possible. We look forward to forthcoming research on the matter of racial discrimination and xenophobia in Russia, as it is such a precarious topic.

Moreover, discrimination is not just limited to ethnicity or skin color. Another major issue of "deviation" in Russia is homophobia, which exploded on the international scene when Putin signed a federal law "for the Purpose of Protecting Children from Information Advocating for a Denial of Traditional Family Values" in June 2013. Widely referred to as the anti-gay propaganda law, the legislation criminalizes homosexuality because it is "morally corrupting."[74] The law punishes ordinary citizens, public officials, foreigners, and even businesses or organizations deemed to promote so-called "gay propaganda" with fines, arrests, detainments, job firings, and even deportation. (All of these government responses have been denounced by the United Nations and other non-governmental organizations [NGOs] as violations of freedoms of speech and assembly.)

Gay pride parades have been frequently denied the right to protest on Russian territory, and those that do occur—lawfully or unlawfully—are typically assaulted by anti-gay protestors. If the police are called to the situation, it is the LGBT (lesbian, gay, bisexual, and transgender) activists who are arrested, rather than the physically violent counterdemonstrators. When it comes to gay parents, Russian courts and social workers are ready to revoke parental rights than they are in situations of drug-abusing or physically abusive parents. It is a further testament to the reality that gay lifestyles and rights are portrayed by the Kremlin as nothing but satanic products of the overly indulgent, amoral West, from whose vileness the Russian people must protect their purer cultural values.[75]

Of course, in official discourse with the international community, the Russian government still pretends to accept all identities and peoples. Just as its migration authorities pretend to welcome Muslims, the Kremlin also assured the world before the 2014 Winter Olympic Games in Sochi that the anti-gay law leaves the rights of sexual minorities intact, insisting that gays "are full-fledged members of our society and they are not being discriminated against in any way." This is a blatant lie. The majority of the Russian population's reaction to gays is a much more accurate indicator of their cultural and political sphere's closed attitude and disrespect for human rights. The fact that even foreigners and Muslims in Russia, who themselves suffer discrimination at the hands of Russian society, also participate in the persecution of gays is crucial. In an ironic twist, they get praised for their encouragement of ordinary people to beat up members of the LGBT community.[76] Somehow, oppressed groups in Russia express no qualms with shouldering the government's line of discriminatory mistreatment and, in turn, oppressing other groups, be they gay, foreign, or Muslim. The lack of solidarity between the groups—none of which are treated with respect by the state or the general Russian population—is striking and only reveals the damaging, isolating, and alienating tactics of a manipulative Russian government and culture.

This all serves as further evidence that the Russian government fabricates a certain biopolitical narrative in order to legitimize its own status as a nation-state (despite its non-ethnically homogenous population) and to impose a biased, state-controlled order upon human nature. That narrative, and that order, also helps to fulfill the Russian government's vision for a conservative, Orthodox nation-state that stands in opposition to the European values of plurality, diversity, and liberalism. Putin has opted to exploit the self-other relationship to identity, through which a state creates a constitutive outside for the purpose of imagining a politically and socially unified inside, artificially demanding unity and national oneness by creating enemies against which its population can bond together. This nationalist siege mentality and demonized biopolitical image of "others" is not just dangerous for those targeted, but it is also dangerous for Russia's fate: such tactics could instigate the violence they imagined, in the first place—except the Russian propagators will be the ones responsible.

PUTINISM AND THE SPECTER OF *HOMO SOVIETICUS*

This real-life evidence of racism, homophobia, and Russian elitism within even the *private* lives of Russian citizens can be attributed to the interruption and alteration of all social relations at the command of the sovereign and the governing ideology.[77] Specifically, Putin can define who is and who is not a citizen, or who is one of "us" and who is one of "them." Those who fit in the former category are considered worthy of the state and granted possession and access to it, whereas those who fit into the latter category are seen as undeserving and often degenerate. Individuals who are not considered to be one of "us" are transformed into nothing more than bare life, to use the term coined by Agamben. Accordingly, they are stripped of dignity and rights by virtue of the fact that the persons in question do not "belong" to Russian society and, therefore, cannot claim the full guarantee of protection under the sovereign.[78]

Putin's selections are largely accepted by his citizenry so long as the justifications he provides fit the national script and can be linked to doing what is best for the nation-state. The states of exception he imposes upon certain strategic groups of people help the Kremlin in its biopolitical endeavor to invent a united population. This project is eerily reminiscent of an infamous phrase from *Animal Farm* (1945), English writer George Orwell's satirical novella lampooning Stalinism: "All animals are equal but some are more equal than others."[79] Orwell's absurd phrase seems as though it must be a joke, a satirical critique, but it turns out to be an accurate reporting on the potential absurdity of human thought.

Similarly, Putin has also taken to manufacturing politically significant categories, which he uses to interpellate people accordingly and pit categories such as "loyal Russian subjects" against Kremlin dissenters, non-Russians, pro-Western sympathizers, gays, and other "threats" to Russia. The Kremlin regulates a person's categorical status and reserves the right to change it at any time, scaring the population into behaving as actively "good" subjects because, as long as everyone has a reason to be afraid, they will act obediently to the state and its commands. In sum, Putin's regime anesthetizes individuals' morals, feelings, and memories in its bid to manage the national consciousness while eroding the ability to think freely.

Putin has opted to exploit the self-other relationship to identity, through which a state creates a constitutive outside for the purpose of imagining a politically and socially unified inside. In other words, the state attempts to artificially demand unity and national oneness by creating active enemies against which its population can bond together. Part of what animates this process is that it always fails to create that desired national oneness, that robust enduring feeling of belonging, which only deepens a vicious cycle of inclusion versus exclusion. This nationalist siege mentality and demonized image of "others" moralizes the subsequent sovereign-mandated exceptions against them, justifying the government's states of exception on the basis that the state has the right—the duty, really—to defend itself from the violence these specific groups of people may unleash.

Through the manipulation of biopolitics, the self-other distinction, and memory regarding the common Soviet imaginary, the Kremlin promotes the worldview that Russia is a superior civilization, the antithesis of the West, and so exceptional that it need not abide by international norms. While the goal is not to revive the Soviet Union, Putinism and its strategies embody Leninism and its flagrant use of violence, propaganda, paranoia, anti-individualism, and promises of a new, superior society. At their cores, they both rule via "criminal enterprises" that are bent on eliminating enemies for the sake of their chosen, loyal population. The likeness between Leninism and Putinism does not translate into the notion that Putin is a socialist or a Communist, but it should be even more disturbing: the defining aspects of one of the most violent, abusive ideological movements in all of history are still alive and well in Putin's equally ideological, non-socialist regime. Parallels like these cannot be taken lightly; they must be admitted for all their incriminating worth.

It is at this point that the term *homo sovieticus* should be advanced. Like all totalitarian experiments, the Soviet Union (particularly under Josef Stalin) dreamed of utopia brought about and populated by the New Man, an ultimate kind of human who was morally and ideologically dedicated to the regime's revolutionary utopian vision. Again, as demonstrated by all totalitarian experiments that have failed throughout history, the New Man is a preposterous concept. Russian satirist Aleksandr Zinovyev coined the term *homo sovieticus*, then, as the more accurate and negatively connotative phrasing for the Soviet project to create their New Man. *Homo sovieticus*, in Zinovyev's eponymously titled book from 1984, knows nothing of individuality and seeks meaning in conformity and the collective. It is because of this type of collectivist and their willingness to aspire to little else except a larger community's utopian goal that the Soviet Union was born and then survived for decades. As Zinovyev put it, *homo sovieticus* represented a "mass phenomenon" that become normalized in Soviet society and played "a dominant role in the process of formation of social consciousness and social psychology" in the totalitarian state.[80]

One of the authors of this book examined this ideological stultification in his 1988 volume *The Crisis of Marxist Ideology in Eastern Europe: The Poverty of Utopia*, in which he wrote, "Mortification of the imagination ... universal acceptance of the dreary climate of blind obedience, compliance with a boundless opportunism: *homo sovieticus* was thus born."[81] Yuri Levada further hypothesized *homo sovieticus* as a believer in a paternalistic state, egalitarian hierarchy, imperialism, conformity, the superiority of *the* ideology, and self-isolation. *Homo sovieticus*, then, was a "perfect creature and subject of the totalitarian state" for its willingness to atomize itself from Man and not to question the contradictory statements that the state made (and, at its core, was based on).[82]

Of course, there were few diehard examples of the Soviet New Man in existence. The Soviet regime was a cruel joke to a sizeable portion of the population by the time of its demise, with most Soviet Men knowing how to work the system to avoid punishment at the hands of corrupt, bureaucratic imbeciles.[83] While not the ideal Soviet New Man, many of those people who skirted some aspects of Soviet rule remained as sufficient examples of *homo sovieticus*, for they still reported on their neighbors, coworkers, friends, and family members; still were content to remain in a totalitarian state; still showed up to participate in workers' parades, and so on, especially before the 1980s and all the uncertainty regarding the future of the Communist state hit.

Putin, in his own way, represents the surviving presence of *homo sovieticus* in today's Russian society. He is not a buffoon, as the satirical *homo sovieticus* has come to be caricatured. But he is a persistent, unyielding remnant of the past, a past that was rotten to its core, contradictory, ideological, and explicitly nationalistic and hateful of the West and pluralism. *Homo sovieticus* was made by and for their Soviet rulers, for a regime that spent more time demanding loyalty and obedience in the face of its many lies than it did actually working toward a better life for all its inhabitants. Putin and Putinism still stand for all of these incriminating characteristics: the only difference is that the name of the regime has changed, and the utopian goal has been made more realistic and attainable (although while the ends of Putinism have been adjusted, its means remain controlling and manipulative). And most eerily, Putin and the Russian population, once only products of the Soviet drive for *homo sovieticus*, now act as its producers, as well.

Not every citizen needs to be a New Man actively obsessed with achieving glory for the Russian state or ready to lay down their life in the name of Russian honor. Rather, it is sufficient if the majority believe that their community is superior to any other in the world; that their way of life is under attack from democratic and Western forces; that their government is working to attain the people's best interests for the future; and that their only duty as individuals is to agree with what the state-controlled media says and to defend their country in even the most seemingly passive of ways (e.g. voting for Putin, defending Putin and Russian policies in ordinary conversations, assuming Western media is all a bunch of lies, glaring at foreigners, flying a Russian flag off of their balcony, etc.). And if the time comes for it, some young men will go off to war in Georgia, Ukraine, or some other country where Russians need to be "liberated," and their mothers will be proud of those sons for serving the state.[84]

In other words, it is enough for today's Russian citizens to continue the trend of *homo sovieticus* and to refrain from questioning their government so long as they are told it is working to meet their needs. This is not to say that the people's support is trivial. On the contrary, it is everything. It is crucial to the success of the Putinist ideology and regime. Just as the Soviet Union needed *homo sovieticus* to survive, so does Putin's Russia need the support of the citizenry. Without their legitimizing effect, the state would have no receptive majority through which to pursue its authoritarian goals with relative ease, nor would it have an audience with which to sustain the national myths it perpetuates. Myths matter little if few abide in them, for a myth by itself has no power to influence mass consciences. A myth needs believers to grow in popularity, moral strength, and the ability to affect judgments about the world and individuals' places in it.

This examination makes clear that Putin is *not* the ultimate decision-maker for the Russian people: a history of instability, a trend of authoritarianism, and the popular consent of the people, all inform a national script by which Putin is expected to perform sovereign power. Putin does not define Russia's animosity toward the West because seeds are already present within his population; he knows the desire is out there, and it fits the national narrative. So, Putin sets out to manipulate it in order to cultivate more legitimacy for himself as head of state and for the Kremlin as an authority deserving of the national population's respect and support. But how has this national script arisen, exactly? How does Putin ensure its stability? The next chapter will explore these questions on the basis that it is not through his personality alone, but through various societal institutions, that Putinism has become the nation's fixed narrative.

Notes

1. Peter Pomerantsev, *Nothing is True and Everything is Possible: The Surreal Heart of the New Russia* (New York: PublicAffairs, 2014), p. 47.
2. In addition to the current Russian population, long-dead historical figures are co-opted by Putin's Kremlin, as well, albeit in a different fashion. For example, Putin has taken to rebuilding the estate of novelist Ivan Turgenev as a monument to Russian national pride, despite the overwhelming evidence that Turgenev would likely despise today's Russia and its ideological

fantasies. After all, according to director of the Turgenev family estate Elena Levina, the famous writer and thinker "never idealized anything and described the reality that he saw," and he freely expressed his belief that Russia was part of Europe and should not pursue its own Russian way. These views do not fit into the Putinist narrative whatsoever; yet Putin's Kremlin and indoctrinated Russian audiences alike nevertheless choose to partake in certain fabricated stories that distort the pasts and images of even the most outspoken Russian figures. In this way, Putin and his Kremlin successfully annex iconic cultural personalities from the past in order to conceal and/or deny their adamant rejection of any form of nationalism. Andrew Higgins, "*Turgenev Dissed Russia but Is Still Lionized as Literary Star by Touchy Kremlin*," New York Times, 11 March 2019.
3. Robert C. Tucker, *Political Culture and Leadership in Soviet Russia: From Lenin to Gorbachev* (New York: W.W. Norton & Company, Inc., 1987), pp. 22 and 45.
4. Brian Whitmore, "Putin vs. Putin," Radio Free Europe/Radio Liberty, 2 September 2016.
5. Robert C. Tucker, "Stalin and the Uses of Adversity," *World Politics*, Vol. 8, No. 4 (July 1956), p. 463.
6. Pier Paolo Pasolini, "What is Neo-Zhdanovism and What is Not," *October*, Vol. 13 (Summer 1980), p. 10.
7. For more on the subject of Zhdanovism, see Vladimir Tismaneanu, *The Crisis of Marxist Ideology in Eastern Europe: The Poverty of Utopia* (New York: Routledge, 1988) and Katerina Clark and Evgeny Dobrenko with Andrei Artizov and Oleg Naumov, *Soviet Culture and Power: A History in Documents, 1917–1953* (New Haven: Yale University Press, 2007).
8. Ferenc Fehér, Ágnes Heller, and György Markus, *Dictatorship Over Needs: An Analysis of Soviet Societies* (New York: St. Martin's Press, 1983), p. 147.
9. Hannah Arendt, *Origins of Totalitarianism* (New York: Meridian Books, 1958), p. xxxvi.
10. Édouard Glissant, *Poetics of Relation*, trans. Betsy Wing (Ann Arbor: the University of Michigan Press, 1997), p. xxii.
11. Tucker, *Political Culture*, p. 31.
12. Arkady Ostrovsky, *The Invention of Russia: From Gorbachev's Freedom to Putin's War* (New York: Viking Press, 2015), p. 307; Naeem Inayatullah and David L. Blaney, *International Relations and the Problem of Difference* (New York: Routledge, 2004), p. 42.
13. Wendy Brown, *Walled States, Waning Sovereignty* (New York: Zone Books, 2010), p. 21; Richard Lourie, *Putin: His Downfall and Russia's Coming Crash* (New York: Thomas Dunne Books, 2017), pp. 78–79.
14. Elena Barabantseva, "How do people come to identify with nations?" in *Global Politics: A New Introduction*, 2nd ed., eds. Jenny Edkins and Maja Zehfuss (New York: Routledge, 2008), p. 261.

15. Nikolai Bukharin, "The International Situation and the Tasks of the Comintern," *International Press Correspondence*, Vol. 8, No. 41 (30 July 1928), p. 727.
16. Étienne Balibar, *We, the People of Europe? Reflections on Transnational Citizenship* (Princeton: Princeton University Press, 2004), p. 15.
17. Lara Ryazanova-Clarke, "Russian with an Accent: Globalisation and the Post-Soviet Imaginary," in *The Russian language Outside the Nation: Speakers and Identities*, ed. Lara Ryazanova-Clarke (Edinburgh: Edinburgh University Press, 2014), p. 256.
18. Official Internet Resources of the President of Russia, speech by Vladimir Putin, "Poslanie Prezidenta Federal'nomu Sobraniju," 4 December 2014.
19. Timothy Snyder, "Fascism, Russia, and Ukraine," *The New York Review*, 20 March 2014; for more details on this subject in the Soviet Union, see Serhii Plokhy, *The Last Empire: The Final Days of the Soviet Union* (London: Oneworld Publications, 2015), pp. 406–407.
20. Lilia Shevtsova, "Implosion, Atrophy, or Revolution?" *Journal of Democracy*, Vol. 23, No. 3 (July 2012), pp. 25–27.
21. Timothy Snyder, *The Road to Unfreedom: Russia, Europe, America* (New York: Tim Duggan Books, 2018), p. 81.
22. Mark Kramer, "Russian Policy Toward the Commonwealth of Independent States: Recent Trends and Future Prospects," *Problems of Post-Communism*, Vol. 55, No. 6 (2008), p. 4; Gleb Bryanski, "Putin, Medvedev praise values of Soviet Union," *Reuters*, 17 November 2011; Vladimir Putin, "Novyj internacionnyj proekt dlja Evrazii – budushhee, kotoroe rozhdaetsja sevodnyja," *Izvestia*, 3 October 2011.
23. Edward Lucas, *The New Cold War: Putin's Russia and the Threat to the West* (New York: St. Martin's Press, 2014), pp. 2–3; Official Internet Resources of the President of Russia, speech by Vladimir Putin, "Poslanie Federal'nomu Sobraniju Rossijskoj Federacii," 25 April 2005.
24. Official Internet Resources of the President of Russia, speech by Vladimir Putin, "Vystuplenie i diskussija na Mjunhenskoj konferencii po voprosam politiki bezopasnosti," 2007 Munich Conference on Security Policy, 10 February 2007.
25. Speech by Vladimir Putin in 2007, cited in *Teaching History and the Changing Nation State: Transnational and Intranational Perspectives*, ed. Robert Guyver (London: Bloomsbury Academic, 2016), p. 195. This speech promoted a Kremlin-approved history textbook which portrays Stalin as a great leader and justifies his terror as an "instrument of development." The book, written by nationalist historian Alexander Filipov, was published in 2007 under the title, *A Modern History of Russia: 1945–2006: A Manual for History Teachers*.

26. Michael McFaul, *From Cold War to Hot Peace: An American Ambassador in Putin's Russia* (New York: Houghton Mifflin Harcourt Publishing Company, 2018), pp. 57–72.
27. Brown, *Walled States*, p. 82.
28. Ostrovsky, *The Invention of Russia*, p. 307.
29. Levada Center, "Foreign Agents," Levada Center: Yuri Levada Analytical Center, 17 December 2015.
30. Leon Aron, "Don't Be Putin's Useful Idiot," American Enterprise Institute, 21 December 2016.
31. Arendt, *Origins of Totalitarianism*, p. 142.
32. Sergey Lavrov, "Istoricheskaja perspektiva vneshnej politiki Rossii," *Russia in Global Affairs*, 3 March 2016.
33. Maxim Shevchenko, "My ne Evropa? I slava bogu!" *Moskovskii Komsomolets*, 10 February 2011; Ostrovsky, *The Invention of Russia*, p. 312; Snyder, "Fascism, Russia, and Ukraine"; Sergei Glazyev, *Genocide: Russia and the New World Order*, trans. Rachel B. Douglas (Leesburg: Executive Intelligence Review, 1999), p. 14.
34. Whatever "overcoming the West" really entails seems to vary from day to day. It might mean debunking Western democracy as a façade, proving Russia as a superior culture, or something else.
35. Official Internet Resources of the President of Russia, "Vystuplenie i diskussija na Mjunhenskoj konferencii."
36. Official Internet Resources of the President of Russia, "Poslanie Prezidenta."
37. Levada Center, "Western Lifestyle," Levada Center: Yuri Levada Analytical Center, 16 October 2015.
38. Anne Garrels, *Putin Country: A Journey into the Real Russia* (New York: Farrar, Straus and Giroux, 2016), p. 186.
39. Vladimir Voinovich, *The Anti-Soviet Soviet Union*, trans. Richard Lourie (San Diego, New York, and London: Harcourt Brace Jovanovich, 1985), pp. 17–18.
40. Official Resources of the President of Russia, speech by Vladimir Putin, "Obrashhenie Prezidenta Rossijskoj Federacii," 18 March 2014.
41. Emilio Gentile, *Politics as Religion*, trans. George Staunton (Princeton and Oxford: Princeton University Press, 2006), p. 139; Anthony Smith, "The 'Golden Age' and National Renewal," in *Myths and Nationhood*, eds. Geoffrey Hosking and George Shöpflin (New York: Routledge, 1997), p. 48.
42. Timothy Snyder, *Bloodlands: Europe Between Hitler and Stalin* (London: Vintage Books, 2010).
43. Timothy Snyder and Thomas Carothers, "The Road to Unfreedom" (presentation at Carnegie Endowment for International Peace, Washington, DC, 18 May 2018).

44. Pomerantsev, *Nothing is True*, p. 66.
45. Snyder, *The Road to Unfreedom*, p. 157.
46. Leon Aron, "The Putin Doctrine: Russia's Quest to Rebuild the Soviet State," *Foreign Affairs*, 8 March 2013.
47. Andrei Soldatov, "Putin Has Finally Reincarnated the KGB," *Foreign Affairs*, 21 September 2016.
48. George Shöpflin, "The Functions of Myths and a Taxonomy of Myths," in *Myths and Nationhood*, eds. Geoffrey Hosking and George Shöpflin (New York: Routledge, 1997), p. 29; Ilya Prizel, "Nationalism in Postcommunist Russia: From Resignation to Anger," in *Between Past and Future: The Revolutions of 1989 and Their Aftermath*, eds. Sorin Antohi and Vladimir Tismaneanu (Budapest and New York: Central European University Press, 2000), p. 351.
49. Gorbachev, *The New Russia*, p. 426.
50. Leon Aron, "Novorossiya! Putin and his dangerous 'new Russia,'" *Commentary Magazine*, 1 December 2014.
51. Snyder, "Fascism, Russia, and Ukraine"; Derek Gregory, *The Colonial Present* (Malden: Blackwell Publishing, 2004), pp. 4 and 21.
52. Voinovich, *The Anti-Soviet Soviet Union*, p. 23.
53. Vladimir Putin, "Rossija i menyayushchiysya mir" [Russia and the Changing World], *Moskovskih novostjah*, 27 February 2012.
54. See Roger Cohen, *Hearts Grown Brutal: Sagas of Sarajevo* (New York: Random House, 1998).
55. Weimar Germany, or the Weimar Republic, is the unofficial term used widely to describe the German government established following its defeat in World War I and the abdication of Kaiser Wilhelm II. This government was in power between 1919 and 1933, ending once Adolf Hitler democratically became Chancellor. Weimar Germany suffered a slew of difficulties since its creation. The Treaty of Versailles, which ended World War I and called upon Germany to make massive concessions and financial reparations for its brazen attempt to ruin European civilization, left many Germans seething under a sense of national humiliation. Not only had their imperialist and supposedly superior empire lost the war, but they also literally had to pay for the destruction they wreaked, too. Rather than force Germany into submission, though, these punishments were demonized by nationalist Germans who had not learned the vital lessons of World War I. Hyperinflation and economic disaster especially were harnessed by fascists like Adolf Hitler to gain notoriety for their rabidly millenarian visions of utopia and their re-ignition of violent nationalism across the German population. A rejection of European values, resistance to democratic transition, economic hardship, fabricated threats of internal enemies, belief in a superior German race, and imperialist views combined at the hands of

right-wing extremists to galvanize a barbaric movement that culminated in World War II. Stephen E. Hanson and Jeffrey S. Kopstein, "The Weimar/Russia Comparison," *Post-Soviet Affairs*, Vol. 13, No. 3 (July–September 1997), pp. 252–283 and Walter Laqueur, *Putinism: Russia and Its Future with the West* (New York: Thomas Dunne Books, 2015).
56. Hanson and Kopstein, "The Weimar/Russia Comparison."
57. Roger Cohen, "Russia's Weimar Syndrome," *New York Times*, 1 May 2014. For more on the ideas of Weimar Germany and Weimar Russia and how they relate to one another, see Alexander Yanov, *Weimar Russia and What We Can Do About It* (New York: Slovo-Word Publishing House, 1995).
58. Michel Foucault, *The Birth of Biopolitics: Lectures at the Collège de France, 1978–1979*, ed. Michael Senellart (New York: Palgrave Macmillan, 2008), p. 317.
59. Giorgio Agamben, *Homo Sacer: Sovereign Power and Bare Life* (Stanford: Stanford University Press, 1995), pp. 12–13.
60. Agamben, *Homo Sacer*, p. 6.
61. Andrey Makarychev, "Putin's Russia: Bare Life, Emptiness and Biopolitical Regulations," PONARS Eurasia, 20 February 2013.
62. Prizel, "Nationalism in Postcommunist Russia," p. 336.
63. McFaul, *From Cold War to Hot Peace*, p. 36; Michael Cox and Peter Shearman, "After the fall: nationalist extremism in post-communist Russia," in *Politics of the Extreme Right: From the Margins to the Mainstream*, ed. Paul Hainsworth (London: Bloomsbury Academic, 2016), p. 232.
64. Serguei A. Oushakine, *The Patriotism of Despair: Nation, War, and Loss in Russia* (Ithaca: Cornell University Press, 2009), p. 124; Makarychev, "Putin's Russia."
65. Ben Judah, *Fragile Empire: How Russia Fell In and Out of Love with Vladimir Putin* (New Haven: Yale University Press, 2013), p. 148.
66. Garrels, *Putin Country*, pp. 58–59; Michael Stuermer, *Putin and the Rise of Russia* (New York: Pegasus Books, 2009), p. 117.
67. Alicja Cecylia Curanović, "Relations Between the Orthodox Church and Islam in the Russian Federation," *Journal of Church and State*, Vol. 52, No. 3 (Summer 2010), p. 539.
68. Garrels, *Putin Country*, pp. 134–153.
69. Garrels, *Putin Country*, pp. 134–153; Lourie, *Putin: His Downfall*, p. 86.
70. Judah, *Fragile Empire*, p. 149; Stuermer, *Putin and the Rise of Russia*, p. 125.
71. Pomerantsev, *Nothing is True*, pp. 48 and 119; Garrels, *Putin Country*, p. 124.
72. Judah, *Fragile Empire*, p. 149; Stuermer, *Putin and the Rise of Russia*, p. 118; Garrels, *Putin Country*, p. 122.

73. Snyder, *The Road to Unfreedom*, p. 61.
74. Amendments to the law protecting children from information harmful to their health and development, Official Internet Resources of the President of Russia, 30 June 2013; Human Rights Watch, "Russia: Anti-LGBT Law a Tool for Discrimination," Human Rights Watch, 29 June 2014.
75. Mark Gevisser, "Life Under Russia's 'Gay Propaganda' Ban," *New York Times*, 27 December 2013; Snyder, *The Road to Unfreedom*, p. 52; Garrels, *Putin Country*, p. 55.
76. Garrels, *Putin Country*, p. 51.
77. Giorgio Agamben, *State of Exception* (Chicago: University of Chicago Press, 2005), p. 65.
78. Oushakine, *The Patriotism of Despair*, p. 126; Agamben, *Homo Sacer*, p. 182.
79. George Orwell, *Animal Farm: A Fairy Story* (London: Secker and Warburg, 1945), p. 123.
80. Aleksandr Zinovyev, *Homo Sovieticus* (London: Polonia, 1984), p. 8; see also Russian émigré writer Mikhail Heller's *Cogs in the Wheel: The Formation of Soviet Man* (Westminster: Alfred A. Knopf, Inc., 1988).
81. Tismaneanu, *The Crisis of Marxist Ideology*, p. 12.
82. Yuri Levada, *Sovetsky prostoy chelovek: Opyt sotsial'nogo portreta na rubezhe 90-kh* (Moscow: publisher unknown, 1993). Cited in Masha Gessen, *The Future is History: How Totalitarianism Reclaimed Russia* (New York: Riverhead Books, 2017), p. 59. For a more detailed yet digestible discussion of Levada's *homo sovieticus* and how his term reflected reality, see Gessen, *The Future is History*, pp. 59–66.
83. Lev Gudkov and Eva Hartog, "The Evolution of Homo Sovieticus to Putin's Man," *The Moscow Times*, 13 October 2017.
84. It should be noted that there are, of course, some groups that refuse to conform in such a manner, such as the Russian NGO called The Union of the Committees of Soldiers' Mothers of Russia. Members of groups like this one protest against the Kremlin for unfairly sending their children off to fight under terrible conditions and for what they understand to be trivial reasons. Unfortunately, their numbers are few, and the Russian government has increased its efforts to counter their protests over the past few years, particularly since the invasion of Ukraine. The aforementioned NGO has been labeled a "foreign agent" and some of its leaders have been harassed and detained in an effort to delegitimize their complaints, and thus keep the Russian government looking heroic and morally correct, in the eyes of the rest of the indoctrinated citizenry. Radio Free Europe/Radio Liberty, "Russian 'Soldiers' Mothers' Activist Detained," Radio Free Europe/Radio Liberty, 18 October 2014.

REFERENCES

Agamben, Giorgio. 1995. *Homo Sacer: Sovereign Power and Bare Life*. Stanford: Stanford University Press.
———. 2005. *State of Exception*. Chicago: University of Chicago Press.
Amendments to the law protecting children from information harmful to their health and development. 2013. Official Internet Resources of the President of Russia. June 30. Accessed 29 January 2019 at http://en.kremlin.ru/events/president/news/18423
Arendt, Hannah. 1958. *Origins of Totalitarianism*. New York: Meridian Books.
Aron, Leon. 2013. The Putin Doctrine: Russia's Quest to Rebuild the Soviet State. *Foreign Affairs*, March 8. Accessed 2 September 2016 at https://www.foreignaffairs.com/articles/russian-federation/2013-03-08/putin-doctrine
———. 2014. Novorossiya! Putin and His Dangerous 'New Russia.' *Commentary Magazine*, December 1. Accessed 13 December 2016 at https://www.commentarymagazine.com/articles/novorossiya/
———. 2016. Don't Be Putin's Useful Idiot. *American Enterprise Institute*, December 21. Accessed 21 December 2016 at https://www.aei.org/publication/dont-be-putins-useful-idiot/
Balibar, Étienne. 2004. *We, the People of Europe? Reflections on Transnational Citizenship*. Princeton: Princeton University Press.
Barabantseva, Elena. 2008. How Do People Come to Identify with Nations? In *Global Politics: A New Introduction*, ed. Jenny Edkins and Maja Zehfuss, 2nd ed., 245–268. New York: Routledge.
Brown, Wendy. 2010. *Walled States, Waning Sovereignty*. New York: Zone Books.
Bryanski, Gleb. 2011. Putin, Medvedev Praise Values of Soviet Union. *Reuters*, November 17. Accessed 2 January 2017 at http://in.reuters.com/article/idINIndia-60590820111117
Bukharin, Nikolai. 1928. The International Situation and the Tasks of the Comintern. *International Press Correspondence* 8 (41): 725–740.
Clark, Katerina, Evgeny Dobrenko, Andrei Artizov, and Oleg Naumov. 2007. *Soviet Culture and Power: A History in Documents, 1917–1953*. New Haven: Yale University Press.
Cohen, Roger. 1998. *Hearts Grown Brutal: Sagas of Sarajevo*. New York: Random House.
———. 2014. Russia's Weimar Syndrome. *New York Times*, May 1. Accessed 21 August 2018 at https://www.nytimes.com/2014/05/02/opinion/cohen-russias-weimar-syndrome.html
Cox, Michael, and Peter Shearman. 2016. After the Fall: Nationalist extremism in Post-Communist Russia. In *Politics of the Extreme Right: From the Margins to the Mainstream*, ed. Paul Hainsworth, 224–246. London: Bloomsbury Academic.

Curanović, Alicja Cecylia. 2010. Relations Between the Orthodox Church and Islam in the Russian Federation. *Journal of Church and State* 52 (3): 503–539.
Fehér, Ferenc, Ágnes Heller, and György Markus. 1983. *Dictatorship Over Needs: An Analysis of Soviet Societies*. New York: St. Martin's Press.
Foucault, Michel. 2008. In *The Birth of Biopolitics: Lectures at the College de France, 1978–1979*, ed. Michael Senellart. New York: Palgrave Macmillan.
Garrels, Anne. 2016. *Putin Country: A Journey into the Real Russia*. New York: Farrar, Straus and Giroux.
Gentile, Emilio. 2006. *Politics as Religion*. Trans. G. Staunton. Princeton/Oxford: Princeton University Press.
Gessen, Masha. 2017. *The Future Is History: How Totalitarianism Reclaimed Russia*. New York: Riverhead Books.
Gevisser, Mark. 2013. Life Under Russia's 'Gay Propaganda' Ban. *New York Times*, December 27. Accessed 29 January 2017 at http://www.nytimes.com/2013/12/28/opinion/life-under-russias-gay-propaganda-ban.html?_r=0
Glazyev, Sergei. 1999. *Genocide: Russia and the New World Order*. Trans. R.B. Douglas. Leesburg: Executive Intelligence Review.
Glissant, Édouard. 1997. *Poetics of Relation*. Trans. B. Wing. Ann Arbor: The University of Michigan Press.
Gregory, Derek. 2004. *The Colonial Present*. Malden: Blackwell Publishing.
Gudkov, Lev, and Eva Hartog. 2017. The Evolution of Homo Sovieticus to Putin's Man. *The Moscow Times*, October 13. Accessed 15 March 2019 at https://themoscowtimes.com/articles/the-evolution-of-homo-sovieticus-to-putins-man-59189
Guyver, Robert. 2016. Speech by Vladimir Putin in 2007. In *Teaching History and the Changing Nation State: Transnational and Intranational Perspectives*, ed. Robert Guyver. London: Bloomsbury Academic.
Hanson, Stephen E., and Jeffrey S. Kopstein. 1997. The Weimar/Russia Comparison. *Post-Soviet Affairs* 13 (3): 252–283.
Heller, Mikhail. 1988. *Cogs in the Wheel: The Formation of Soviet Man*. Westminster: Alfred A. Knopf, Inc.
Higgins, Andrew. 2019. Turgenev Dissed Russia But Is Still Lionized as Literary Star by Touchy Kremlin. *New York Times*, March 11. Accessed 11 March 2019 at https://www.nytimes.com/2019/03/11/world/europe/russia-turgenev.html?rref=collection%2Fbyline%2Fandrewhiggins&action=click&contentColle ction=undefined&region=stream&module=stream_unit&version=latest&cont entPlacement=1&pgtype=collection
Human Rights Watch. 2014. Russia: Anti-LGBT Law a Tool for Discrimination. *Human Rights Watch*, June 29. Accessed 29 January 2017 at https://www.hrw.org/news/2014/06/29/russia-anti-lgbt-law-tool-discrimination

Inayatullah, Naeem, and David L. Blaney. 2004. *International Relations and the Problem of Difference*. New York: Routledge.
Judah, Ben. 2013. *Fragile Empire: How Russia Fell In and Out of Love with Vladimir Putin*. New Haven: Yale University Press.
Kramer, Mark. 2008. Russian Policy Toward the Commonwealth of Independent States: Recent Trends and Future Prospects. *Problems of Post-Communism* 55 (6): 3–19.
Laqueur, Walter. 2015. *Putinism: Russia and Its Future with the West*. New York: Thomas Dunne Books.
Lavrov, Sergey. 2016. Istoricheskaja perspektiva vneshnej politiki Rossii [A Historical Perspective of Russia's Foreign Policy]. *Russia in Global Affairs*, March 3. Accessed 20 January 2017 at https://www.globalaffairs.ru/global-processes/Istoricheskaya-perspektiva-vneshnei-politiki-Rossii-18017
Levada, Yuri. 1993. *Sovetsky prostoy chelovek: Opyt sotsial'nogo portreta na rubezhe 90-kh* [The Simple Soviet Man: A Social Portrait's Experience of the 1990s]. Moscow: Publisher Unknown.
Levada Center. 2015a. *Foreign Agents*. Levada Center: Yuri Levada Analytical Center. December 17. Accessed 12 January 2017 at http://www.levada.ru/eng/foreign-agents
———. 2015b. *Western Lifestyle*. Levada Center: Yuri Levada Analytical Center. 16 October. Accessed 12 January 2017 at http://www.levada.ru/eng/western-lifestyle
Lourie, Richard. 2017. *Putin: His Downfall and Russia's Coming Crash*. New York: Thomas Dunne Books.
Lucas, Edward. 2014. *The New Cold War: Putin's Russia and the Threat to the West*. New York: St. Martin's Press.
Makarychev, Andrey. 2013. Putin's Russia: Bare Life, Emptiness and Biopolitical Regulations. *PONARS Eurasia*, February 20. Accessed 29 January 2017 at http://www.ponarseurasia.org/article/putin%E2%80%99s-russia-bare-life-emptiness-and-biopolitical-regulations
McFaul, Michael. 2018. *From Cold War to Hot Peace: An American Ambassador in Putin's Russia*. New York: Houghton Mifflin Harcourt Publishing Company.
Official Internet Resources of the President of Russia. Speech by Vladimir Putin. 2005. *Poslanie Federal'nomu Sobraniju Rossijskoj Federacii* [Annual Address to the Federal Assembly of the Russian Federation]. April 25. Accessed 7 January 2017 at http://en.kremlin.ru/events/president/transcripts/22931
———. 2007. *Vystuplenie i diskussija na Mjunhenskoj konferencii po voprosam politiki bezopasnosti* [Speech and the Following Discussion at the Munich Conference on Security Policy]. 2007 Munich Conference on Security Policy, February 10. Accessed 7 January 2017 at http://en.kremlin.ru/events/president/transcripts/24034

———. 2014a. *Poslanie Prezidenta Federal'nomu Sobraniju* [Presidential Address to the Federal Assembly]. December 4. Accessed 7 January 2017 at http://en.kremlin.ru/events/president/news/47173
———. 2014b. *Obrashhenie Prezidenta Rossijskoj Federacii* [Address by the President of the Russian Federation]. March 18. Accessed 26 September 2018 at http://kremlin.ru/events/president/news/20603
Orwell, George. 1945. *Animal Farm: A Fairy Story*. London: Secker and Warburg.
Ostrovsky, Arkady. 2015. *The Invention of Russia: From Gorbachev's Freedom to Putin's War*. New York: Viking Press.
Oushakine, Serguei A. 2009. *The Patriotism of Despair: Nation, War, and Loss in Russia*. Ithaca: Cornell University Press.
Pasolini, Pier Paolo. 1980. What Is Neo-Zhdanovism and What Is Not. *October* 13: 7–10.
Plokhy, Serhii. 2015. *The Last Empire: The Final Days of the Soviet Union*. London: Oneworld Publications.
Pomerantsev, Peter. 2014. *Nothing Is True and Everything Is Possible: The Surreal Heart of the New Russia*. New York: PublicAffairs.
Prizel, Ilya. 2000. Nationalism in Postcommunist Russia: From Resignation to Anger. In *Between Past and Future: The Revolutions of 1989 and Their Aftermath*, ed. Sorin Antohi and Vladimir Tismaneanu, 332–356. Budapest/New York: Central European University Press.
Putin, Vladimir. 2011. Novyj internacionnyj proekt dlja Evrazii—budushhee, kotoroe rozhdaetsja sevodnyja [A New Integration Project for Eurasia: The Future in the Making]. *Izvestia*, October 3. Accessed 2 January 2017 at http://www.russianmission.eu/en/news/article-prime-minister-vladimir-putin-new-integration-project-eurasia-future-making-izvestia-3-
———. 2012. Rossija i menyayushchiysya mir [Russia and the Changing World]. *Moskovskih novostjah*, February 27. Accessed 1 July 2018 at http://www.mn.ru/politics/78738
Radio Free Europe/Radio Liberty. 2014. Russian 'Soldiers' Mothers' Activist Detained. *Radio Free Europe/Radio Liberty*, October 18. Accessed 17 February 2017 at https://www.rferl.org/a/detention-bogatenkova-soldiers-mothers-russia-ukraine/26643664.html
Rusanov, Dmitrii. 2014. Vojna nachalas'! Prizyvat' k miru – predatel'stvo! Aleksandr Dugin [The War Has Begun! The Call to Peace – Betrayal! Aleksandr Dugin]. *ANNA*, May 6. Accessed 10 January 2017 at http://old.anna-news.info/node/15794
Ryazanova-Clarke, Lara. 2014. Russian with an Accent: Globalisation and the Post-Soviet Imaginary. In *The Russian language Outside the Nation: Speakers and Identities*, ed. Lara Ryazanova-Clarke, 249–281. Edinburgh: Edinburgh University Press.

Shevchenko, Maxim. 2011. My ne Evropa? I slava bogu! [We Are Not Europe? And I Thank God!] *Moskovskii Komsomolets*, February 10. Accessed 9 January 2017 at http://www.mk.ru/politics/2013/02/10/810258-myi-ne-evropa-i-slava-bogu.html

Shevtsova, Lilia. 2012. Implosion, Atrophy, or Revolution? *Journal of Democracy* 23 (3): 19–31.

Shöpflin, George. 1997. The Functions of Myths and a Taxonomy of Myths. In *Myths and Nationhood*, ed. Geoffrey Hosking and George Shöpflin, 19–35. New York: Routledge.

Smith, Anthony. 1997. The 'Golden Age' and National Renewal. In *Myths and Nationhood*, ed. Geoffrey Hosking and George Shöpflin, 36–59. New York: Routledge.

Snyder, Timothy. 2010. *Bloodlands: Europe Between Hitler and Stalin*. London: Vintage Books.

———. 2014. Fascism, Russia, and Ukraine. *The New York Review*, March 20. Accessed 9 September 2016 at http://www.nybooks.com/articles/2014/03/20/fascism-russia-and-ukraine

———. 2018. *The Road to Unfreedom: Russia, Europe, America*. New York: Tim Duggan Books.

Snyder, Timothy, and Thomas Carothers. 2018. *The Road to Unfreedom*. Presentation at Carnegie Endowment for International Peace, Washington, DC, May 18.

Sokolov, Maksim. 2007. Putin absoljuten [Putin Is Absolute]. *Izvestia*, October 5. Accessed 10 July 2018 at https://iz.ru/news/329407#ixzz4MJ1Pft7u

Soldatov, Andrei. 2016. Putin Has Finally Reincarnated the KGB. *Foreign Affairs*, September 21. Accessed 21 September 2016 at http://foreignpolicy.com/2016/09/21/putin-has-finally-reincarnated-the-kgb-mgb-fsb-russia/

Stuermer, Michael. 2009. *Putin and the Rise of Russia*. New York: Pegasus Books.

Tismaneanu, Vladimir. 1988. *The Crisis of Marxist Ideology in Eastern Europe: The Poverty of Utopia*. New York: Routledge.

Tucker, Robert C. 1956. Stalin and the Uses of Adversity. *World Politics* 8 (4): 455–483.

———. 1987. *Political Culture and Leadership in Soviet Russia: From Lenin to Gorbachev*. New York: W.W. Norton & Company, Inc.

Voinovich, Vladimir. 1985. *The Anti-Soviet Soviet Union*. Trans. R. Lourie. San Diego/New York/London: Harcourt Brace Jovanovich.

Whitmore, Brian. 2016. Putin vs. Putin. *Radio Free Europe/Radio Liberty*, September 2. Accessed 15 October 2016 at http://www.rferl.org/content/putin-vs-putin/27962888.html

Yanov, Alexander. 1995. *Weimar Russia and What We Can Do About it*. New York: Slovo-Word Publishing House.

Zinovyev, Aleksandr. 1984. *Homo Sovieticus*. London: Polonia.

CHAPTER 6

Russian Nationalism in Education, the Media, and Religion

Nationalism in Russia has become an inescapable everyday influence that constantly reminds Russian citizens, consciously or subconsciously, of how their country is special and destined for greatness. It comes in many forms, such as television, national holidays, official ceremonies, education, religion, military might, the Kremlin, Putin as head of state, and so on. Those included in the nation's identity are indoctrinated by nationalist propaganda from the state, media, and fellow citizens to, above all, see their state as a superior world superpower—just as the Soviet Union contended during the Cold War. Nationalism is a crucial element of Russian ideology, and it is another vehicle through which Putin's Kremlin is able to curry popular favor.

The Kremlin's most important demand is for patriotism, and it seems to be doing well on this front: in November 2015, polls showed that 85 percent of Russian citizens were at least "somewhat proud" of the Russian armed forces, and 88 percent responded similarly when it came to Russian history. Fifty-nine percent agreed that Russia is better than most other countries in the world.[1] The people are not to be mere Russian citizens, but *loyal* Russian citizens. What this entails was demonstrated at a rally commemorating the armed forces on 23 February 2013 in Moscow's Luzhniki Stadium: Putin asked the crowd, "Do we love Russia?" and then encouraged the 130,000 people present to vocally respond. As a Russian journalist commented, Putin uttered in his speech the word "'death' exactly four times … he was calling on us to die in his name, for Russia personified."[2]

© The Author(s) 2020
K. C. Langdon, V. Tismaneanu, *Putin's Totalitarian Democracy*,
https://doi.org/10.1007/978-3-030-20579-9_6

This kind of mobilizing nationalism is related to Russia' superiority complex and functions as another pillar of the Kremlin's greater ideology. Ultranationalism in Russia serves to celebrate its mighty, powerful, and successful moments, while forgetting others. This means that the state ideological machine is fully geared to promote selective memory and its reverse, selective amnesia. Aided by officially sanctioned remembrance and the process of historical revisionism, Russia can further convince its population that the country, with its past glorifying history, is destined for future greatness. It is a celebration of Russia as a higher civilization, one that has a special mission in the world and is not bound to the same international rules all other nation-states are expected to obey because it is so exceptional. A poll conducted in January 2016 by the Levada Center asked Russian citizens, "What kind of democracy does Russia need?" 46 percent of respondents selected the option "A completely special kind that is appropriate to Russia's national traditions and unique characteristics"— emphasizing how the view of an extraordinary Russia significantly influences a substantial part of the citizenry. It leads them to believe Russia is so unlike any other nation that it must govern itself differently, as well.[3]

But how and why does such a large portion of the population ever come to believe this narrative? Again, we turn to Robert C. Tucker's illuminating analysis of Soviet Russia and his emphasis on societal behavior:

> Through socialization (or acculturation), the young are inducted into the culture by training and experience. They learn both the ideal culture patterns or accepted principles and, also, especially as they graduate into adulthood, the prevalent practices. Where discrepancies exist, socialization works toward training the new generation into acceptance of them. If slavery, for example, is an established set of practices in a particular society although incongruent with certain religious principles held by most people in that society, the generality of the society's members, slaves included, may be socialized into believing in the rightness of the institution so long as slaves are treated according to certain rules.[4]

It is true that the magnitude of this kind of managed socialization in today's Russia might not be as totalizing or as violent as it was during Soviet times. And this is not to say that all Russians fall (or all Soviets fell, for that matter) for ideologically manipulative lies. Still, many post-Soviets and Russians alike, hailing from all classes and backgrounds, did grow up to be conformists who rationalized the otherwise illogical system. Take, for example, the Russian media that often complain about how U.S. air strikes in Syria violate international law, yet applaud President Putin for illegally annexing Crimea in the most brazen imperialist act since Adolf Hitler's time. Tucker's iteration about forced socialization, then, remains highly relevant.

The Soviet Union has disintegrated, but ideological state apparatuses and societal institutions have not. The intensity with which propagandistic, Russocentric thoughts are shared and reproduced throughout Russian society indicates the significant power ideological state apparatuses still wield in largely successful attempts to socialize the national population. In Russia, three of the most important ideological state apparatuses, as French Marxist philosopher Louis Althusser coined them, happen to be the national education system, the media, and the Russian Orthodox Church. All three of these institutions function to indoctrinate Russian citizens on a daily, personal basis into the ideological tenets examined in Chap. 5. Simultaneously, they also close off new lines of flight, peremptorily obstructing rational explorations which may cause individuals to see the world in an alternate dimension and to question their government's policies.

IDEOLOGY AND YOUTH EDUCATION IN RUSSIA

Education grooms and provides tools with which children learn to understand the world. A national education system is an effective mechanism by which to install hegemony over a people, as education can be directly involved in the self-identification process of individuals, particularly young ones. The Russian government, like many others, is well aware of this and manages schools throughout the country so as to promote nationalism.

In Putin's own words at the National Russian Conference of Humanities and Social Sciences Teachers in June 2007, he ordered new Kremlin-approved history textbooks for the purpose of "mak[ing] our citizens, especially the young, proud of their country."[5] Recently appointed Russian Minister of Education and Science Olga Vasilyeva concurred with Putin's goal, saying at a youth forum in 2016, "It is impossible to build the future without a foundation, and that foundation is patriotism—anything else is unimaginable."[6] She has no qualms with the fact that the textbooks positively refer to Stalin and commend him for (what she deems to be nothing more sinister than) reviving patriotism.[7] The books even equate Stalin's genocides—from the Holodomor, a planned starvation of somewhere between 2.5 and 7.5 million Ukrainian peasants in 1932–1933,[8] to the famous order No. 00447 in 1937, which demanded the mass execution of any harmful elements of society in the Soviet Union—to racial segregation in the United States.

While all were hideous crimes, regionwide genocide (and the repression, systematic killing, and exile that accompany it) is far more beyond the pale than other offenses. Still, textbooks are influential when it comes to distorting the past: they can trivialize, or outright deny, the murderous belligerence that a country has exuded in its history. Putin's new books take advantage of this function of historical distortion. They portray Russia's past and present as topics to celebrate and revere, particularly because Russia has inherited the Soviet Union's noble mission for global social justice. Crucial to this supposed success and unity is a long history of autocracy; the books stretch back to include tsarist times as centuries of impressive expansion, military bravery, and social peace via state cooptation under the rule of authoritarian leaders. In celebrating some of the most egregious Stalinist falsifications, this version of history sends primordial messages to its readers.[9] It prompts the duplication of norms and attitudes that characterized previous times, which lead readers to believe that instability arises in the absence of dominating leadership. For example, Mikhail Gorbachev lamented in his book *The New Russia* (2016) that "at the time of Perestroika we were slow in coming to see the need for strong presidential power"—as if the lack of such a figure was the reason why the country suffered.[10]

Assumptions made on the basis of historical events, especially those which occurred centuries before, are dangerous in the present. The fixed social imaginary they inspire results in a narrow, falsified common perspective that prevents students of Russian history from seeing life beyond their one cultural lens. Modern Russia's education system takes a note from that of tsarist times, when education was strictly limited to certain topics and one pro-Russian narrative. These schoolbooks harp on the advantages of autocracy. They subliminally stunt children's growth in understanding the evolving world, the diverse opinions within it, and the potential alternatives to a nationalistic, authoritarian state—which turns out to seriously benefit Putin.

These pieces of state propaganda teach students from an early age that their nation is next to infallible and, by virtue of being the nation's leader, so is Vladimir Putin. The new history textbook rather unsubtly convinces students of this when it states, "We see that practically every significant deed is connected with the name and activity of President V. V. Putin."[11]

In this manner, the Russian education apparatus serves as a creative form of indoctrinating practice that molds young Russians in their formative years, disconnecting them from alternative ways of seeing the world. It is also a form of reconciliation without truth, which is a dangerous game to play in a world where societies are increasingly adopting postmodern views, in which truths becomes indistinguishable from fictions, accountability becomes a lost concept, and blanket attitudes of indifference replace the quest to balance tolerance and respect for human dignity with punishment of intolerance.[12] These distortions are not just taught in classrooms or textbooks, either: they are also perpetuated by the adults who were shaped by the same education system, by the media and religious forces that influence everyday life in Russia (as will be described in the upcoming pages), and by specially formed political youth organizations such as the *Nashi* [Ours],[13] *Mestniye* [Locals], [Network], and *Molodaya Gvardiya Yedinoi Rossii* [Young Guard of United Russia]. Such organizations have been suspected of receiving the majority of their funding from the Russian government and essentially promote their young members to harass opposition groups that might challenge Putin and Russia's conservative traditional values.[14] Through this long process of indoctrination both inside and outside of the education system proper, Putin's regime—in addition to other regimes across the globe—can claim whatever glorifying versions of history they wish with little resistance.

Ideology and the Media in Russia

Russian media reinforce this totalizing lie and continue the state's ideological education program for those who have graduated from youthdom. The media have essentially become subservient to the state. They spew the Kremlin's narrative of events, as a fair number of in-depth studies have already proven.[15] Television channels are the most popular sites from which average Russians get their news. Since Vladimir Putin ascended to the presidency and promptly raided, threatened, or altogether shut down any stations that reported criticisms of him or his inner circle, TV media programs have become shrill megaphones for anti-Western conspiracy theories and condemnations.[16] In his book *Nothing is True and Everything is Possible: The Surreal Heart of the New Russia* (2014), Soviet-born British journalist Peter Pomerantsev documented the typical newsroom antics in one of Russia's largest propaganda outlets, RT News (formerly known as Russia Today). When his acquaintance composed a piece that referenced the Soviet Union's occupation of Estonia in 1945, the writer was chewed out by his boss, who maintained the belief that Russians *saved* Estonia. Any other descriptions of the events of 1945 were unacceptable assaults on Russia's integrity, apparently, so the boss demanded that he amend his text.

Pomerantsev also included a story that perfectly sums up the Russian media's reaction to the Russo-Georgian War of August 2008: as the conflict began, Russia Today broadcast a continuously scrolling alert on its television programs which biasedly told viewers, "Georgians commit genocide in Ossetia."[17] It should be noted that the Russo-Georgian War was instigated by the Russian military and involved a serious breach of Georgian sovereignty (not to mention the fact that no evidence of genocide perpetrated by Georgians was ever unearthed). The Russian media's immediate, shrill Russocentric reaction to contemporary conflict—as well as a hypersensitivity toward denouncing different, unofficial narratives of historical events—demonstrate how the press is just another tool to portray Russia as the brave savior of weaker states and oppressed peoples.

As it did during Soviet times, the media continue to function as a propaganda machine for the state. It has become all about the daily spectacle of the news and the emotions those spectacles evoke within the media's audience. After all, as prominent Russian TV journalist Dmitri Kiselev said in 1999, "people will, of course, swallow anything" the news tells them.[18] Thus, the Russian media's goal is not to depict reality, but to create it. It plays into the Kremlin's security imaginary and follows its predetermined lines of cultural and political difference, which then ingrain themselves upon the worldviews of those who watch and believe.[19] It has the ability to mobilize masses of people: media consumers become so panicked by the alarming propaganda of media outlets that the entire nation ultimately takes part in Russia's struggles and triumphs. It should be noted that the term *mobilize*, as employed here, does not suggest that millions of Russians spring to their feet and take to the streets; rather, it is meant to demonstrate how vast portions of the Russian population hear the Kremlin's stories and remain actively loyal to their government by remaining complicit, voting for the government, dismissing the West and its values, or even going off to war for Russia.[20]

At the same time, it cannot be argued that Russian citizens are simply victims of the Kremlin's propaganda. As a population, they have sought stability for generations. The Kremlin first began to seize independent media when the population spasmed in fits and starts regarding faith in its leadership, economic woes, corruption scandals, and more, until it had gobbled up all space for alternative approaches to the news and intimidated outlets with non-sanctioned perspectives into silence. The Russian people did not react to the seizure with vehemence; they ate it up. The Kremlin-controlled media, then, spits out stories that are both satisfactory to Russian consumers and Putin's regime. It controls the story and, by extension, the public's reaction and mood.[21]

And the Russian people have fallen for it repeatedly. They could choose, with a bit of effort, to find alternative sources of information on the Internet, or to make and talk to friends outside of Russia; they could wrack their brains to understand potential opposite perspectives and ask what pieces of data or analysis are missing from Russian media stories.[22] But this does not happen with many Russians, nor does it happen often enough to cultivate a strong opposition or create a new media outlet outside of the state's control. Instead, Russians will merely insist that American media is full of lies because it is American (actually, this case extends to any Western nation not friendly with Russia), whereas Russian media is trustworthy because it is Russian.

There is no objectivity here. American human rights lawyer Dan Kovalik's book, *The Plot to Scapegoat Russia: How the CIA and the Deep State Have Conspired to Vilify Russia* (mentioned in Chap. 1), asserts the very same preposterous tale. With little conclusive evidence, he writes of how awful the American media is and how Americans readily believe their lies; in defense of Russian news outlets, however, Kovalik assuages the guilt of RT News by saying that anyone who watches it *knows* it is the Russian view: thus, they cannot be blind believers, and it cannot be propaganda. This logic makes absolutely no sense—people watching American news know it is American, yet still fall for its lies, in Kovalik's opinion, yet apparently they can suddenly accurately judge press when they know it is Russian.[23]

On top of this nonsense reasoning, Kovalik fundamentally fails to understand what propaganda is. It is not just some secret, brainwashing subliminal message. The most effective propaganda can be blatant and loud. It can proclaim itself to be Russian and still convince its audience that its stories are true. This is how the Russian media succeeds in garnering support for the illegal annexation of Crimea: it can tell viewers that all the inhabitants of Crimea, including the Tartar minority, are happier under Russian governance than under Ukrainian governance.[24] And the majority will believe this. It is that simple and that unsupported by evidence, much less evidence of a factual nature arising from multiple, trustworthy sources.

After all, it is easier to just accept the Kremlin's news. It is more pleasant to view your own country as an innocent, morally correct entity and to hate outsiders than it is to question all you have believed since childhood—or, perhaps more precisely, all your parents have believed since childhood. A poll conducted in October 2015 reveals that over 50 percent of Russian citizens do not feel they are being deceived or supplied with false information by their news sources.[25] A Soviet-born art history professor in St. Petersburg confessed this sentiment when he told his class of American students, of which I [KL] was a part, in the fall of 2015: "It was better in Soviet times. At least then we all knew the TV and radio were lying. Today, people just believe." Russian media fails to inform its viewers, much less allow them to understand their own country or the world of which they are a part.[26] It perpetuates a vicious cycle of disinformation and public support.[27]

When it comes to the material and narratives allowed to exist within Russian borders, the government does not stop at news outlets or radio broadcasts. In January 2018, Russia's Ministry of Culture banned director Armando Ianucci's film *The Death of Stalin* from being screened in theaters. A black comedy about the power struggle between power-hungry and idiotic Soviet leaders that ensued after Josef Stalin's death in March 1953, Minister of Culture Vladimir Medinsky accused the film of "blackening the memory of our citizens who conquered fascism" and of lampooning Russia's history. Other ministry officials and professors called the film "despicable," suspected that is might be part of a "western plot to destabilise Russia by causing rifts in society," and favored the ban because the film insulted "our historic national symbols."[28] Only one theater in the entire country, Pioner Cinema, chose to move forward with their screening of *The Death of Stalin*; in response, Russian police officers raided the building and fined the business, and the Ministry of Culture threatened other theaters with the prospect of "temporary closure" if they also tried to show the banned film.[29]

Medinsky refused to admit that the ban amounted to censorship. Instead, he justified it as a moral act meant to protect the good name of Russia.[30] The intense, personal degree of insult generated in response to the film demonstrates the highly sensitive nature of nationalist ideology in Russia today. To begin with, the film takes place years after the end of World War II, and so does not make a farce of wartime Soviet conduct.

Even if *The Death of Stalin* did, it would be absurd of any government to ban a movie for supposedly insulting historic memory in relation to events that transpired 70 years prior.

Yet this is exactly what occurred. Clearly, the government and society are both sensitive to national memory and pride. Perhaps they also see the links between Stalin and Putin and take offense at the perceived mocking of their modern-day leader. No matter what the exact reason behind the decision to ban the film was, it is evident that ideological views of contemporary Russian society and the sacredness of Russian national glory influence major aspects of media and entertainment in Russia.

Ideology and Religion in Russia

The third major source of ideological control is the Russian Orthodox Church. It serves as a mechanism by which the Kremlin's narrative can delve furthest into each individual's private realm. It is the second-most respected institution in Russia as of 2015, with a poll rating of 75 percent (behind the presidency, with a poll rating of 91 percent).[31] Similar to how right-wing American evangelists heavily impact politics in the United States, Russian Orthodoxy also distorts Russian politics—but on a much larger scale. The Church has played a crucial role in Russian history, from supporting the tsars to being co-opted by the Soviet and modern Russian governments. No matter which political leaders it served, the Orthodox Church has functioned to preserve a stable, conservative, paternalistic, nationalistic order in Russia, an order often beloved by the majority of the population.

As M. Steven Fish, a political scientist at UC Berkeley specializing in post-Communist regime change, puts it, Putin's Kremlin has successfully leveraged the Church by assuming de facto control over its properties, funding, and high-level appointments. It also has buddied up to the head of the Russian Orthodox Church (his full title being Patriarch Kirill of Moscow and All Rus') in the most personal of ways; for example, the Kremlin reacted to his complaints against Timofey Kulyabin, the director of the Novosibirsk Opera and Ballet Theater who had arranged for a "blasphemous" performance of Richard Wagner's *Tannhäuser* in 2015, by outright firing Kulyabin and replacing him with Kirill's suggested candidate.[32] In fact, security expert Marcel van Herpen asserts that in the last two decades, Vladimir Putin has co-opted the Church into expressing "unconditional support for his aggressive neo-imperialist policies" and backing him in his endeavors to proclaim the shared values of the state and of the Church in order to further distance Russia from the modern, European nation-state.[33]

From the standpoint of *practicality*, it *matters not* that Putin does not adhere to any religious doctrine. The Kremlin and the Church have cultivated a strategic and ideological partnership that has no bearing whatsoever to a shared religion or faith. Like Putin and his Kremlin, the Church emphasizes its suspicion of Western values, namely individualism, liberalism, and democracy. To counter them, the Church makes a concerted effort to produce a Russian national consciousness composed primarily of dynastic legends, territorial pride, and Orthodox faith—fundamentally referring to a culture that distinguishes itself from, and is superior to, that of the West.[34]

From the standpoint of *content*, it *does matter* that Putin does not adhere to any religious doctrine. To present Russia as a theophoric, God-carrying nation (a prophetic notion introduced by Fyodor Dostoyevsky during a speech he delivered in Moscow at the June 1880 unveiling of a monument to Russian poet Alexander Pushkin[35]) without actually believing in a religion signals that the Russian government's collaboration with the Russian Orthodox Church is part of an ethnonationalist project and obsession. As Vladislav Surkov, the First Deputy Head of the Administration of the President (aka the Kremlin's chief strategist), uttered during a lecture at the Russian Academy of Sciences in June 2007, "Culture is fate. God made us Russians, citizens of Russia."[36] In a 2013 interview with RT News, Putin told his audience, "Russians have different, far loftier ambitions; more of a spiritual kind. It's more about your relationship with God," thereby hailing all Russian subjects as faithful, moral subjects of a higher religious power, as well.[37] This mentality plays perfectly to Putin's ideology, adding a solid spiritual, God-granted dimension to the beliefs that Russia is a superior culture and must protect itself from the West. In other words, this connection between church and state is one of an ethnic nature, one that places itself in fundamental opposition to the ideals of a pluralistic, diverse society based on equal human rights and dignity.

The term "Holy Russia" is difficult to avoid hearing or reading on the streets of St. Petersburg and Moscow. Average Russian citizens make statements in interviews, newspapers, news videos, and so on such as, "we must rescue the soul of Holy Russia." They also warn of "how the great Orthodox Empire (to which Russia is the successor) was brought low by a mix of oligarchs and the West." Therefore, they say Russia must resist the "self-love [that] is at the root of Western rationality" because it allows for individualism that splits a community apart. This is not the Russian way, they say, since in the kingdom of God, "all is one," and this unity is exactly "why the Russian soul is holy. It can unite everything. Like in an icon. Stalin and God."[38] Some people even refer to Putin, the leader of their great country, as *batyushka* [holy father]. As Putin campaigned for reelection in 2012, Patriarch Kirill referred to his first two presidential terms as a "miracle from God."[39]

Religious justification such as this is popular among the citizenry. It advocates for essentially the same societal ends as the Kremlin does. In particular, it aids Putin's regime in its conservative denunciation of all potentially destabilizing forms of protest. Archpriest Dmitrii Smirnov laid this pro-government theme on thick to the Russian population during the infamous (and since then unheard of) 2012 protests against Putin when he warned, "One needs to remember that the first revolutionary was Satan."[40] His statement is just one instance among many in which the Church perpetuates the Kremlin's line and traditional conservatism in Russia. Russian conservatism "promotes the status quo and hates anything that might be a source of instability."[41] In short, it represses free, pluralist activity and prevents civil action, immediately demonizing them as occasions of rabble-rousing. Democracy, then, is not celebrated in the Orthodox Church or in Putin's Russia: as of a 2013 survey, 37 percent of Orthodox bishops insisted that democracy was entirely "not for Russia."[42] As discussed in Chap. 3, Putin has been especially wary of any public protest since he witnessed the anti-Soviet revolution in Dresden as a mediocre KGB officer in December 1989; so, Russian conservatism enjoys a symbiotic relationship with Putinism. The added input of the conservative Russian Orthodox Church, therefore, further cements conservatism and Putinism.

In keeping with Russia's post-Soviet religious revival, the Eastern spiritual image of St. George[43] has resurfaced under Putin as a patriotic symbol of modern Russia. The original St. George's ribbon dates back to 1769 and was bestowed as the highest military decoration in Imperial Russia, owing to St. George's legendary bravery in combat. It features orange and black stripes meant to represent fire and gunpowder, the death and resurrection of St. George, and the colors of the imperial Russian coat of arms.

The ribbon's usage and meaning began to fade with the Soviet Union's turn to atheism—until late 2004, when it reemerged as the emblem of those who opposed Ukraine's Orange Revolution.[44] The Kremlin feared a color revolution could spread to Russia and threaten the stability of Putin's regime. So, it preemptively denounced the Orange Revolution as a conspiracy with fascist undertones masterminded by the CIA. In 2010, popular Russian news outlet *Perviy Kanal* [Channel One] aired a "documentary" (a propaganda film, in actuality) by the name of *The Orange Children of the Third Reich*.[45] All the while, the St. George's ribbon steadily grew in popularity among Russian nationalists, signifying the might of the Russian state. The ribbon became the symbol for the pro-Russian separatists in Ukraine who protested against the 2013–2014 Euromaidan in Kyiv.

In the fall of 2015 in St. Petersburg, an American peer of mine [KL] asked our Russian-American professor what "that orange and black ribbon" (a St. George's ribbon) hanging on the rearview mirror of a nearby van was, as she had "seen it everywhere." The professor answered in front of myself and ten other students, "oh, it's something that will get you killed in Ukraine." In his mind, this ribbon embodied Russia, its purity, its faith, its glorious history, and its destiny; contrastingly, Ukrainians were apparently so vile and wanted to destroy Russia so badly that they would immediately murder anyone who supported it. His confidence that Russia was "the good guy" surrounded by enemies of lesser moral value completely ignored the fact that no such murders of Russians by Ukrainians had been documented by official sources—except, of course, when referring to the fighting in Ukraine's Donbas region, at which point his logic would also hit another snag: Ukrainians were not simply murdering Russians for the fun of it. It had been Russia that first broke international law, invaded another sovereign nation-state, and instigated hostilities by entering into war and killing Ukrainians who tried to protect their communities.

The words of sociologist Neil Smelser are particularly relevant in analyzing this situation: "one of the most profound aspects of evil is that he who does the evil is typically convinced that evil is about to be done to him. He regards the world or at least part of it as dangerous or bent on destruction and therefore something justifiably to be destroyed."[46] This professor had been so indoctrinated by the Kremlin's ideology that he could not fathom how his country had committed any wrongdoing which might warrant disobedience (or "evil," in his mind) from another country. All he could think of was Russia's integrity. The (il)logic of this imaginary tainting of national identity at the hands of savage Ukrainians demonstrates how Russian ideology grooms its subjects into viewing the world from a single, state-determined perspective, and how objects like the St. George's ribbon serve as reinforcing reminders of this thought pattern.

On 28 April 2016, about 20 ultranationalists sporting the St. George's ribbon (and military-style uniforms) attacked an awards ceremony held in Moscow by human rights and political opposition organization Memorial. The ceremony was organized to honor a group of high school students for their excellent essay submissions on twentieth-century Russian history. Their attackers threw eggs and green slime at the attendees, angered that the essay submissions "diminish[ed] the Soviet Union's role in the victory over Nazi Germany in World War II" by focusing on the crimes the Soviet Union had perpetrated during the time. The protestors called the youths "whores, not students" and justified their actions by saying, "We're exorcising demons from these Jewish kids. These kids have been converted. They're off their rockers. They need medical help."[47]

These words were of anti-Semitic, misogynistic, patriarchal, and a slew of other offensive natures. Yet the ultranationalist perpetrators of this bizarre crime wore the St. George's ribbons because they believed they were on a holy mission for the betterment of Russian society. Their conviction—and their understanding of the St. George's ribbon—makes it all too clear how the Kremlin's ideology warps the minds of individuals by combining religion and nationalism to claim Russia's values to be superior to all others. Worse still, it exemplifies the horrific power of a conservative ideology: it is not that Russians cannot act in public at all, but that their actions must align with the goals of the Kremlin. An attack on anti-Semites, feminists, political opposition, or others who seem to threaten the Putinist cause on a similar scale as the April 2016 brutalization is unimaginable because Putinist ideology is not about mass mobilization for democratic or liberal causes.[48] Rather, it is about imparting its values on the population in ways that continue to strengthen the authoritarian regime without risking destabilization of its projects. The story of the St. George's ribbon's rise from an imperial military honor to an everyday, nationalist reminder to all citizens reveals the danger of how this sort of ideology can evolve into something horrifically bloody and judgmental that cuts off avenues for other forms of friendly, culturally tolerant encounters.

How Individuals Reproduce the Kremlin's Ideology

It is a slippery slope from this sort of antidemocratic conservatism to a society characterized by an intense hatred of gays, of Islamic traditions, of multiculturalism, of women's equality, and of other natural human rights that are deemed as dangerous elements of decadent Western liberalism.[49]

In this way, the choice to respect or to soil human rights gets nationalized through ideology and the reproduction of its message in individuals' actions.

Symbols play a huge role in all of this. The nationalist myth promotes several symbols that affect citizens' daily lives, associates those symbols with certain Kremlin-sponsored narratives, and evokes certain emotions among the population. All of this occurs in a feedback loop that repeats at every stage and cycle. Ultimately, it generates a story that deepens in intensity and widens in breadth as the story accumulates more believers and symbols. The myth, then, becomes more and more compelling as individuals establish closer ties to it and to the greater community that also believes the same story.

It is true that all collective identities need and use symbols, be they at the local, regional, national, or international levels. But what separates fascist identities from non-fascist identities is the instigation of hatred. Some presidencies notwithstanding, and assuming that the current Trump administration's policies have not supplanted the vision of the United States of America vis-à-vis 1776 (or 1863, or 1964, for that matter), the American flag stands for freedom, individuality, opportunity, and democracy. It does not represent a closed society's desires for global military conquest. Neither does the Canadian flag, or the French flag, or many others. In the same vein, nor does the Spanish flag represent an oppressive monarchical empire out to destroy Catalan traditions and success, as much as Catalan separatists might complain it does. Though all of these symbols bear their share of responsibility for historical injustices (in addition to comparatively minor ones), they have at no point stood for outright hatred of other nationalities.

The swastika, on the other hand, will forever remain as a symbol of the militant belief in German racial superiority backed by rabid anti-Semitism and other violent, imperialist hatreds of non-Aryans or "imperfect" Aryans. Reich Minister of Public Enlightenment and Propaganda Joseph Goebbels was particularly adept in regard to the usage of the swastika and other symbols. In fact, Goebbels created an entire Nazi cult of traditions and rituals in order to introduce more symbols to the German population that associated Nazism with ethnic greatness and emotional pride.[50] They functioned to normalize Nazi ideology in the overwhelming majority of their audiences' minds. In other words, they helped to normalize hatred against whatever groups of people whom the government identified to be "the enemy."

It is this invocation of hatred, this arbitrary yet nevertheless lethal distinction between friend and foe, that signifies a fascist government; if the call is heeded, then it signifies a successfully indoctrinated fascist society, as well.[51] In healthy modern-day communities, hatred on the national scale is no longer socially acceptable unless otherwise ideologically justified and directed at a specific enemy of the entire community at large. But in nation-states that can justify the suspicions they espouse on an ideological level, then hatred, violence, fascism, and totalitarianism might take root if enough individuals in the larger population choose to allow them and believe the rationale for actively disliking certain groups of people on the bases of national security and purity. Symbols and myths and government-controlled versions of both history and current events are prime avenues through which to instigate hatred and feed mass desires for authoritarianism with no regard for human dignity.

More dangerous still is the fact that these hateful symbols can operate at both the individual and collective levels. For example, in Russia, where the nationalist myth is effectively and creatively cultivated, a symbol such as a statue of Stalin comes to signal more than just the historical existence of Stalin the man: it also begins to represent subjective associations with leadership and national power in the international sphere, serving as inspiration for many individual citizens to develop a desire for strong leadership tendencies and over-the-top security policies, among other things. Maybe that same person also sees a St. George's ribbon tied to a uniformed policeperson's wrist, simultaneously reminding them that Russia is under attack from external forces and that Ukraine does not deserve to be its own country.

Russian citizens can be constantly bombarded by symbols that promote fear and suspicion of non-Russians in their daily lives. They might become so inspired by those symbols and the narrative meanings associated with them that they, as individuals, begin to actively campaign for the election of a leader like Putin, or to defend him in casual conversations or on international television. Individuals, then, can become so engrossed in government-sponsored symbolism that they begin to sponsor it themselves.

Once a state has intensified its ideology so much that other lines of flight are precluded—or at least much more difficult to access—by restricting sources of knowledge and diverse opinions, it can almost certainly count on its population to reproduce its thought pattern. To help explain this situation, we cite British historian Norman Cohn's observation in his book, *Europe's Inner Demons: An Enquiry Inspired by the Great Witch-*

Hunt (1975), that "not only the waking thoughts but the trance experiences of individuals can be deeply conditioned by the generally accepted beliefs of the society in which they live."[52] And those most helpful in duplicating the Kremlin's ideology belong to what Hannah Arendt referred to as "the mob." The term describes a group "in which the residue of all classes are represented" and "always will shout for the 'strong man,' the 'great leader'" to take power and fulfill his promises to them. Members of the mob see the strong man as their ticket to a better life and are willing to turn out "of necessity to extra-parliamentary action," if it means the leader can enact policies that increase their prosperity.[53] Thus, the mob actually calls for states of exception, which grant their authority figure more and more power. Simply because the people have asked their sovereign to do so, this leader also benefits by gaining more legitimacy in the citizens' eyes. The more legitimacy a sovereign has, the easier it becomes for said sovereign to act without crossing over the line of acceptability, upsetting the people, or risking the claim to power. Essentially, the sovereign is freer to fake truths and facts.

This leader is thus able to engage in an increasing number of actions which are excused by believers but might otherwise alarm a non-engaged population. For example, Putin can preside over a notoriously corrupt regime with low-quality public services, yet his personal popularity ratings remain high because his faithful subjects continue to accept his position as the leader Russia "needs." Hence they obey him. They defend Putin with arguments such as, "at least people are actually getting their wages paid, unlike during the chaotic Yeltsin years," or "the policing isn't as bad as Stalin's was" (which people somehow take as proof that Putin is still a good guy whose potential to develop a unified Russian superpower forgives his "half-crimes" of stealing from the state or violating personal freedoms of speech). Other common excuses are: "Putin inherited chaos and needs to overcompensate on forcefulness in order to rebalance the country," and "Putin *had* to bomb Chechnya because they posed a threat to us Russians, and our nation is not guilty for any deaths." All of these examples are paraphrased, yet unaltered in meaning, versions of arguments heard daily from ordinary citizens in Russia.

This exoneration of the sovereign Putin for corruption, restrictions of freedoms, and policy failings is yet another feature of the Kremlin's ideology. Mikhail Gorbachev summed up this protective sphere when he argued in his recent book, "Even the president only has two hands and one head: God makes no exceptions."[54] Gorbachev's words allude to those of the early social contract theorists Hobbes and Locke, when they described the religious reverence with which a community of subjects treats their sovereign. As this person is entrusted with the power of the state and the security of everything within it, they automatically receive a guarantee for indemnity. Here, the power of the sovereign is the "no-man's land between law and political fact" which cannot be questioned, in part because an extra-juridical action escapes the sphere (e.g. rules and punishments) of juridical law. Like Nazi-supporting political theorist Carl Schmitt asserted, political sovereignty "imitate[s] God's power—supreme and temporally infinite" and indisputable, unless something totally egregious were to occur on the sovereign's orders.[55]

When Putin first began to be accused of corruption early in his presidential career, those loyal to him (meaning most of the Russian population) waved the law-breaking away. They argued it was a non-issue because corruption is nothing new—the Soviet Union ran on corruption, and even in the democratic Russian Federation, Yeltsin rigged the 1996 presidential vote.[56] Putin and his cronies in business, media, and government even openly admit to corruption and bribery. So long as they present themselves as powerful patriots who serve the state's interests by virtue of *being* the state, and so long as ordinary citizens continue to receive their salaries and consume on the free market, then the average Russian views racketeering as only fair: these authorities work for the state's benefit, after all, so why not help themselves to national riches?

Putin and other Russian government officials likely feel no guilt or shame when it comes to corruption because it fits the ideological script of cultural superiority, disrespect for the rule of law, and reverence for strong, protective leadership.[57] With a historical foundation of Leninism, Putin's Kremlin has accordingly mutated the state into both a financially and morally corrupt entity.[58] Various estimates from Swedish business analysts, the CIA, and Bill Browder—the CEO of Hermitage Capital Management, one of the largest investment funds to ever operate in Russia—have estimated Putin's personal wealth to be between $40 billion and $200 billion. This range is obviously huge but still puts him in at least the top 20 wealthiest people in the world, if not *the* wealthiest person overall.[59] Such a ranking for an elected official who himself has never been a business owner or financial expert screams corruption of astronomical proportions. Yet the people are silent.

When a public fails to protest, or to simply acknowledge the illegality of, official crookedness, it is a sign that the people accept their status as lesser individuals with unequal opportunities when compared to ruling and/or business elites (although they likely would not explain their tolerance in these words). Additionally, it signals that the rule of law is lacking and incapable of restraining the sovereign from acting as they please.[60] Corruption is also a coerced form of dependency on the state: according to *The Dictator's Handbook* (2011), "the easiest way to compensate [supporters] for their loyalty—including their willingness to oppress their fellow citizens—is to give them free rein to be corrupt." They are ready to resign themselves to meager official pay because they know it is not only acceptable in their society, but also necessary for them to be corrupt in order to survive. By the same token, they become obliged to continue this loyalty, or else they run the risk of having the government revoke their privileges and perhaps of being legally punished for trying to introduce fairness into the system.[61] In fact, anyone who dwells on the criminality of corruption (or other less-than-desirable aspects of the Kremlin's policies) risks their own private access to political spoils. Furthermore, according to Kremlin ideologist Vladislav Surkov, this person also becomes publically branded as someone who defies the President of the Russian Federation and is, therefore, "an enemy of the great God of 'stability.'"[62] This is public humiliation for having an outspoken conscience.

The famous case of oligarch Mikhail Khodorkovsky, once the owner of Yukos Oil Company and the wealthiest oligarch in Russia, embodies Surkov's threat. In a televised interview in February 2003, Khodorkovsky accused Putin and his regime of serious corruption. One of the most damning charges was that state officials were plotting to legally attack oligarchs who did not share their wealth with them and/or entered into politics. Within months, Khodorkovsky's business partner had been arrested. Come October 2003, so was Khodorkovsky himself, on charges of fraud and tax evasion.

His trial has been described as Kafka-esque, in that the court was trying him on activities that were only made illegal after Khodorkovsky had concluded them. He was convicted and sentenced to nine years in a penal colony. Once released in 2013, he fled to Switzerland, knowing that if he set foot in Russia again, the government would no doubt find some new charge for which to arrest him.[63] Khodorkovsky's fate made it clear: Putin is not to be touched (and no one in Russia is innocent). This president will not take any criticism. Should any arise, he will bend the judicial system in order to suppress it[64]—and the public will accept it. They believe Putin *is* the law, so how could he act illegally?

Such a thought process was best described by Polish philosopher Leszek Kołakowski, when he wrote, "the devil ... invented ideological states, that is to say, states whose legitimacy is grounded in the fact that their owners are owners of truth. If you oppose such a state or its system, you are an enemy of truth."[65] Putin has the benefit of deciding what such "truth" is and using it as a shield which allows him to deflect criticisms of the Kremlin right back at the critic. Once the Kremlin issues a policy, "there is no question of right or wrong, but only absolute obedience, the blind conformism," as Hannah Arendt so perceptively put it.[66] This strong ideological dependence on the sovereign exhibited in modern Russia leads to the constant excusing of Putin's actions. He is so fetishized that in 2011, a first-year journalism student at Moscow State University named Alisa Kharcheva decided to pose in lingerie for an erotic calendar to be given to Vladimir Putin on his birthday. Her reasoning was that he deserved to be thanked, since "we are well off because of Putin."[67]

Putin's image is inseparable from that of the state and its citizens. In 2014, Deputy Chief of Staff Vyacheslav Volodin spelled out this symbolic overlap at the annual meeting of the Valdai Discussion Club[68] in Sochi, declaring, "there is no Russia today if there is no Putin." He followed his statement up with the results of a recent poll which showed that 66 percent of Russians "could not see any candidates besides Putin running for president in 2018." They agreed that, therefore, "any attack on Putin is an attack on Russia" because he represents the entire country's will.[69]

Putinism has succeeded to the degree that Russian citizens and small businesses take it upon themselves to promote the ideology, whether they realize this or not. In 2014, an average candymaking business based in St. Petersburg, called Shokobox, decided to produce their own line of Putin chocolate bars. One is a dark chocolate bar, the wrapping of which sports a picture of Putin after he won the 2012 presidential election; his portrait is complete with a single tear falling down his cheek, which Putin later attributed to the wind (and still later to his overwhelming love for the country). Another is a milk chocolate bar, wrapped in an image of Putin cuddling a puppy. The back of each of these bars features the same quote of Putin's: "I dream we will all be happy, each of us, but how do we do this?"[70] In 2014 yet another Russian company, Chocolate Traditions, decided to produce chocolate bars that feature a map of Russia—but not just any map. The wrapper, complete with a legend, highlighted not only the land officially recognized by the international community as belonging to the Russian state but also "new territories" including Crimea and, worse still, large swaths of "perspective territories" in Scandinavia, Eastern Europe, Central Asia, China, and Alaska. Though this bar is likely just a joke and not a serious call for Russia to engage in an ultra-aggressive imperialist expansion that would undoubtedly trigger World War III, its mere existence—and the notion that such an idea could be humorous—is indicative of the darker themes that are evidently present in Russian citizens' minds.[71]

These commodities sell Putin's image. They make him appear as though he were the kind, benevolent, and thoughtful caretaker of Russia. One must realize that this is propaganda, but in a form different from the kind Hannah Arendt observed in, say, Stalin's favorite film *Circus*, or in Soviet anti-fascist posters of the early 1940s. The Russian state had not ordered these particular companies, or the individuals making the decisions, to create pro-Putin products, unlike the Soviet state had done for decades. The candymakers themselves buy into the idea of Putin as a commodity desired by those living in the state. This instance demonstrates how the Kremlin's propaganda has done its work. It has successfully raised a loyal mob, which can be counted on to reproduce the state's message.

At the same time, the candymakers' decisions to contribute to celebrating the nation's sovereign also note an important aspect of Russia's national script: the Kremlin alone does not have total control over the narrative. The people (and businesses) can influence and shape it, as well. Of course, if the people are indoctrinated well enough, then the Kremlin need not worry too much about sustaining the image of a strong, united, nationalist Russia. The population's ideas would almost certainly complement those already promoted in the state's script. Still, this is a crucial aspect of Russian politics to understand: the state *needs* the general population to follow along and bring its desires to fruition.

It is at this advanced stage of ideological indoctrination that the Kremlin has achieved its dream of dominating all modes of political discourse. Successful interpellative programs mean that independent movements can hardly develop within Russia's boundaries, especially without the government's knowledge. Putinism manipulates the language of the nation-state and has gobbled up any and all spaces that may have given oppositionists even the most minute chance of forming and expressing their own ideas. Putin has closed off avenues for diverse thought and herds the citizenry down a government-approved path, which "help[s] the Kremlin rewrite the narrative of protestors from political injustice and corruption to one of Holy Russia versus Foreign Devils, deflecting the conversation from the economic slide and how the rate of bribes that bureaucrats command has shot up 15 percent to 50 percent of any deal."[72]

Indoctrination crawls from the top echelons of Putin's administration to the masses. Such practices are so ingrained now that they are both top-down *and* bottom-up, circulating throughout the population as citizens come to reinforce the Kremlin's ideology among one another through their own daily practices. The result is little different than from Soviet times, when political, military, and social sectors—be it the Communist Party, the Komsomol, the Committee for State Security (KGB), military groups, factories, kolkhozes, schools, hospitals, and so on—all created or reiterated propaganda that served the state.[73] Today, most of the aforementioned groups have different names, but the basic theme endures: both state and societal institutions continue to reinforce the government's narratives.

Putin has effectively molded the people's desires to match his own. As of a 2015 survey, 57 percent of Russian citizens would like to see Russia as "powerful," compared to only 30 percent for "just" or seven percent for "diverse."[74] Never mind judicial ethics, fairness, or the benefits of multicultural richness. The people have been prompted in all facets of life, from religion to education to media to holidays, to want Russia to become the superpower they have heard about for their entire lives. The Kremlin no longer has to bear the full burden of imposing its ideology on the Russian population, as they themselves echo its messages.

Sure, opposition parties *do* exist, and some citizens *do* vocalize their disgust with the Kremlin, and elections *are* held regularly. Russian officials often cite these facts in an effort to refute claims that Russia is totalitarian and repressive—but these tidbits fool the Russian citizenry into believing they live in a free country. Actually, they live in a country where the government manages the opposition closely enough to limit their success while still appearing as a multiparty democracy.[75] As Graeme B. Robertson accurately put it:

> Rulers in these regimes face a singular dilemma: how to accommodate significant political freedoms without allowing dangerous levels of opposition that might signal weakness to potentially disaffected members of the elite. Moreover, this needs to be achieved while drawing as little attention as possible to the authoritarian nature of the regime in order to avoid undermining perceptions of its democratic legitimacy.[76]

The trick is that repression thrives within the abstract, intangible ideology of Putinism, planting its invisible seeds within the minds of Russian citizens and breeding a majority willing to drown out anti-Kremlin protestors. Russia calls itself a democracy by virtue of majority rule, but democracy cannot, in fact, exist when people's minds have been abused from the start and denied a wide variety of knowledge. This is a form of intellectual violence often overlooked in studies of Russian governance, which usually deny the notion that Russia is totalitarian. Their modes of analyses are inherently flawed, missing the most important point: Putin aims to create a national condition in which it becomes impossible to think differently than the state. In monopolizing historical perspectives and current views of the rest of the world, as well as in silencing dissent, Putin's regime has forcefully driven the minds of millions of Russian citizens into a single furrow. With this act, the Kremlin destroys their ability to make free decisions or fairly evaluate the alternatives.[77] At the same time, this also means that the stakes are higher than ever for the Kremlin: if it creates the "monster," it must be certain it can tame it. In other words, if Putin's government is to allow the mirage of democracy, then it must be completely sure that its techniques of social control are far-reaching, predictable, and effective (e.g. totalitarian, a charge that will be best elaborated upon in Chap. 8).

It is this lack of choice that comprises the core of totalitarian regimes. It is the reason why non-Jewish civilians living in Nazi Germany, for the most part, responded with the same complete passivity to the otherwise inhumane policies involving the extermination of Jewish population, of other human beings.[78] Such an ideology isolates its believers from the rest of the human race, subtly or unsubtly infusing violence and fear into everyday rhetoric. As Hannah Arendt wrote, their atomization and assumptions of external threats result in dissociation. When the time comes for the government to target a certain group of people who do not fit the profile of a loyal subject and to assign to them the sanitized label of worthless, dangerous bodies, interpellated citizens simply cannot recognize enough of themselves in those to-be victims to warrant protest or hesitation.[79]

Indoctrinated subjects have become so used to life under the current regime, in which the spaces, liberties, and rights they have been promised by their sovereign increasingly inscribe each person's life inside the state apparatus. This solidifies their subordination to, and enhances the justification for, the sovereign power—the same power that limits their identity, aspirations, and global perceptions. Citizens are left to live in a world where whatever the sovereign declares to be reality, *is* reality. In that world, atrocious acts can be committed with the support of political, military, and civilian communities who simply do not know any better than to give in to the desire to kill (be it another human, culture, or someone's own individuality and politically aware soul) so as to supposedly secure oneself.[80]

This is not to say that no Russian citizen has any choice in the matter of whether or not they support the Putinist narrative. No one, not even in a totalitarian society, is technically stripped of the basic chance to choose where they metaphysically or politically stand. No German was forced to vote for the National Socialist Party. No German housewife was forced to devote her life to the Nazi cause. No Christian Pole in the village of Jedwabne was forced by German Nazis to round up nearly all 1600 of their Jewish neighbors, humiliate them, and brutally burn them in a barn in 1941.[81] But many did. Sure, defiance of the Nazis and their goals might have cost your life, but in such a hopeless reality filled with mass murder, people with principles could—and did, like philosopher, Walter Benjamin, writer Joseph Roth, writer Stefan Zweig, and others—still refuse to comply with an unprecedented killing machine.

Thus, every Nazi or anti-Nazi *did* make a choice, even if those choices were artificially limited by the authorities, and even if the outcomes of either choice had essentially already been decided for them. Likewise, every Russian today—just like every American, every Argentine, every Brit, every Italian today—constantly has the chance to support or deny their government. Most people today probably have more choices to choose between than just a life of collaboration with authoritarianism or death in defiance of authoritarianism, but the basic principle still holds.

The only difference is that in Russia, the Kremlin has made it much easier for individuals to overlook the moral consequences of its nationalist outlook and not to question the inconsistencies of its narrative. In large part, the Kremlin's control mechanisms over society are to blame; at the same time, Russians also play into the narrative on their own volition and choose not to exercise their ability to distinguish between, as Timothy Snyder puts it, "what is true and what they want to hear."[82] Observers, then, must understand just how susceptible the human mind can be toward propaganda which portrays imagined glories and intoxicatingly (but falsely) appeals to their personal dreams of prosperity, while simultaneously portraying alternative choices or ideologies as sources of enmity.

Now that we have explained how indoctrination occurs in Russia, we return to the idea of Weimar Russia mentioned in Chap. 5. To that discussion we will add the penetrating judgment of Galina Starovoitova. A dissident against both the Soviet and post-Soviet regimes, Starovoitova became a member of the Russian Parliament, where she continued to fight for human rights, minority protections, and democracy. For that work, she was assassinated in her apartment building—like Russian journalist Anna Politkovskaya was—on 20 November 1998.[83] Despite the fact that Starovoitova never had the opportunity to write during Putin's presidencies, her comparison between Weimar Germany and post-Soviet Russia offers an alarmingly accurate diagnosis through 2019 (and likely beyond). In an article she published in 1993, Starovoitova observed,

> The danger of an extreme-nationalist revolution is real, as the state of things in Russia comes more and more to resemble the plight that Germany's Weimar Republic faced in the 1920s. The widespread persistence of imperial thinking, the humiliation of a proud people, discrimination against its members living in bordering states, and the continual broadcasting of the concept of a "divided nation" all helped to pave the way for fascism. In the case of "Weimar Russia," we may add to this list economic deterioration, indifference and misunderstanding on the part of the West, and the sinister union that extreme right-wingers have formed with ex-communist hard-liners ....
>
> ... Russians have been unwilling to heed the sad lesson of German history because of our unexamined conviction that our country, having defeated a fascist regime in war, has thereby automatically become immune to fascism. This conviction, alas, is not necessarily true. The spiritual vacuum resulting from the collapse of communism is being rapidly filled by a Russian nationalism that is spreading throughout various strata of society—from the lowest levels up to the military officers and intelligentsia. The national idea itself has traditionally been associated more closely with the territorial greatness of Russia than with its historical traditions.[84]

Starovoitova's words do not, of course, justify Russia's grievances or supposed rationale behind its imperial, nationalist ideology. But they are a useful tool by which to understand the more basic societal impression of the average Russian and thereby to explain why the overwhelming majority believes the Kremlin's myths. Ultimately, the fantasy of a superior Russian civilization is another crucial pillar in garnering mass public support for a nationalist government like Putin's.

Starovoitova was rightly concerned about the power of nationalism in Russia in 1993. Over two decades later, its power has grown through the Kremlin's propagandistic policies and the exploitation of already existing sensitivities encompassed by the Weimar Russia syndrome. Three major social institutions—the education system, the media, and the Russian Orthodox Church—have become mouthpieces for the government, ensuring that many of those who come in contact with them take Weimar syndrome and all its paranoia to heart. Thus, these three apparatuses and the indoctrinated population continue to feed off of one another and help the Putinist regime to manipulate themes that otherwise might not provoke so much hatred, violence, or ideological devotion.

When bombarded by state propaganda on a daily basis, Russian citizens are essentially brainwashed[85] by the Kremlin—perhaps not fully, and perhaps not every individual, but enough so "the choice between good and evil becomes distilled" and feelings of nationalist aggression can multiply and then reign over other desires.[86] This is a necessity of the Putin Phenomenon: indoctrinated subjects are constantly exposed to the Kremlin's propaganda in both public and private settings, and the permeation of life's two main sides functions to steer thoughts and discussions *away* from corruption within their nation and *toward* frustrations with foreign cultures (or wherever else Putin wants to direct the masses' attention).

As Anna Arutunyan documented in her book *The Putin Mystique: Inside Russia's Power Cult* (2015), this is what makes it possible for a Russian citizen to say, "'America has attacked us. Putin is our sovereign. We are for him, with all our soul. And *body*.'"[87] It marks the ebbing away of the ability to make informed, individual choices in favor of unhesitatingly supporting the country as a whole. This is the greatest danger posed by ideological regimes that deny citizens their right to question truth, their right to recognize and improve upon their own vulnerabilities as humans, and their right to discover avenues of friendly cultural encounter. As the following chapter investigates, these ideological constraints are most visible in regard to the Kremlin's foreign policy, which serves to domestically reinforce the entire cycle of public obedience to Putin the sovereign.

Notes

1. Levada Center, "Pride and Patriotism," Levada Center: Yuri Levada Analytical Center, 9 December 2015. We emphasize this particular survey in our text because its questions are the most direct and applicable to our research. A few other studies have been conducted since this 2015 poll, of

course, and readers are encouraged to look them up, but they are not mentioned here because the wordings are not nearly as relevant to the sociological phenomenon around which we have written this book.
2. Anna Arutunyan, *The Putin Mystique: Inside Russia's Power Cult* (Northampton: Olive Branch Press, 2015), pp. 276 and 278.
3. Levada Center, "Democracy in today's Russia," Levada Center: Yuri Levada Analytical Center, 20 January 2016.
4. Robert C. Tucker, *Political Culture and Leadership in Soviet Russia: From Lenin to Gorbachev* (New York: W.W. Norton & Company, Inc., 1987), p. 17.
5. Official Internet Resources of the President of Russia, speech by Vladimir Putin, "Stenograficheskij otchet o vstreche s delegatami Vserossijskoj konferencii prepodavatelej gumanitarnyh i obshhestvennyh nauk," 21 June 2007.
6. Anna Plotnikova, "Russia's New Education Minister Gives Stalin a Nod," Voice of America, 25 August 2016.
7. Eva Hartog, "God, Stalin, and Patriotism—Meet Russia's New Education Chief," *The Moscow Times*, 25 August 2016.
8. For more on this subject, see Anne Applebaum, *Red Famine: Stalin's War on Ukraine* (London: Allen Lane, 2017).
9. Vladimir Tismaneanu, *The Devil in History: Communism, Fascism, and Some Lessons of the Twentieth Century* (Berkeley and Los Angeles: University of California Press, 2012), p. 218.
10. Mikhail K. Gorshkov, "The Sociology of Post-reform Russia" in *Russia: The Challenges of Transformation*, eds. Piotr Dutkiewicz and Dmitri Trenin (New York: New York University Press, 2011), p. 147; Mikhail Gorbachev, *The New Russia* (Cambridge: Polity Press, 2016), p. 425.
11. Plotnikova, "Russia's New Education Minister"; Peter Pomerantsev, *Nothing is True and Everything is Possible: The Surreal Heart of the New Russia* (New York: PublicAffairs, 2014), p. 198.
12. Tismaneanu, *The Devil in History*, p. 218; Leszek Kołakowski. *Freedom, Fame, Lying and Betrayal: Essays on Everyday Life*, translated by Agnieszka Kołakowska (London and New York: The Penguin Group, 1999), pp. 36–37.
13. Though it is true that *Nashi* is now defunct, it is nevertheless mentioned here because it made enormous impacts on Russia's youth. Different youth organizations, including the others also listed in our text, operate using similar tactics, methods, principles, and structures as *Nashi* did.
14. Tom Balmforth, "Network, Son Of Nashi: New Youth Group Seeks To Woo Russia's Middle Class," Radio Free Europe/Radio Liberty; Molodaya Gvardiya, "Napravlenia," Molodaya Gvardiya.

15. Sarah Oates, "Russia's Media and Political Communication in the Digital Age," in *Developments in Russian Politics*, 8th ed., eds. Stephen White, Richard Sakwa, and Harney E. Hale (Durham: Duke University Press, 2014), pp. 130–144.
16. Anne Garrels, *Putin Country: A Journey into the Real Russia* (New York: Farrar, Straus, and Giroux, 2016), pp. 182–183.
17. Pomerantsev, *Nothing is True*, p. 48.
18. Arkady Ostrovsky, *The Invention of Russia: From Gorbachev's Freedom to Putin's War* (New York: Viking Press, 2015), p. 313. It is unsurprising to note that Putin later appointed Kiselev to head Russia's latest government-owned international news agency Rossiya Segodnya in 2013.
19. Timothy Snyder, "Fascism, Russia, and Ukraine," *The New York Review*, 20 March 2014.
20. Hannah Arendt, *Origins of Totalitarianism* (New York: Meridian Books, 1958), p. 109.
21. Michael McFaul, *From Cold War to Hot Peace: An American Ambassador in Putin's Russia* (New York: Houghton Mifflin Harcourt Publishing Company, 2018), pp. 242, 297, and 435.
22. Garrels, *Putin Country*, pp. 185–186.
23. Dan Kovalik, *The Plot to Scapegoat Russia: How the CIA and the Deep State Have Conspired to Vilify Russia* (New York: Skyhorse Publishing, 2017), pp. 25–27.
24. Kovalik, *The Plot to Scapegoat Russia*, p. 128.
25. Levada Center, "Trust in the Mass Media," Levada Center: Yuri Levada Analytical Center, 26 October 2015.
26. Francesca Borri inspired this connection in her book *Syrian Dust: Reporting from the Heart of the War* (2016). Though it is specifically a brave condemnation of the international community's utter failure when it comes to the Syrian people, Borri's book recounts the ails of society, in general. This journalist's lament of the state of today's media is more than applicable to Russia. Francesca Borri, *Syrian Dust: Reporting from the Heart of the War*, trans. Anne Milano Appel (New York: Seven Stories Press, 2016), p. 130.
27. For more on how the Russian government's propaganda spreads to the West, see Timothy Snyder's fifth chapter, "Truth or Lies," in *The Road to Unfreedom: Russia, Europe, America* (New York: Tim Duggan Books, 2018), pp. 159–216.
28. Marc Bennetts, "Russia considers ban on Armando Iannucci's film The Death of Stalin," *The Guardian*, 20 September 2017; Marc Bennetts, "Russia pulls 'despicable' Death of Stalin from cinemas," *The Guardian*, 23 January 2018; "Death of Cinema?" *Russian Life*, Vol. 61, Iss. 2 (March/April 2018), pp. 7–8.

29. "Kinoteatru 'Pioner' grozit shtraf do 300 tysjach rublej za pokaz 'Smerti Stalina,'" *NewsRu*, 19 February 2018.
30. Bennetts, "Russia pulls 'despicable' Death of Stalin."
31. Levada Center, "Institutional Trust," Levada Center: Yuri Levada Analytical Center, 16 October 2015.
32. M. Steven Fish, "The Kremlin Emboldened: What is Putinism?" *Journal of Democracy*, Vol. 28, No. 4 (October 2017), p. 63; Mikhail Zygar, *All the Kremlin's Men: Inside the Court of Vladimir Putin* (New York: Public Affairs, 2016), p. 235.
33. Marcel Van Herpen, *Putin's Propaganda Machine* (New York: Rowman and Littlefield, 2015), pp. 129 and 149: Ostrovsky, *The Invention of Russia*, p. 312.
34. Stella Rock, "Russian Piety and Orthodox Culture 1380–1589" in *Eastern Christianity*, ed. Michael Angold (Cambridge: Cambridge University Press, 2006), p. 275; Thomas Bremer, "How the Russian Orthodox Church Views the 'Russian World'" *Occasional Papers on Religion in Eastern Europe*, Vol. 35, No. 3 (2015), p. 43.
35. Steven Cassedy, *Dostoevsky's Religion* (Stanford: Stanford University Press, 2005), p. 80.
36. Emil Pain, "Socio-Cultural Factors and Russian Modernization" in *Waiting for Reform Under Putin and Medvedev*, eds. Lena Jonson and Stephen White (London: Palgrave Macmillan, 2012), p. 98.
37. RT News, Vladimir Putin interviewed by RT News, "Putin Q&A on RT: President on 1st visit to RT's state-of-the-art HQ," RT News, 12 June 2013.
38. Edward Lucas, *The New Cold War: Putin's Russia and the Threat to the West* (New York: St. Martin's Press, 2014), p. 157; Yegor Kholmogorov, "Atomnoe pravoslavie," *Russkii Obozrevatel*, 31 August 2008; Pomerantsev, *Nothing is True*, pp. 184–188.
39. Sandra Bjelica, "Discourse Analysis of the Masculine Representation of Vladimir Putin" thesis, Free University of Berlin, Berlin, 2014; Leon Aron, "Novorossiya!" *Commentary Magazine*, 1 December 2014; Cheng Chen, *The Return of Ideology: The Search for Regime Identities in Postcommunist Russia and China* (Ann Arbor: University of Michigan Press, 2016), p. 80.
40. Peter Pomerantsev, "Putin's God Squad: The Orthodox Church and Russian Politics," *Newsweek*, 10 September 2012; M. Steven Fish, "What Has Russia Become?" *Comparative Politics*, Vol. 50, No. 3 (April 2018), p. 330.
41. Fish, "What is Putinism?" p. 61.
42. Ben Judah, *Fragile Empire: How Russia Fell In and Out of Love with Vladimir Putin* (New Haven: Yale University Press, 2013), p. 152.

43. St. George is known as the man who, according to Christian tradition, slayed a terrifying dragon and saved countless human lives and has since become one of the most often-depicted saints in Christian religious icons.
44. The Orange Revolution is one of the several color revolutions of the early 2000s. These were popular movements formed by citizens that sought to promote democracy and to fight corruption. They occurred in former Soviet states, for the most part.
45. Andreas Umland, "New Extremely Right-Wing Intellectual Circles in Russia: The Anti-Orange Committee, the Isborsk Club and the Florian Geyer Club" *Russian Analytical Digest*, Vol. 135 (August 2013), p. 3. The brazen association made by the Russian state between *all* Ukrainians who protested for transparent governance and the Nazi regime is an egregiously apparent attempt at slandering the cause of the color revolutions as a whole.
46. Neil Smelser, *The Social Edges of Psychoanalysis* (Berkeley: University of California Press, 1998), p. 87.
47. Radio Free Europe/Radio Liberty, "Russian Nationalists Attack Event for High-School History Students," Radio Free Europe/Radio Liberty, 28 April 2016.
48. For more on the difference between mass mobilization and the supervision of stability among the Russian population, see Fish, "What is Putinism?" p. 62.
49. Fish, "What is Putinism?" p. 64.
50. Zdzisław Mach, "The concepts of culture and civilization," European Civilization (class lecture, Jagiellonian University, Kraków, Poland, 4 October 2018).
51. Snyder, *The Road to Unfreedom*, p. 61.
52. Norman Cohn, *Europe's Inner Demons: An Enquiry Inspired by the Great Witch-Hunt* (New York: Basic Books, Inc., 1975), p. 224.
53. Arendt, *Origins of Totalitarianism*, pp. 107–108.
54. Gorbachev, *The New Russia*, p. 425.
55. Giorgio Agamben, *State of Exception* (Chicago: University of Chicago Press, 2005), pp. 10–11.
56. Lucas, *The New Cold War*, pp. 8–9. The election has never officially been declared fraudulent, but it is common knowledge that as the election approached, Yeltsin's popularity was sinking. The vote counts reported from various regions of the Russian Federation did not seem to jibe with this pattern. According to the data, Yeltsin won absurd percentages of votes in places like Chechnya, which he had just spent the last few years viciously bombing as a part of the First Chechen War.
57. Karen Dawisha, *Putin's Kleptocracy: Who Owns Russia?* (New York: Simon and Schuster Paperbacks, 2014). We refer readers to Karen Dawisha's

excellent examination of the shocking depth of corruption embedded within the Russian state at the behest of its top leaders.
58. Dawisha, *Putin's Kleptocracy*, p. 323.
59. Richard Lourie, *Putin: His Downfall and Russia's Coming Crash* (New York: Thomas Dunne Books, 2017), p. 220; Voice of America, "'Terrible Crimes' Made Putin World's Richest Person, Financier Testifies," Voice of America, 27 July 2017.
60. Lucas, *The New Cold War*, p. 18; Graeme Gill, "Russia and the Vulnerability of Electoral Authoritarianism?" *Slavic Review*, Vol. 75, No. 2 (Summer 2016), p. 372; Sarah Henderson, "Review Essay," *Slavic Review*, Vol. 75, No. 2 (Summer 2016), p. 447.
61. Bruce Bueno de Mesquita and Alastair Smith, *The Dictator's Handbook: Why Bad Behavior is Almost Always Good Politics* (New York: PublicAffairs, 2011), p. 140.
62. Pomerantsev, *Nothing is True*, p. 66.
63. Masha Gessen, "The Wrath of Putin," *Vanity Fair*, April 2012.
64. McFaul, *From Cold War to Hot Peace*, p. 70.
65. Leszek Kołakowski, *Modernity on Endless Trial* (Chicago: University of Chicago Press, 1990), p. 189.
66. Arendt, *Origins of Totalitarianism*, p. 141.
67. Arutunyan, *The Putin Mystique*, p. 215.
68. The Valdai Discussion Club is an organization established by several Russian educational and research-oriented institutions in 2004 to share (rather biased) information about Russia with intellectuals and foreign experts all over the world.
69. *The Moscow Times*, "'No Putin, No Russia,' Says Kremlin Deputy Chief of Staff," *The Moscow Times*, 23 October 2014.
70. *The Moscow Times*, "Russian Candymaker Hopes Putin Chocolate Bars Are a Recipe for Success," *The Moscow Times*, 26 November 2014.
71. Graham H. Roberts, *Consumer Culture, Branding and Identity in the New Russia: From Five-year Plan to 4x4* (London and New York: Routledge, 2016), pp. 82–83.
72. Pomerantsev, *Nothing is True*, pp. 67, 126, and 148.
73. Vladimir Voinovich, *The Anti-Soviet Soviet Union*, trans. Richard Lourie (San Diego, New York, and London: Harcourt Brace Jovanovich, 1985), p. 38.
74. Pomerantsev, *Nothing is True*, p. 66; Levada Center, "Is Russia a superpower?" Levada Center: Yuri Levada Analytical Center, 3 December 2015.
75. Luke March, "Managing Opposition in a Hybrid Regime: Just Russia and Parastatal Opposition," *Slavic Review*, Vol. 68, No. 3 (Fall 2009), p. 527.
76. Graeme B. Robertson, "Managing Society: Protests, Civil Society, and Regime in Putin's Russia," *Slavic Review*, Vol. 68, No. 3 (Fall 2009), p. 546.

77. Agamben, *State of Exception*, p. 33; Mariana Budjeryn, "Violence, Power, and Nuclear Putin," *The World Affairs Journal*, 15 May 2014.
78. Arendt, *Origins of Totalitarianism*, p. xxxiii.
79. Joanna Bourke, "Why does politics turn to violence?" in *Global Politics: A New Introduction*, 2nd ed., eds. Jenny Edkins and Maja Zehfuss (New York: Routledge, 2008), pp. 475–476; Arendt, *Origins of Totalitarianism*; Judith Butler, *Precarious Life: The Powers of Mourning and Violence* (New York: Verso, 2004), p. 41; Franz Fanon, *Wretched of the Earth* (New York: Grove Press, 1961), p. 17.
80. Giorgio Agamben, *Homo Sacer: Sovereign Power and Bare Life* (Stanford: Stanford University Press, 1995), p. 121; Pomerantsev, *Nothing is True*, p. 86.
81. For more on the pogrom that occurred in Jedwabne, Poland, see Jan T. Gross, *Neighbors: The Destruction of the Jewish Community in Jedwabne, Poland* (Princeton: Princeton University Press, 2001).
82. Snyder, *The Road to Unfreedom*, p. 249.
83. While the two men who attacked Galina Starovoitova were arrested and jailed, it is widely believed that the Russian state security services ordered her murder. Amy Knight, *Orders to Kill: the Putin Regime and Political Murder* (New York: Thomas Dunne Books, 2017), pp. 57–78.
84. Galina Starovoitova, "Weimar Russia?" *Journal of Democracy*, Vol. 4, No. 3 (July 1993), pp. 108–109.
85. "Brainwashed" should be acknowledged as a contentious term. Is it actually "brainwashing" if the person or entity advocating for a certain topic believes in it? Do Russian state officials truly believe in the unrivaled superiority of their nation and all the ideological assumptions that accompany it? This is an intriguing topic that deserves to be explored in an opus of its own. Without such a detailed analysis, and for lack of a better term, "brainwashed" is used here in our research. George Orwell, "Notes on Nationalism," *Polemic*, October 1945.
86. Bourke, "Why does politics turn to violence?" p. 480.
87. Arutunyan, *The Putin Mystique*, p. 9.

References

Agamben, Giorgio. 1995. *Homo Sacer: Sovereign Power and Bare Life*. Stanford: Stanford University Press.
———. 2005. *State of Exception*. Chicago: University of Chicago Press.
Applebaum, Anne. 2017. *Red Famine: Stalin's War on Ukraine*. London: Allen Lane.
Arendt, Hannah. 1958. *Origins of Totalitarianism*. New York: Meridian Books.

Aron, Leon. 2014. Novorossiya! Putin and His Dangerous 'New Russia'. *Commentary Magazine*, December 1. Accessed 13 December 2016 at https://www.commentarymagazine.com/articles/novorossiya/

Arutunyan, Anna. 2015. *The Putin Mystique: Inside Russia's Power Cult*. Northampton: Olive Branch Press.

Balmforth, Tom. 2019. *Network, Son Of Nashi: New Youth Group Seeks To Woo Russia's Middle Class*. Radio Free Europe/Radio Liberty. Accessed 12 March 2019 at https://www.rferl.org/a/network-russian-youth-group-nashi-/25444358.html

Bennetts, Marc. 2017. Russia Considers Ban on Armando Iannucci's Film The Death of Stalin. *The Guardian*, September 20. Accessed 5 October 2018 at https://www.theguardian.com/world/2017/sep/20/russia-considers-ban-armando-iannucci-film-death-of-stalin

———. 2018. Russia Pulls 'Despicable' Death of Stalin from Cinemas. *The Guardian*, January 23. Accessed 5 October 2018 at https://www.theguardian.com/world/2018/jan/23/russia-urged-to-delay-death-of-stalin-release-until-summer

Bjelica, Sandra. 2014. *Discourse Analysis of the Masculine Representation of Vladimir Putin*. Thesis, Free University of Berlin, Berlin. Accessed 11 October 2016 at http://www.academia.edu/11590578/Discourse_Analysis_of_the_Masculine_Representation_of_Vladimir_Putin

Borri, Francesca. 2016. *Syrian Dust: Reporting from the Heart of the War*. Trans. A.M. Appel. New York: Seven Stories Press.

Bourke, Joanna. 2008. Why Does Politics Turn to Violence? In *Global Politics: A New Introduction*, ed. Jenny Edkins and Maja Zehfuss, 2nd ed., 472–495. New York: Routledge.

Bremer, Thomas. 2015. How the Russian Orthodox Church Views the 'Russian World'. *Occasional Papers on Religion in Eastern Europe* 35 (3): 43–49.

Budjeryn, Mariana. 2014. Violence, Power, and Nuclear Putin. *The World Affairs Journal*, May 15. Accessed 3 November 2016 at http://www.worldaffairsjournal.org/article/violence-power-and-nuclear-putin

Bueno de Mesquita, Bruce, and Alastair Smith. 2011. *The Dictator's Handbook: Why Bad Behavior Is Almost Always Good Politics*. New York: Public Affairs.

Butler, Judith. 2004. *Precarious Life: The Powers of Mourning and Violence*. New York: Verso.

Cassedy, Steven. 2005. *Dostoevsky's Religion*. Stanford: Stanford University Press.

Chen, Cheng. 2016. *The Return of Ideology: The Search for Regime Identities in Postcommunist Russia and China*. Ann Arbor: University of Michigan Press.

Cohn, Norman. 1975. *Europe's Inner Demons: An Enquiry Inspired by the Great Witch-Hunt*. New York: Basic Books, Inc.

Dawisha, Karen. 2014. *Putin's Kleptocracy: Who Owns Russia?* New York: Simon and Schuster Paperbacks.

"Death of Cinema?". 2018. *Russian Life* 61 (2): 7–8.

Fanon, Franz. 1961. *Wretched of the Earth*. New York: Grove Press.
Fish, M. Steven. 2017. The Kremlin Emboldened: What Is Putinism? *Journal of Democracy* 28 (4): 61–75.
Fish, M.Steven. 2018. What Has Russia Become? *Comparative Politics* 50 (3): 327–346.
Garrels, Anne. 2016. *Putin Country: A Journey into the Real Russia*. New York: Farrar, Straus and Giroux.
Gessen, Masha. 2012. The Wrath of Putin. *Vanity Fair*, April. Accessed 8 January 2017 at http://www.vanityfair.com/news/politics/2012/04/vladimir-putin-mikhail-khodorkovsky-russia
Gill, Graeme. 2016. Russia and the Vulnerability of Electoral Authoritarianism? *Slavic Review* 75 (2): 354–373.
Gorbachev, Mikhail. 2016. *The New Russia*. Cambridge: Polity Press.
Gorshkov, Mikhail K. 2011. The Sociology of Post-reform Russia. In *Russia: The Challenges of Transformation*, ed. Piotr Dutkiewicz and Dmitri Trenin, 145–190. New York: New York University Press.
Gross, Jan T. 2001. *Neighbors: The Destruction of the Jewish Community in Jedwabne, Poland*. Princeton: Princeton University Press.
Hartog, Eva. 2016. God, Stalin, and Patriotism—Meet Russia's New Education Chief. *The Moscow Times*, August 24. Accessed 25 August 2016 at https://themoscowtimes.com/articles/god-stalin-patriotism-meet-russias-new-education-minister-55090
Henderson, Sarah. 2016. Review Essay. *Slavic Review* 75 (2): 446–453.
Judah, Ben. 2013. *Fragile Empire: How Russia Fell In and Out of Love with Vladimir Putin*. New Haven: Yale University Press.
Kholmogorov, Yegor. 2008. *Atomnoe pravoslavie* [Atomic Orthodoxy]. *Russkii Obozrevatel*, 31 August. Accessed 12 July 2018 at http://www.rus-obr.ru/idea/594
"Kinoteatru 'Pioner' grozit shtraf do 300 tysjach rublej za pokaz 'Smerti Stalina'" [Pioner Cinema Faces a Fine of up to 300, 000 Rubles for Showing "The Death of Stalin"]. 2018. *News Ru*, February 19. Accessed 5 October 2018 at https://www.newsru.com/russia/19feb2018/thedeathofstalin.html
Knight, Amy. 2017. *Orders to Kill: The Putin Regime and Political Murder*. New York: Thomas Dunne Books.
Kołakowski, Leszek. 1990. *Modernity on Endless Trial*. Chicago: University of Chicago Press.
———. 1999. *Freedom, Fame, Lying and Betrayal: Essays on Everyday Life*. Trans A. Kołakowska. London/New York: The Penguin Group.
Kovalik, Dan. 2017. *The Plot to Scapegoat Russia: How the CIA and the Deep State Have Conspired to Vilify Russia*. New York: Skyhorse Publishing.

Levada Center. 2015a. *Institutional Trust*. Levada Center: Yuri Levada Analytical Center, October 16. Accessed 12 January 2017 at http://www.levada.ru/eng/institutional-trust
———. 2015b. *Is Russia a superpower?* Levada Center: Yuri Levada Analytical Center, December 3. Accessed 12 January 2017 at http://www.levada.ru/eng/russia-superpower
———. 2015c. *Pride and Patriotism*. Levada Center: Yuri Levada Analytical Center, December 9. Accessed 12 January 2017 at http://www.levada.ru/eng/pride-patriotism
———. 2015d. *Trust in the Mass Media*. Levada Center: Yuri Levada Analytical Center, October 26. Accessed 12 January 2017 at http://www.levada.ru/eng/trust-mass-media
———. 2016. *Democracy in Today's Russia*. Levada Center: Yuri Levada Analytical Center, January 20. Accessed 12 January 2017 at http://www.levada.ru/eng/democracy-todays-russia
Lourie, Richard. 2017. *Putin: His Downfall and Russia's Coming Crash*. New York: Thomas Dunne Books.
Lucas, Edward. 2014. *The New Cold War: Putin's Russia and the Threat to the West*. New York: St. Martin's Press.
Mach, Zdzisław. 2018. *The Concepts of Culture and Civilization. European Civilization*. Class Lecture at Jagiellonian University, Kraków, Poland, October 4.
March, Luke. 2009. Managing Opposition in a Hybrid Regime: Just Russia and Parastatal Opposition. *Slavic Review* 68 (3): 504–527.
McFaul, Michael. 2018. *From Cold War to Hot Peace: An American Ambassador in Putin's Russia*. New York: Houghton Mifflin Harcourt Publishing Company.
Molodaya Gvardiya. 2019. Napravlenia. *Molodaya Gvardiya*. Accessed 12 March 2019 at http://www.molgvardia.ru/projects
Oates, Sarah. 2014. Russia's Media and Political Communication in the Digital Age. In *Developments in Russian Politics*, ed. Stephen White, Richard Sakwa, and Harney E. Hale, 8th ed., 130–144. Durham: Duke University Press.
Official Internet Resources of the President of Russia. Speech by Vladimir Putin. 2007. *Stenograficheskij otchet o vstreche s delegatami Vserossijskoj konferencii prepodavatelej gumanitarnyh i obshhestvennyh nauk* [Excerpts from Transcript of Meeting with Participants in the National Russian Conference of Humanities and Social Sciences Teachers]. June 21. Accessed 25 August 2016 at http://en.kremlin.ru/events/president/transcripts/24359
Orwell, George. 1945. Notes on Nationalism. *Polemic*, October.
Ostrovsky, Arkady. 2015. *The Invention of Russia: From Gorbachev's Freedom to Putin's War*. New York: Viking Press.
Pain, Emil. 2012. Socio-Cultural Factors and Russian Modernization. In *Waiting for Reform Under Putin and Medvedev*, ed. Lena Jonson and Stephen White, 96–116. London: Palgrave Macmillan.

Plotnikova, Anna. 2016. Russia's New Education Minister Gives Stalin a Nod. *Voice of America*, August 25. Accessed 25 August 2016 at http://www.voanews.com/a/russia-education-minister-refers-positively-stalin/3481067.html

Pomerantsev, Peter. 2012. Putin's God Squad: The Orthodox Church and Russian Politics." *Newsweek*, September 10. Accessed 2 July 2018 at http://www.newsweek.com/putins-god-squad-orthodox-church-and-russian-politics-64649

———. 2014. *Nothing Is True and Everything Is Possible: The Surreal Heart of the New Russia*. New York: PublicAffairs.

Radio Free Europe/Radio Liberty. 2016. Russian Nationalists Attack Event for High-School History Students. *Radio Free Europe/Radio Liberty*, April 28. Accessed 28 April 2016 at http://www.rferl.org/a/russian-nationalists-attack-event-for-high-school-history-students-ulitskaya/27704871.html

Roberts, Graham H. 2016. *Consumer Culture, Branding and Identity in the New Russia: From Five-year Plan to 4x4*. London/New York: Routledge.

Robertson, Graeme B. 2009. Managing Society: Protests, Civil Society, and Regime in Putin's Russia. *Slavic Review* 68 (3): 528–547.

Rock, Stella. 2006. Russian Piety and Orthodox Culture 1380–1589. In *Eastern Christianity*, ed. Michael Angold, 251–175. Cambridge: Cambridge University Press.

RT News. Vladimir Putin interviewed by RT News. 2013. Putin Q&A on RT: President on 1st Visit to RT's State-of-the-Art HQ. *RT News*, June 12. Accessed 7 January 2017 at https://www.rt.com/news/putin-rt-interview-full-577/

Smelser, Neil. 1998. *The Social Edges of Psychoanalysis*. Berkeley: University of California Press.

Snyder, Timothy. 2014. Fascism, Russia, and Ukraine. *The New York Review*, March 20. Accessed 9 September 2016 at http://www.nybooks.com/articles/2014/03/20/fascism-russia-and-ukraine

———. 2018. *The Road to Unfreedom: Russia, Europe, America*. New York: Tim Duggan Books.

Starovoitova, Galina. 1993. Weimar Russia? *Journal of Democracy* 4 (3): 106–109.

The Moscow Times. 2014a. 'No Putin, No Russia,' Says Kremlin Deputy Chief of Staff. *The Moscow Times*, October 23. Accessed 11 January 2017 at https://themoscowtimes.com/articles/no-putin-no-russia-says-kremlin-deputy-chief-of-staff-40702

———. 2014b. Russian Candymaker Hopes Putin Chocolate Bars Are a Recipe for Success. *The Moscow Times*, November 26. Accessed 16 February 2017 at https://www.themoscowtimes.com/2014/11/26/russian-candymaker-hopes-putin-chocolate-bars-are-recipe-for-success-a41731

Tismaneanu, Vladimir. 2012. *The Devil in History: Communism, Fascism, and Some Lessons of the Twentieth Century*. Berkeley/Los Angeles: University of California Press.

Tucker, Robert C. 1987. *Political Culture and Leadership in Soviet Russia: From Lenin to Gorbachev*. New York: W.W. Norton & Company, Inc.

Umland, Andreas. 2013. New Extremely Right-Wing Intellectual Circles in Russia: The Anti-Orange Committee, the Isborsk Club and the Florian Geyer Club. *Russian Analytical Digest* 135: 1–9.

van Herpen, Marcel. 2015. *Putin's Propaganda Machine*. New York: Rowman and Littlefield.

Voice of America. 2017. 'Terrible Crimes' Made Putin World's Richest Person, Financier Testifies. *Voice of America*, July 27. Accessed 2 July 2018 at https://www.voanews.com/a/terrible-crimes-made-putin-world-richest-person-financier-tells-senators/3961955.html

Voinovich, Vladimir. 1985. *The Anti-Soviet Soviet Union*. Trans. R. Lourie. San Diego/New York/London: Harcourt Brace Jovanovich.

Zygar, Mikhail. 2016. *All the Kremlin's Men: Inside the Court of Vladimir Putin*. New York: Public Affairs.

CHAPTER 7

Russian Foreign Policy: Freedom for Whom, to Do What?

Foreign policy is typically defined as a government's strategy for dealing with other states in an attempt to safeguard its own national interests. In line with this understanding, Vladimir Putin argues that he pursues a realist sort of foreign policy solely meant to "ensur[e] one's own security," which "is the right of any sovereign state."[1] Our research agrees that Putin's international actions revolve around security concerns but contends that the well-being of the state and its population is not the ultimate target of securitization: Vladimir Putin does not treat foreign policy (or national security from external forces) as an end in itself, but rather as a tool designed to reinforce the Kremlin's ideology, galvanize the Russian citizenry in solidarity against external security threats, and ultimately legitimize his claim to authority in the eyes of the polity he relies upon to democratically elect him. After all, in the poignant words of prominent Russia scholar Leon Aron, "The tiger of patriotic mobilization needs to be fed."[2] Thus, Russia's foreign activities are engaged as a part of President Putin's strategy for achieving internal ambitions. He seeks to preserve his power largely through externally focused means. Foreign policy, then, is yet another key factor of Putinism.

The Kremlin's foreign policy serves to "prove" Putinism to be correct. It manifests the key factor discussed in Chap. 5: the imaginary of a hostile Western world from which Russia must defend itself, which necessitates the presence of a strong leader (Putin) and unifies the nation-state and its entire population as one against a globe filled with others. Without a foreign policy to generate the impression of dangerous security threats, no other or besieged-fortress mentality would exist via which to unify this Russian entity. The state would have little concrete basis for shared identity, and without this the state could not hope to fulfill any grand predestined mission begun back in ninth-century Kyivan Rus'.[3] The domestic would not be stabilized upon one unique identity, enemy, or goal. Putin's paternalistic role as the nation's authoritative caretaker would not exist as a top societal priority, since security would not be the state's central issue—simply defining itself would be.

Thus, the Kremlin's foreign policy is created in a way that allows Putin to channel the desires and fears of the Russian citizenry. In perpetuating the old yet familiar Soviet idea of a hostile world and the need for states of exception, this foreign policy blurs the line between the foreign and domestic spheres. It transforms the world in the eyes of interpellated Russians into one giant domestic space where non-indoctrinated individuals would ordinarily see an international space. This fear-mongering allows the Kremlin to gradually lead the public (likely unconsciously) into becoming a defensive (or is it offensive?) machine of destruction, prioritizing security so much that the population tolerates the usage of foreign policing methods in domestic affairs at any cost.[4] Essentially, this foreign policy helps Putin to secure the domestic sphere: it ensures that his role as the authority figure is seen as the nation's top necessity and, thusly, that he is continuously granted political power—which may just be the ultimate duplicitous purpose of the Kremlin's foreign policy in the first place.

Russia's foreign policy does more than just ensure the physical security of the nation. It distracts the public from economic woes, human rights violations, and questions of Russian identity, diverting their attention across the nation's borders and away from domestic failures that could potentially lead to protests, disunity, and challenges to the Russian government itself. Russia's foreign policy functions to fulfill the Kremlin's ideological goals. It presents the celebratory image of a unified Russian state whose values are superior to other, invariably less-moral Western states and, therefore, has special permission to act outside of international law.[5] This illusion of success in the name of doing "what is best" for the Russian people provides a pretext for Russian police to silence dissent at home, functions as a defining factor of Russian identity, and helps to incorporate the populace as loyal subjects of the state. In short, Russia's foreign policy is just another ideological strategy by which Putin retains his domestic popularity, his spurious legitimacy, and, thus, his claim to power.

This chapter will explore how Vladimir Putin uses foreign policy to manipulate national security appeals as a mobilizing force for public support. An examination of Russia's invasion of eastern Ukraine and subsequent illegal annexation of the Crimean Peninsula, as well as its violent actions in Syria, will demonstrate how President Putin manages to maintain his domestic popularity ratings through the totalitarian practice of espousing states of exception that artificially unite the country against "the foreign." This support comes not just from a Russian population excited to continue the imperialist legacy that was once so dear to the Soviet Union,[6] but a nationalist population looking to Russia's grand future.

The analysis of these Russian aggressions in Ukraine and Syria will also highlight how foreign policy has expanded the Kremlin's target base for interpellation beyond Russia's borders, thereby granting Putin proportionately more power to exercise in the name of protecting these specific populations. Investigating the Russian citizens' subsequent receptions of their state's foreign policies, as well, should provide further evidence of the psychologically manipulative techniques employed by the Kremlin in an attempt to persuade its citizenry into believing that Russia's history entitles the state to act above international law, claim physical land, and declare itself as the global superpower with an ideology superior to the West's.

With the help of Kremlin-controlled media (which essentially covers all media outlets in Russia), the Russian citizenry is mobilized by such ideas into an artificial reality in which Russian values, people, and lands are in constant danger. Therefore, not only must Russia always be on the offensive, but it also must always be guided by a strong leader capable of protecting it. Here the principles of autocracy and geopolitics loom in the background, just as they did in the sixteenth century when the Russian population bowed to the power of the first tsar, Ivan IV, and in the twentieth century when the Soviet population felt its existence jeopardized by Western enemies. In scholar of post-Communist societies M. Steven Fish's words, the practice of "slaying dragons abroad to generate mass support at home" has been a favorite of regimes across time and space.[7]

In the face of all these threats and duties purported by the Kremlin's media, the citizenry is intensely convinced that security has to be Russia's upmost concern. They are told they must preserve the Russian culture from an inimical West. They come to perceive the benefits of Putin's foreign gambits as outweighing the negatives. This justification somehow absolves the Kremlin's behaviors, or at least distracts Russian citizens from dwelling on the economic (not to mention human) costs of Putin's actions, Putin's prioritizing of international endeavors over the rescue of Russia's failing domestic economy, and the basic fact that Russia has withdrawn from a majority of these foreign engagements without ever accomplishing a specific concrete goal (e.g. Russia has militarily stalemated eastern Ukraine in a state of paralytic de facto partition, rather than de jure annexation). In this respect, Russia's foreign policy and the practices associated with it perpetuate a culture of insecurity that calls upon ideological citizens to blindly trust their state and their sovereign.

Putin's Foreign Policy, the "Near Abroad," and Beyond

Russia is not embroiled in some fantastic ideological struggle involving nuclear weapons, as it was during the Cold War. Still, memory can be a battlefield and there are several continuities between the two eras that cannot be ignored, namely their shared ambition to become *the* geopolitical superpower.[8] The obsession with finding constant enemies in Western nations is found in both Soviet history and the Russian present. The Kremlin desires to keep the West politically, economically, and ideologically out of the (ex-)Soviet sphere. This signals that irredentism holds a significant place in Russian ideology and goals. The semi-irredentist Russian nation-state legitimizes itself as a regional successor-power to the USSR, for it feels the need to control states that were a part of a larger Soviet history (including Ukraine, Georgia, Moldova, etc.). Control over former Soviet republics is crucial to today's Russia because, as some grow closer to the West and thrive off of international economic deals that boost living standards, average Russians might wonder why they do not see the same opportunities in their beloved Motherland. The Kremlin works to destroy the seed for any reason for protest, and thusly it seeks to prevent these states from appearing better off than Russia.

Not only does the geopolitically-focused Russia spread the fear of the imaginary pollution of national identity in the face of Western encroachment on Russia's own sovereign borders, but it also feels insecure in the notion that ex-Soviet countries once dependent on the Russian Soviet Republic could find their own independence and prosper without Russia's help (or, perhaps more accurately, without Russia's consent). To compensate for this perceived weakness, Putin has frequently sabotaged attempts of ex-Soviet satellites to Westernize on the basis of the violent cartographies imagined by the Russian state, from Russia's launch of the Russo-Georgian War in 2008 when Georgia hoped it would join NATO to Russia's 2014 invasion of eastern Ukraine in opposition to Ukraine's hopeful accession to the EU.

Russia decides it alone has the right to decide the futures of its neighboring countries and their populations—and those countries have no license to protest Russia's plans for them.[9] Somehow, even when violating other nation-states' sovereignties so blatantly, Russia portrays itself to its subjects as a benevolent actor by claiming to be the regional successor-power to the USSR and therefore responsible for looking after the "near abroad." The Kremlin further justifies its interventions by arguing that these post-Soviet countries still cannot make rational decisions or act in their own best interests because they "lack[ed] independence for decades" under Soviet rule and apparently have not yet achieved functionality after more than 25 years of otherwise sovereign statehood.[10]

This Russocentric perspective is perfectly encapsulated in Mikhail Gorbachev's indignant complaint (specifically made in regard to the Kremlin's attempts at limiting NATO expansion in Eastern Europe), "it was said Russia had no right to veto decisions involving other countries."[11] Such commitment to stories of the nation's historical trajectory as the paternalist authority over not just the current Russian citizenry, but the once-Soviet populations living in other countries, as well, testifies to the collective coherence and supposedly legitimate foundation of Russia. In the end, the Russian population is led to believe Russia is an exceptional nation on a great mission—one that traverses across territorial borders and unfairly attracts many enemies.

While the rest of this chapter will focus on Russian foreign policy on Ukraine and Syria, it is imperative to keep in mind that Russia's international gambits are not limited to just these two countries. Belarus, China, Cuba, the Czech Republic, Estonia, Finland, Georgia, Greece, Hungary, Iran, Italy, Kazakhstan, Kyrgyzstan, Latvia, Lithuania, Macedonia, Moldova, Nicaragua, North Korea, Norway, Poland, Romania, Serbia, Sweden, Tajikistan, Turkey, Turkmenistan, Venezuela, and others have all experienced some sort of meddling from Russia. Forms vary, but Russia has been most known to launch cyberattacks, to fund Internet trolls who would publically disparage Western values and disseminate lies, to interfere in "democratic" elections, to (often illegally) finance anti-Western and anti-liberal parties, to back genocidal leaders, to support breakaway regions like Transnistria and South Ossetia, to build military bases, to threateningly direct submarines and bomber planes into their national waters and airspaces, to exploit cultures of corruption that have survived the Soviet regime from which they were born, to hold energy supplies hostage and thus allow hundreds of people in the targeted areas to freeze to death, and more.[12]

It would also be remiss to remain silent on Russian influence in regard to the platforms, funding, and support of specific political parties including France's National Front, Germany's Alternative for Germany (AfD), Greece's Syriza and Golden Dawn, Hungary's Fidesz, Spain's Podemos, and the United Kingdom Independence Party (UKIP), to name a few. Putin and Putinism is a huge source of this populist avalanche. There is also the monumental issue of Russian hacking of the 2016 elections in the United States; and worse still, there is the damning point of the various murders for which the Kremlin has called (most recently in the United Kingdom with the failed assassination attempt of ex-Soviet military intelligence officer Sergei Skripal[13]). The diverse geographic bases of Putinism's reach, from post-Communist spaces to Western Europe and even across the Atlantic Ocean, demonstrate how Russia's influence extends far beyond just surrounding former Soviet satellites. Douglas E. Schoen and his co-author Evan Roth Smith uncover one of the most alarming factors in all this in their book *Putin's Master Plan: To Destroy Europe, Divide NATO, and Restore Russian Power and Global Influence* (2016): as bad as the West's negligence is when it comes to these atrocious behaviors, it is even more shocking that the political parties targeted for Russian influence run the full spectrum of political beliefs, from Greece's leftist, socialist Syriza and to Greece's extreme rightist, neo-fascist Golden Dawn.[14]

One might perceive this to mean that Russia's tactics are not ideological at all, then, if they play both sides. But this thinking could not be more incorrect. Recall our discussion of Peronism in Chap. 4; also consider that ideology still radiates from the core of Russia's decision to influence political parties regardless of their political affiliation. This is what makes Russia's actions abroad so heinous: the ability of an illiberal—not to mention foreign—power to gain influence over diverse opinions across an array of countries is in itself a feat of ideological manipulation. Not only are those living in Russia at risk of falling for these manipulations, but so are those living on the far side of Europe (and on entirely different continents), most of whom are not even Russian.

And while Putinism is Russocentric in most ways, the goal of the above-described ideological luring is not necessarily to convince a person or a political party that they should support Putin's Russia. Support is always helpful—especially in international debates—but part of what makes Putinism so dangerous is that it is also content to simply sow discord against democratic, pluralist values in areas that the Russian government otherwise could not reach. American historian Timothy Snyder discussed this tactic in his presentation at the Carnegie Endowment for International Peace in May 2018, telling audiences that it is enough for the Kremlin to publicize the narrative that homosexuality is an international conspiracy against traditional values, in order to encourage a group like Front National in France to grasp onto this rhetoric and then use it for themselves.[15]

Putin might not garner explicit, direct support through idea-sharing, but the Kremlin definitely succeeds in that it gets to disseminate its ideas to distant circles. The spreading of such ideas opens up questions about identity and rifts between "Us" (in this case, conservative homophobes) and "Them" (who end up being demonized in a catch-all category of gay-loving liberals) that, in the long run, help to lay the groundwork for doubts about human dignity and democracy. It is a sly maneuver reminiscent of the snake in the Garden of Eden, slowly poisoning opinions across the globe and making people feel like they need to choose sides against others.

Thus, Russia's long legacy of imperialism, a concept that many world historians relegate to the centuries predating that of the twenty-first, has more than survived under Putin: it thrives, building up the national ego and levels of trust in Putin's Kremlin (or its themes) much to the detriment of the rule of law and liberal democratic potentials. The cases of Russian aggression in Ukraine and Syria especially attest to this situation and prove Russia scholar Vladislav Inozemtsev's stance that Putinism maintains "deep roots in Russia's political traditions and imperial history"—roots that indicate a fundamental disrespect for democracy and human rights and a fundamental propensity for fascism and totalitarianism, as will be discussed in the final sections of this chapter and book.[16]

The Case of Ukraine and Expanding Biopolitics

Perhaps the most compelling basis upon which Putin justifies his international interventions is the claim that he is acting in the best interests of Russian national security not just for current citizens, but also for fellow ethnic Russians living abroad. Exactly this transpired when Russia invaded eastern Ukraine in February 2014. The invasion and the later illegal annexation of Crimea were met with high approval among Russian citizens, due in large part to their narrow understanding, already warped by the state's narratives, of these aggressive actions as measures that "had" to be taken by the Russian military in order to, as Putin said, "defend the rights of Russians, our compatriots abroad."[17]

The territory now belonging to the modern nation-state of Ukraine saw the creation of Kyivan Rus' in the ninth century, a land that is considered to be the heart and origin of the Russian Empire. In Russia's nationalist myth, such territory and historical memory is key to preserving Russia's glory. As Ukraine was pursuing its Association Agreement with the European Union in 2014, the Western-phobic, semi-irredentist Russian government sought to (1) mar Ukraine's efforts to drift Westward, and (2) retain the imperial Russian sphere of influence which generates so much historical and geopolitical respect for Russia among its citizenry. The Kremlin invented a violent cartography which held that, in eastern Ukraine, the Ukrainian government was violating the human rights of Russians. In this manner, Russia invoked itself as both the determiner of who was biologically considered to be Russian and the protector of these "biological Russians"' rights.

The Kremlin saw an opportunity to preserve its sphere of post-Soviet influence by sounding the alarm that ethnic Russians in Ukraine were endangered because the Western-leaning Ukrainian Parliament was considering the repeal of a 2012 law on minority languages. This legislation had granted Russian's status as a second official government language in areas with a certain percentage of Russian speakers. (The repeal movement was never signed into law or de facto enacted, it should be noted.[18]) With this, the Kremlin announced an emotionally charged state of exception which transformed the supposed violation of the rights of a vague set of Russian-identified people living in Ukraine into a national catastrophe that blurred the foreign and the domestic. It created a "sense of imminent or proximate danger, which in turn eased the way for any state measure" to pass. On the basis of imagined danger, the Kremlin deemed that a specific population of Russians living in foreign countries were in harm's way and decided that these people were suddenly also members of the population that Russia declared it must protect.[19]

At first, Russia began to politically undermine Ukrainian authority by reaching across borders to issue passports to Russian-identified Ukrainian citizens. This constitutes a major violation of the traditional understanding of nation-state sovereignty. Then, like the physical walls built between Palestine and Israel or Mexico and the United States, the physical invasion of Ukraine by Russian military forces helped to "project an image of sovereign jurisdictional power and an aura of the bounded and secure nation"—that is, the Russian nation—onto lands that, according to most of the world's perspective, legally belonged to the Ukrainian nation-state but, to the Russian perspective, provided the basis for the delegitimization of Ukrainian sovereignty.[20]

The (il)logic of Russia's aggressive behavior in Ukraine further evidences the contrived nature of the Russian security imaginary. It leads citizens to believe the nation-state is the most sovereign form of political community and, therefore, that the state should be respected as the ultimate authority for its citizens. The Russian state champions itself as such a sovereign nation-state. However, the invasion of Ukraine—also a sovereign nation-state—shows that the Russian people and state are simultaneously willing to disrespect the sanctity of other nation-states in the name of their own sovereignty. This is a paradox that has the potential to endanger the universal legitimacy of the same type of nation-state upon which Russians rely. If one sovereign nation-state can destabilize another, then why should the sovereignty of any nation-state be respected?

The Russian government had an answer to this conundrum in the violent cartography[21] it trumpeted for Ukraine. Putin presented Ukraine as lacking the legitimacy to the land, people, and authority associated with a nation-state, at the same time praising Russia for its superior culture and destiny as a superpower. According to Westphalian principles, without territory sanctified by a political map of the Earth, a nation-state has no sovereignty, no relevancy, and no existence. Putin captured this belief when he said to President of the United States George W. Bush at the 2008 NATO Summit in Bucharest, Romania, "You don't understand, George, that Ukraine is not even a state. What is Ukraine? Part of its territories is Eastern European, but the greater part is a gift from us [Russia]."[22] By severing Ukraine from its territory, Russia also destroyed Ukraine's sovereignty. Like the tragic case of Native Americans in the United States, Ukraine was deemed by a colonizing outside power to be a space lacking in political sovereignty and therefore full of political savages—and Russia then used this notion to justify its right to set foot in what it viewed to be illegitimate Ukrainian lands.[23] In the words of professor of intellectual history Marci Shore, "Putin found instability in Ukraine desirable."[24]

To the chagrin of virtually every Russian citizen, it is tempting to add that such a (ir)rationale was a favorite of the fascist Nazi regime, the supposed sworn enemy of the Soviet Union. Take, for example, the Nazi argument that Poland was merely "a bit of earth inhabited by ungoverned and undefined beings," so their takeover was more than acceptable. To Nazi believers, it was a form of salvation.[25] Outraged Putinists, for whom comparisons between Russians and Nazis are the worst insults they could possibly hear, will likely retort that the United States frequently engages in this same logic and point to controversial events like the bombing of Hiroshima or the Iraq War, pretending that Russia's actions are for some reason disparate from those undertaken by the West and therefore "not so bad."

Here, the Putinists are partly correct when they argue that Russia's crimes *cannot* be compared to events like the bombing of Hiroshima and the Iraq War: the difference is that the latter two controversies resulted from incompetent democratization attempts, whereas Russian behaviors are born out of imperial conquest. Putinists constantly try to evade direct comment on Russia's actions by deflecting criticisms to the West, but these are just attempts to distract from the real issue at hand: that Russia is a repeat offender of international law and sovereign borders, and it is not excusable.

Another line of reasoning for Russia's violent cartography of Ukraine stems from the reanimation of the geopolitically inclined Soviet imaginary discussed in Chap. 5. Russia sounds repeated demands for solidarity across the post-Soviet sphere, much to the detriment of the sovereign nations that comprise the region because those states are part of a larger Soviet history through which a semi-irredentist Russia legitimizes itself as a regional successor-power to the USSR. By design, Russia's violent cartography minimizes the authority wielded by the Ukrainian state while maximizing the Russian state's authority. It is a form of modern colonialism that splits Russia into a civilized "Us" (which also claims the right to geopolitical conquest) and Ukraine into a barbaric "Them."

The violent cartography not only vilified the Ukrainian government but also omitted mention of its nuanced sociopolitical intricacies (i.e. its status as a nation long-tormented by a regional controlling power—Russia—but now reclaiming its sovereignty and choosing to befriend the West). By neglecting the existence of these complexities, this Russian perspective encouraged the demonization of those within Ukraine's physical borders. Tightly controlled by statist elites, the media of Russia are well-trained in administering the most manipulative political technologies, designed to demoralize the Ukrainian "enemy" and win misguided hearts and minds—but, most importantly, *control*—in the territory Russia had occupied.

It made use of these skills by branding civil society leaders of the Euromaidan movement like Kyiv's Mayor Vitali Klitschko as "gay iconoclast[s]" and stigmatizing all Ukrainians as fascists.[26] Both of these traits—homosexuality and fascism—are highly offensive to Russia's prevailing Orthodox faith and keen memory of World War II, thus transforming Ukrainians into godless villains in the mind of the average Russian citizen. This performative practice plays off of the politics of paranoia, or the usage of conspiracy theories that strike fear into a population and help mobilize them against whatever group of people their government claims is the next threat.[27] It amplifies feelings of animosity against Ukrainians and provokes more violent behaviors, leading the Russian citizenry to accept Putin's decision to invade Ukraine when he decided it was becoming too close to the Western society that sponsored sexual "decadence" and perversion. Consequently, when Putin declared "that the situation in Ukraine has evolved in such a way that we have to start work on returning Crimea to being a part of Russia," the Russian population, having already been primed for aggression, stood by him.[28]

In fact, the Russian Public Opinion Research Center (VCIOM) released polls showing that 95 percent of citizens in Russia in March 2014 appreciated Russia's seizure of the Crimean peninsula from "fascist" Ukrainians who "threatened" the culture and lives of ethnic Russians.[29] But why did Russian citizens suddenly perceive the need to ensure the protection of the rights of ethnic Russians abroad as a top priority at that particular moment in 2014? There were no reports of systematic violence perpetrated by the Ukrainian state against ethnic Russians living in Ukraine; however, this reality was made irrelevant by Putin's government and the security imaginary it had constructed to convince citizens that their state was being victimized by the West and that their existence was threatened outside of Russian borders. While Putin's domestic approval rating had been hovering just above 60 percent in the months leading up to the March 2014 invasion, it shot up to over 80 percent once news of the (illegal) annexation broke.[30]

Typically, when a country sends its own troops into dangerous entanglements, the public reacts negatively once death tolls rise. Vladimir Putin tried to skirt around this issue by denying the presence of Russian troops in Ukraine—until a Russian made-for-TV documentary, entitled *Crimea: Path to the Motherland*, was aired one year later, in which Putin triumphantly detailed the plan for Crimea's takeover. The public was not enraged by the fact that their president had lied, however—after all, no deaths had been reported. Of course, there were no reports because Vladimir Putin had previously declared any Russian casualties "in peacetime" to be a matter of state secrecy.[31] But the TV documentary distracted from this ugly aspect of war and instead focused on the bravery of Russian troops and the glory they were bringing to the Russian Federation by reincorporating its "lost land" of Crimea.[32]

The Kremlin's cover was blown when a bureaucratic slip later in 2015 resulted in the publication of sensitive information in a routine military report. The text, which was promptly redacted by government censors, read: "In all, as of February 1, 2015, monetary compensation had been paid to more than 2,000 families of fallen soldiers and to 3,200 military personnel suffering heavy wounds and recognized as invalids." But even this evidence of the human costs of Russian's aggression in Ukraine did not shake support for the annexation of Crimea. Kremlin supporters merely toed the Kremlin's line, claiming the leaked document was fake. Those few who actually considered that it could have been a real report shrugged off the deathly implications: they continued to support Putin's decision to invade, choosing to see the situation as one in which the troops had been injured or killed while honorably performing their duty to better the entire state. They had transformed the soldiers into martyrs, distorting fact to fit the fiction espoused by the Kremlin.[33]

Thus, the Russian citizenry does not believe, for the most part, that Russia has violated any international laws on account of the "fact" that it had a legitimate cause to act (i.e. the protection of human rights). Some do not even believe international law is valid at all because Russia is such a superior civilization and has been excluded from global alliances altogether. Instead of international law, most Russians believe in the Kremlin's security imaginary and violent cartography. Since the Kremlin portrayed Ukraine's actions as being so dangerous to Russia's culture, the population of Russia felt their nation was warranted to act above the law and to respond exceptionally.

The population not only approves of its state's actions in Ukraine and Crimea; it also makes a point to celebrate them as instances of national pride. In early March 2017, the Russian State Duma drafted a bill seeking to change the date of the 2018 presidential election. The Russian Constitution states that the election is to be held on the second Sunday of the month in which the previous election cycle was held (which happens to be March), but this time there was a popular movement to postpone the election until the third Sunday, 18 March 2018. The date is significant because it marked the fourth anniversary of the day that the Crimean Peninsula "officially" signed an agreement to "liberate itself" and join the Russian Federation.[34] Evidently, this is what Russian citizens and lawmakers concern themselves with: making the effort to change their constitution for the very nationalist desire of celebrating Crimea's "rightful return" to the nation.

To indoctrinated Russian citizens, what is perceived as the encroachment of Westernization threatens their sovereign nation-state's power to command its population's loyalty. The Russian government can act as the ultimate authority of the Russian political community, but at the end of the day it always requires the complicity of ordinary people. Their support comes in the actions of belief, of vocalizing approval, of silencing dissent, and of taking part in the state's actions, whether they do so implicitly or explicitly. Their loyalty stands with the Kremlin, thanks to its intensive ideological indoctrination that leaves subjects with little room to think in ways different from their domineering state. They are essentially cogs in a machine.

THE CASE OF SYRIA AND EXAGGERATING RUSSIA'S ROLE IN GLOBAL ANTI-TERRORISM

Unlike in Ukraine, biopolitics do not play the central role in the Kremlin's Syrian intervention. Still, Russia's engagements in Syria reinforce Putin's ideology by portraying Russia as the superior culture and the non-Russian world as full of evil. Putin's strategy in Syria has been twofold: he can demonize the West (which has been backing anti-Bashar al-Assad and anti-ISIS [Islamic State of Iraq and Syria, or the Islamic State of Iraq and the Levant] forces) to make Russia appear cooperative and as though it were responsible for leading ceasefire negotiations and bringing peace to the Middle East while also destroying the pro-democracy movements in Syria, working to secure a pro-Kremlin sphere of influence in Assad's Syria, cultivating a tighter relationship with a powerful Iran, and strengthening support for Russia throughout the Middle East.[35]

Russia has long sought an ally in Assad for a variety of reasons, including: ensuring stable economic trade with Syria in regard to profitable arms deals (sales of which surpassed $4 billion in 2011 alone) and oil production, presenting the nation as militarily successful, securing the allegiance of at least one nation-state in the Middle East in order to prevent the entire sphere from becoming a Western, democratic sphere of influence, preventing jihadists from filtering into Russia, sabotaging potentially successful revolutions and regime changes, and challenging the West's (the United States', more specifically) perceived role as *the* global fighter of terrorism.[36] All of these interests share a common denominator in "play[ing] upon Russia's desire to be considered a major power," a concept directly associated with the Kremlin's promotion of a national narrative focusing on the nation's superiority.[37]

Russia has been active in the Syrian Civil War since it began in 2011 but launched its airstrike campaign on 30 September 2015, in keeping with Putin's statements to the United Nations General Assembly just two days prior, through which he maintained that "Russia has always been firm and consistent in opposing terrorism in all its forms," including that of ISIS.[38] The airstrikes lasted for six months, ending on 14 March 2016 when Foreign Minister of the Russian Federation Sergey Lavrov triumphantly declared Russian forces would begin withdrawing from Syria because Russia had "radically change[d] the situation in fighting international terrorism."[39]

Of course, little evidence existed to prove this point. The territories ISIS held in September 2015 had only shrunk by 22 percent as of March 2016 (and largely because of Kurdish efforts in the north and north-east of Syria, where Russia had not focused its strikes). Within the first two weeks of the campaign, the United Nations and U.S. State Department told press that "greater than 90 [percent] of the strikes that we've seen to date have not been against ISIL, or al-Qaida-affiliated terrorists." This trend continued throughout Russia's strike period.[40] By the middle of the campaign, analyses had proven nearly five-sixths of the Russian Defense Ministry's claims of "successful" airstrike results to be *incorrect*. In fact, most Russian bombs had not been destroying (much less targeting) ISIS forces at all: instead they were aiming for opponents to the Assad regime and civilians sympathetic to anti-Assad forces, as well as American CIA units. By the end of the Kremlin's six-month airstrike run, its "operation destroyed the capabilities of the only credible non-jihadist alternative to Assad's regime," which were backed by the West. Yet Putin nevertheless declared, "mission accomplished."[41]

If Putin had specified "mission accomplished" on the basis of preserving Assad's hold on Syria's future, he would have had arguable proof. But he made his reference to the Russian military's valiant fight against terrorist forces. While news outside of Russia "expose[d] the false claims that Russia targeted ISIS or defeated international terrorism," inside, Russia's actions in Syria were widely celebrated. For all the Russian citizenry knew, Putin's claims were truthful, since the state-controlled media outlets had been constantly reporting Russian successes as part of a huge disinformation strategy.[42] The whole six-month period was just another way in which Putin relied on "lift[ing] the country up with marvelous military conquests" and encouraging pride in its strong, defensive state. A Levada Center poll from October 2016 shows over 68 percent of the Russian population supported Putin's decision to initiate the air campaign, and 69 percent of citizens believe Russia accomplished the goals it set out to achieve through the military intervention.[43]

At the same time, the "successes" announced by the Kremlin to its citizenry also benefit the Kremlin in two other manners. First, they function to prolong Putin's favorite theme that no revolution is an acceptable revolution. The Free Syrian Army is full of its own extremists and terrorists, but essentially all the people in Syria who have not surrendered or collaborated with the barrel bomb- and chemical weapons-happy Assad have been forcibly transformed into fighters against the regime in their own right.[44] They want, not to mention deserve, a free Syria, but their narrative is ignored in the Russian media. Instead, it portrays them as either helpless citizens desperate for stability (i.e. for Assad, in the Kremlin's purview) or as "revolutionary" terrorists who want a new regime (i.e. instability) and must be eliminated. The Russian people can get behind this story because they themselves know that long, instability-fearing history of Russia, as has been described in greatest detail in Chap. 2.[45] There is an odd affinity, then, for the Russian public with the unstable Syria, one that Putin's Kremlin can manipulate to champion the values of conservatism.

The second benefit of Russia's so-called successes in Syria is that they allow Russia to portray the West as militarily impotent and even terrorist-friendly. What is more, Russia has accused the United States and European nations of purposefully bombing pro-Assad forces in Syria. This is a prime example of the Kremlin-driven, ever-deepening cycle of polarization between Russia and the West. In this way, Russia can condemn the West morally, ideologically, and practically. Putin blames the West for the violence in Syria while attempting to present the Russian state itself as the destroyer of legitimate Syrian targets and as the "true" mediator of peace in the region. The Putinist line ignores a number of incidents where Russia has instead aimed for civilians, American CIA operatives, and even humanitarian aid convoys.[46] When French President François Hollande pointed out these omitted cases in October 2016 and suggested that Russia was guilty of war crimes within Syria, Putin simply canceled his upcoming diplomatic mission to France and projected this idea of guilt onto the West, in general. He argued that the West "prefer[ed] to make sweeping accusations against Russia," rather than own up to its responsibility in the failure of Syria's most recent ceasefire attempt.[47]

In this manner, Putin dismisses the West's opinions within Russian society as hypocritical (which plenty are, but this does not mean that they hold no grains of truth) and therefore nullifies the weight of any Western-launched criticisms of Russia as an authoritarian violator of human rights. It should be noted that Human Rights Watch and several other human rights NGOs have documented and denounced Russia for frequently using internationally banned cluster munitions in its air campaign (in one instance, at least 37 civilians were killed and many others wounded)—but the Kremlin simply denied and ignored the accusation.[48] This discrediting also allows Putin to blame the West for perpetuating violence in the Middle East, in contrast emboldening Russia and portraying it as the more competent, more effective fighter of global terrorism which has an unwritten license to engage in brazen international violence.

These portrayals of the West's "meddling" in "Russia's" international affairs primarily perpetuate the familiar Cold War paranoia that Russia is "menaced by an external force" with the "greatest threats coming from NATO and the United States," as Foreign Minister Sergey Lavrov declared in a March 2016 speech.[49] Not only did Lavrov appeal to cultural nationalism, but also to biopolitics, stating that it is "in the genes of the Russian people" to defeat "attempts of the European West to completely subjugate Russia, and to deny [Russia] its national identity and religious faith."[50] Thus, the performative practices of the security imaginary, combined with state-tailored foreign policy narratives like that of Syria, galvanize the collective notion that the West is a deceitful, evil, and less-moral opponent of the Russian state.

These state-led practices command allegiance from their citizen audiences who are deprived of access to credible information originating from outside of Russia. This ensures that the domestic population will continue to support Vladimir Putin because they believe he is capable of fending off the imaginary enemies constantly seeking to destabilize Russia. In the fall of 2015 in St. Petersburg, a twenty-something-year-old Russian tour guide argued for this logic, telling her group of American students, "Putin says they [anti-Assad Syrians] are terrorists, and I don't like war, but ... We should bomb them because Putin said so." Perhaps in a roundabout way, foreign policy is manipulated to lead subjects of Russia to a single conclusion about domestic politics: Putin's Russia is the best nation-state out there; therefore, this particular sovereign is to be granted power.

Foreign Policy and the Internal Policing of the Enemy

This mass approval for Russia's foreign policy doubly benefits the Kremlin. Aggressive foreign policy garners public support and respect while also reinforcing the Russian citizenry's belief that their nation-state must defend itself from Western encroachment. The following anecdote, witnessed by one of this book's authors [KL], describes how both of these ideas combine to further enforce the Kremlin's ideology: in the fall of 2015 in St. Petersburg, about forty elderly women (and a few men) gathered in quiet prayer just outside of the famous Russian Orthodox Kazan Cathedral. None of them tried to make a scene or speak to passersby. The only clue that they were opposed to the Kremlin's policies were the small blue and yellow Ukrainian flag pins they wore—and the fact that at least 60 Russian police officers, dressed in full riot gear, had formed a ring around them. The officers would intimidate any pin-wearers who chatted with a group of more than three or four fellow protesters. One police officer would walk up to the group and get in their faces, trying to silence their already-quiet, private conversations, while another officer would hold a camcorder above the circle (no doubt any blurry footage he caught would be used as "evidence," should any violence or arrests ensue, to blame the protesters for inciting aggression and to legally justify any actions by the police).

Also present at the scene were five anti-protesters holding massive St. George's ribbon-patterned flags. They also carried a sign that read "USA, get your hands out of Ukraine" and displayed an edited image of President Barack Obama—his face monkey-fied, his teeth sharp, and his mouth dripping with blood—holding the geographical outline of Ukraine, out of which a massive, bleeding bite had been taken. One must ask: what gives these pro-Kremlin nationalists the right to complain about American involvement in the supposedly sovereign Ukraine, when they wouldn't think twice about Russia's right to exert a controlling influence there? Of course, these nationalists would not think to ask themselves this double-edged question or perceive the situation in such a way, for they have been indoctrinated into believing that Russia is *saving* Ukraine from the United States and the rest of the West.

The Russian nationalists were yelling and singing to the Russian anthem, but the riot police did not bother them. Apparently they felt that the quiet, calm pro-Ukrainian independence protestors were disturbing the peace more so than the obnoxiously loud Russian nationalists. Though I [KL] personally observed this scene, I left the area after about two hours for fear of an incident, foolishly thinking I would just read about the end of this event in the next day's Russian news—but as it turns out I could not find a single mention of it online or in print. Though the authors of this book cannot inform readers as to how this scenario ended, we can at least use it as an epitomizing example of how Russian ideology and foreign policy gambits work together to silence dissent at home, promote Russian glory, and generate support for Putin. It shows how normative law, including the idea that no sovereign nation-state may intrude upon another sovereign nation-state's territory or affairs, can be contradicted, hijacked, and altogether decimated by the very government that claims to define itself by such rules. This governmental brutishness uncaringly violates international laws. It creates a permanent state of exception; this is why it goes unpunished and has the gall to insist that it is adhering to the sacred letter of the law and guaranteeing the best interests of the citizenry (as defined by the Kremlin).[51]

As previously discussed in Chaps. 4 and 5, the Kremlin copes with its schizophrenic history of various radical movements, ethnic incorporation (and loss), and the partial destruction of individual identities under Soviet rule by defining external enemies in order to define the Russian identity and consolidate it for the sake of security. It follows that Russia's foreign policy can enact a besieged-fortress mentality, creating a widespread illusion that convinces citizens that their nation is being attacked but is really a ploy to boost the regime's claims to legitimate power at the moment when it most needs support. It serves as a rather efficacious arm for fortifying internal unity against a world it chooses to represent as eternally dangerous and out to subjugate the Russian nation.[52] The Kremlin's policy of demonizing and delegitimizing Ukraine's status as a sovereign nation with a right to existence does just this.

In personifying external evils, however, the Kremlin can better define its own nationalism, indoctrinating its subjects to the point where they take it upon themselves as citizens to police the actions and ideas of other citizens who may not be so nationalistic. Putin's current government has become equated with all of Russia: those who are against Putin may as well be internal enemies of the state, in the eyes of his loyal subjects. Thus, to these pro-Kremlin believers, the group of older women and men who peacefully prayed outside of Kazan Cathedral to communicate their respect for Ukrainian sovereignty was transformed into potentially dangerous, protesting dissenters who must be prevented from damaging the country. Through this channel, foreign policy becomes another tool the Kremlin manipulates to control domestic actions and opinions and to ensure Putin retains his access to power via popular support.

There are some doubters, such as Russian-American journalist Keith Gessen, who argue that Putin's exploitation of foreign policy will lead to his regime's violent demise because its military expeditions cost Russia too much both in terms of finances and stability.[53] Gessen's approach, however, tends to overlook the powerful inner logic of Putinism. The Kremlin has a strong interest in manipulating certain foreign policies for the purposes of fabricating a reality in which the ideology it purports—that of a superior Russian culture constantly under attack from the West—lends itself to more and more credibility. The cycle is so vicious that the public has little ability but to fall for it. Given the public's consent, the Putinist government's one-sided narratives generate effective anomie which justify states of exception as necessary measures. As Italian philosopher Giorgio Agamben wrote, the stage is then set for a sovereign to begin "to free himself from all subordination to the law" and to replace universal morality with national egoism and indifference toward others. In this way, nationalism and aggressive foreign policies have become hugely important exercises of the Kremlin's authority in Russia.[54] It is not likely, as Gessen would predict, that Putin's foreign gambits will backfire, especially when Putin himself knows the importance of not overstepping the country's military limits: regime change, or at least major protests, ensued following defeat in the Crimean War of 1856, in the Russo-Japanese War of 1905, and in the Soviet's Afghan War between 1979 and 1989.[55] From history, Putin knows that defeat is not an option, and thus he will not be keen to risk failure or backfiring. He will continue to ride foreign policy in ways that his administration can model as victories that only promote the Russian nation-state.

Anomie, therefore, makes states of exception acceptable, and uninteresting, for the population who merely trusts that their sovereign's actions are legitimate and for their own good.[56] In this case, Putin and other similar sovereigns can exercise more and more power on their own volition, without obstruction from any protesting citizens, by arguing that the state *must* engage in certain behaviors or else risk its survival. This invocation of national security sets the precedent that Putin can act with impunity outside of Russia's borders—but it also can be manipulated into a power that allows him to enact these same methods internally.

When an expectation of national security is associated with Putin, he is automatically permitted a monopoly on violence and killing, so long as his actions guarantee the safety of his own population. As in Chap. 6, we revisit the general phenomenon which Hannah Arendt so insightfully articulated in her theories of authoritarianism and totalitarianism because the Russian state's laws allow for "no question of right or wrong, but only absolute obedience, the blind conformism" of the society which believes it must support their state in return for protection.[57] As such, it is not that Putinism is *anti*-constitutional, but that it is *supra*-constitutional, building constant loopholes and states of exceptions in which Putin can find justifications for both expanding his power across Russia's borders and cracking down on supposed security threats within its borders. All of these states of exception are imagined on the basis of foreign identity.

For the Russian state, it is paramount to control information and the nation's interpretation of said information.[58] With the arrest of Putin-critic and media tycoon Vladimir Gusinsky (who was essentially forced by the government to sell his largest private news outlets and then flee the country) in June 2000, the Kremlin effectively strangled the media into submission. Thus Putin's opposition faces the assured fate of having no (competent and credible) voice in the media, of being arrested at voting booths, of suffering harassment from both the judicial system and the governmental bureaucracy, and of living with the fear of physical threats. This is a fate designed to discourage anyone from sharing or acting upon their negative views of the Kremlin and its leader.[59] By seizing control of information sources and either silencing them or pumping state-approved narratives into them, the Kremlin can counterfeit legality and expand its powers.

The State Duma (Russian legislature) mandated that all protests must be approved and registered by the federal government; without the proper authorizations, protestors would face penalties. Denials of freedoms of speech and association accelerated when Putin returned to the presidential office in 2012, and public protests of over 30,000 people took to the streets and main squares to complain about electoral fraud. In response, the State Duma enacted a law raising fines for unauthorized protesters and organizers up to 300,000 rubles ($9000) and 1,000,000 rubles (over $27,000), respectively (although the law was updated in July 2014, raising the fine for the former group to roughly one million rubles, as well—a cost which is absurdly far beyond the financial means of a majority of Russian citizens).[60] Putin merely justified the law to outraged human rights NGOs as a necessary measure to prevent radicalism and the intrusion of Western saboteurs that could destroy Russian values and, with this, their nation-state as a whole.

That same year, Putin targeted those troublesome NGOs by signing Federal Law No. 18-FZ, "On Introducing Changes to Several Legislative Acts of the Russian Federation." Also known as the "foreign agent law," this legislation made it particularly difficult for NGOs receiving any funding from outside Russia (i.e. from the Western "jackals," as Putin himself called them in 2011) to exist, dooming them to quarterly tax audits and activity reports for which even one hardly noticeable error or incomplete (in the subjective opinion of Russian tax officials, known for their meticulous efforts of "discovering" mysterious and rather contrived violations) answer could garner up to a $15,000 fine each, or perhaps a lawsuit.

While this law may not explicitly deny freedom of speech, it serves as an efficient method of doing so. Within one year of Federal Law No. 18-FZ's passage, over 2000 NGOs had been raided, and thousands had packed up and left the country due to fear, financial disaster, and the realization that the law disgraced their activities in the eyes of Russian citizens so much that they were demonized by the average citizens they had been trying to help in the first place. As the Russian government granted itself the literal ability to license civil society, anything considered to be related to the West, democracy, or human rights essentially became despised as vehicles of foreign subversion.[61]

In this manner, Putin's government has transformed the judiciary and prison into a political institution—a blatant example of the state's desire to literally control human bodies in order to ensure its own political power. The arrests and "voluntary" exiles of both media magnate Vladimir Gusinsky and former oil giant Mikhail Khodorkovsky teach two lessons that are of particular importance to our research: (1) it is imperative to refrain from critiquing Putin and his regime, and (2) his regime is more than capable of stealing your property, ideas, and life.[62] The imprisonment of Pussy Riot members after the stunt their musical band pulled in a Russian Orthodox Church to protest Putin and Russian conservatism also teaches citizens not to dare cross Russian tradition.[63]

The list of infamously unfair arrests goes on endlessly. Its length explains how the Russian government has managed to create a legal system which forces citizens to ask, "Who will be next?"[64] In other words, they wonder who the next *exception* will be, a worry which instills order throughout society by virtue of the fact that no one wants to become the next government target. Thousands of regular civilians are arrested and released from jail after several months in Russia per year; they usually have not done anything wrong (or at least wrong enough to have warranted such a sentence), but it is a way for the government to tell its citizens that even if they are relatively good, they may still get punished for any behavior of which the government disapproves. For example, a middle-class businesswoman named Yana Yakovleva—the finance chief of a small cleaning-chemical business, one of the products for which the government placed restrictions on without announcing the fact—was retroactively charged for selling a certain chemical that was perfectly legal to sell when she had made the transactions in question; when she refused to pay bribes to the police to clear up the issue, she was imprisoned for seven months.[65]

Stories such as hers circulate and scare Russian citizens into adopting the attitude of living their lives as safely and apolitically as possible, and of paying bribes when they are cornered into it, so as not to potentially offend the Kremlin and draw its ire—a tactic that sounds eerily reminiscent of the Stalin era. The situation is accurately captured in Hannah Arendt's remark:

> the preponderance of the police not merely answers the need for suppressing the population at home but fits the ideological claim to global rule. For it is evident that those who regard the whole earth as their territory will stress the organ of domestic violence and will rule conquered territory with police methods and personnel rather than with the army.[66]

In Russia, the police monitor the country in a fashion similar to how the military enforces Russian foreign policy abroad. Huge OMON prison vans the size of traditional American school buses, as well as the presence of Russian police officers dressed in classic military arctic camouflage and wielding assault rifles at the ready, are common sights in St. Petersburg, or at least they were from August 2015 through December 2015, when I [KL] ran into one few days on my travels around the city. Putin even created his own new National Guard (or is it a praetorian guard?) in the fall of 2016, designed to unite all public security forces together under one command: Putin's. Putin argues the reform is necessary to better combat terrorism, organized crime, and "illegal" protests, but he conveniently omits the overwhelming likelihood that it will also protect himself and his hold on power.[67] He also has failed to comment on the structure's uncanny similarity to the military branches, which are also controlled by Putin, since the Russian Federation's President is also its Supreme Commander-in-Chief.

Under Putin's watch, Russia's military security forces and its domestic police forces have routinely come together for joint training exercises. One of the most important drill scenarios is that the military must quell violence just beyond Russia's borders (i.e. in some other sovereign nation-state's territory), and domestic FSB units are trained to sweep and secure the rear areas, following the military's route further and further outside of the Russian state's boundaries.[68] This is a quite literal example of how Putin's Russia has embarked on a mission of blurring the foreign and the domestic, using whatever forms of violence it can—from physical to intellectual to psychological—for the purpose of formulating internal order.

Main legal theorist of the Third Reich Carl Schmitt referred to this scenario in several of his writings, particularly in *Political Theology: Four Chapters on the Concept of Sovereignty* (originally published in 1922), as the achievement of sovereignty that has been fully realized by a strong leader. Anything that is not a part of this expected order, that is not "recognizable," is treated as a disturbance that could threaten the very security of the nation-state.[69] It is a sign that violence is a constitutive element of the Russian nation-state, and the sovereign has the flexible right to invoke it. Few spaces are truly private. This is eerily redolent of Franz Kafka's terrifying observations of authoritarianism in his 1925 book *The Trial*, which revealed how any space can (inappropriately) become a (rigged) courtroom, and privacy is not a universal right.[70]

Yet, as French historian Alain Besançon attests, today's Russia is an even more complete police state than it ever was under Soviet rule: whereas the KGB was once at least subject to the Soviet regime's rules, now "the police are in power. It is literally a police state." There is no Party anymore, only Putin, oligarchs, security services, and other corrupt cronies embedded in bureaucracy, business, the media, and so on. And as long as Putin, the man from whom Russian security authorities take orders because he is, in fact, the leader of the police at the same time as he is the leader of the country, is on your side, you might as well be part of that police state, as well.[71] The spidery web continues to spin ever thicker with each day, each election, each supposed security risk, each supposed fascist junta in Ukraine and Syria, and each supposed threat from the international community.

Russia's foreign policy not only lands beyond the political borders of its nation-state, but also its domestic space because the foreign has become a term used to describe any person, product, organization, lifestyle, or idea not aligned with Russian values, serving as the baseline for what is deemed to be an unsavory element that must be distrusted within the nation-state. Since Putin's foreign policy is a major element in this process of shaping the population's beliefs of the world, foreign policy should, in fact, be considered to be a fundamental tool for the state's ability to command discipline internally and to demand the population's support. All of the aforementioned tactics of blurring and policing compel Russian citizens to obey the law—and even embrace it—in order not to be punished by Putin's regime. Foreign policy, then, is both a national disciplinary tactic and a social philosophy. Putinism effectively exploits this narrative production and enforces allegiance to the government in order to unify the nation-state, forcing consolidation via the manipulation of historical fears, popular cultural desires for authoritarianism, and an intense nationalist ideology.

Notes

1. Official Internet Resources of the President of Russia, speech by Vladimir Putin, "Vystuplenie i diskussija na Mjunhenskoj konferencii po voprosam politiki bezopasnosti," 2007 Munich Conference on Security Policy, 10 February 2007.
2. Leon Aron, "The Kremlin Emboldened: Putinism After Crimea," *Journal of Democracy*, Vol. 28, No. 4 (October 2017), p. 78.
3. On a related note, the assumption that Kyivan Rus' was the seed from which Russian culture began is flawed in itself. While Russian history textbooks (and some Western ones, as well) argue that Kyivan Rus' marked the earliest manifestation of Russian identity, they are sure not to mention the birth of other identities, such as Ukrainian. Russian ethnonationalists might assert that this speaks to their position that Ukraine and Russia are one nation. Of course, theirs is an absurd claim, even if one considers from the most basic level that, by twenty-first-century international law, the two

states are separate. And their ethnonationalist acceptance of the notion that Kyivan Rus' was the beginning of Russian identity (and Russian identity, only) also fails to recognize the idea that perhaps the Kremlin's version of history is distorted. In fact, it is: Ukrainians, too, can claim that Kyivan Rus' was crucial to their cultural formation. The unquestioning agreement, though, that Kyivan Rus' solely belongs to the Russian tradition is just another example of an ethnocentric, ultranationalist ideology at play. Czesław Porębski, "General Introduction: Political Philosophy, Philosophy of History, Russian History," Russian Thought on Europe (class lecture, Jagiellonian University, Kraków, Poland, 3 October 2018).
4. Giorgio Agamben, *State of Exception* (Chicago: Chicago University Press), p. 86.
5. Leon Aron, "Drivers of Putin's foreign policy," American Enterprise Institute, 14 June 2016.
6. Serhii Plokhy, *The Last Empire: The Final Days of the Soviet Union* (London: Oneworld Publications, 2015), p. 406.
7. M. Steven Fish, "What Has Russia Become?" *Comparative Politics*, Vol. 50, No. 3 (April 2018), p. 339.
8. Luisa Passerini, "Memories Between Silence and Oblivion," in *Memory, History, Nation: Contested Pasts*, eds. Katharine Hodgkin and Susannah Radstone (New Brunswick: Transaction Publishers, 2006), p. 241.
9. Edward Lucas, *The New Cold War: Putin's Russia and the Threat to the West* (New York: St. Martin's Press, 2014), p. 147.
10. Mikhail Gorbachev, *The New Russia* (Cambridge: Polity Press, 2016), p. 307.
11. Gorbachev, *The New Russia*, p. 307.
12. Douglas E. Schoen with Evan Roth Smith, *Putin's Master Plan: To Destroy Europe, Divide NATO, and Restore Russian Power and Global Influence* (New York: Encounter Books, 2016), pp. 15–26 and 90–91; Timothy Snyder, *The Road to Unfreedom: Russia, Europe, America* (New York: Tim Duggan Books, 2018), p. 100.
13. BBC News, "Russian spy: What happened to Sergei and Yulia Skripal?," BBC News, 27 September 2018. While the Kremlin of course denies involvement in the Skripal case and in many others, the authors of this book are confident in assigning overall responsibility to the Russian government because of the heavy hand it plays in the spread of Putinism. Even if the men who tried to kill Sergei Skripal really were just acting as "private Russian citizens" (a claim that various investigate sources have already debunked, anyway, finding that at least one of the attackers was a decorated Russian colonel) and had not been directly ordered by anyone in the Kremlin to murder Skripal, the issue remains that they live in a society in which such behaviors are encouraged through a myriad of already-discussed

methods. The Kremlin is responsible for spinning this ideology, just as those would-be killers are responsible for acting on this ideology. Radio Free Europe/Radio Liberty, "Report: Third Alleged Russian Agent Involved In Skripal Mission Identified," Radio Free Europe/Radio Liberty, 28 September 2018.

14. Schoen, *Putin's Master Plan*, pp. 23 and 112–120.
15. Timothy Snyder and Thomas Carothers, "The Road to Unfreedom" (presentation at Carnegie Endowment for International Peace, Washington, DC, 18 May 2018).
16. Vladislav Inozemtsev, "The Kremlin Emboldened: Why Putinism Arose," *Journal of Democracy*, Vol. 28, No. 4 (October 2017), p. 80.
17. Official Internet Resources of the President of Russia, speech by Vladimir Putin, "Konferencija rossijskih poslov i postojannyh predstavitelej," Official Internet Resources of the President of Russia, 1 July 2014; David M. Herszenhorn, "Putin Vows to 'Actively Defend' Russians Living Abroad," the Atlantic Council, 2 July 2014.
18. While the Russian government and media fabricated much of the hateful discourse around Ukraine and its language laws, we feel compelled to remind readers that Ukraine is certainly not perfect. It still struggles with its Communist past and all the corruption and stunted civil society that accompanies it. There was, in fact, uncertainty about the legal future of the Russian language in official capacities in Ukraine. The 2012 bill that sparked heated debate about the idea of the marginalization of the Russian language, entitled "On the principles of the state language policy," proposed to allow languages besides Ukrainian to appear as additional official languages wherever the regional population comprised at least 10 percent of speakers. Language and identity is a complicated discussion, and certainly so in the post-Soviet space. The bill was rather favorable to Russian minorities, considering that the threshold was 10 percent and not at all unrealistically set. When the traitorous former president of Ukraine Viktor Yanukovych fled the country in February 2014, the national parliament voted in favor of abolishing that 2012 law. However, no Ukrainian president either signed or vetoed the decision to abolish the 2012 law; hence, it remained in effect. On top of that, certain minority language provisions still existed under the Ukrainian Constitution even without the "repealed" law. The Russian government's decision to abuse this confusing set of events and legal parameters, then, demonstrates that it was keen to create a serious, definitive problem where there had not been one. In this case, that fabrication was illegitimate and meant to rally the Russian population to support the Kremlin's "defense" of their compatriots abroad. In the interest of full disclosure, though, we inform readers that in February 2018, Ukraine declared that 2012 bill was, in fact, unconstitutional; what

the country will do now regarding its language laws remains to be seen. Perhaps it will end unfairly for Russian speakers, or perhaps not. While this is important to understand for 2019, this discussion admittedly veers from the main topic at hand because it cannot retroactively legitimize the Russian aggression over the matter. There is a basic truth to the events of 2014: the Kremlin illegitimately fostered conflict about Russian-torturing Ukrainians in order to mobilize Russian nationalists both at home and abroad in support of what became a very illegal, unprecedented endeavor—the seizure of Crimea and invasion of eastern Ukraine. Tetyana Ogarkova, "The Truth Behind Ukraine's Language Policy," the Atlantic Council, 12 March 2018.

19. Carl Schmitt, *Dictatorship: From the Beginning of the Modern Concept of Sovereignty to the Proletarian Class-Struggle*, 7th ed. (Berlin: Duncker and Humblot, 2006); Agamben, *State of Exception*, p. 67; Wendy Brown, *Walled States, Waning Sovereignty* (New York: Zone Books), p. 77; Mark Mardell, "Does Hitler's legacy still cast shadow over the world?" BBC News, 21 October 2016. As more food for thought, Hillary Clinton, David Cameron and Prince Charles of Wales have all made the point that Hitler occupied Czechoslovakia using the excuse of the mistreatment of ethnic Germans, while Putin cited the fate of ethnic Russians in Ukraine and Crimea to justify his own military actions.

20. Brown, *Walled States*, pp. 25 and 44; Masha Gessen, *The Future is History: How Totalitarianism Reclaimed Russia* (New York: Riverhead Books, 2017), p. 435.

21. Derek Gregory, *The Colonial Present* (Malden: Blackwell Publishing, 2004), p. 28.

22. James Marson, "Putin to the West: Hands off Ukraine," *TIME*, 25 May 2009.

23. Brown, *Walled States*, p. 44; Michael McFaul, *From Cold War to Hot Peace: An American Ambassador in Putin's Russia* (New York: Houghton Mifflin Harcourt Publishing Company, 2018), p. 394.

24. Marci Shore, "The Poet Laureate of Hybrid War," *Foreign Policy*, 26 October 2017.

25. Timothy Snyder, *Black Earth: The Holocaust as History and Warning* (New York: Tim Duggan Books, 2015), pp. 105 and 106.

26. Timothy Snyder, "Fascism, Russia, and Ukraine," *The New York Review*, 20 March 2014; Snyder, *The Road to Unfreedom*, p. 133.

27. Jan-Willem van Prooijen and Paul A. M. van Lange, "Power, Politics, and Paranoia: An Introduction," in *Power, Politics, and Paranoia: Why People are Suspicious of Their Leaders*, eds. Jan-Willem van Prooijen and Paul A. M. van Lange (Cambridge: Cambridge University Press, 2014), pp. 1–14; Charles M. Blow, "The Political Uses of Paranoia," *New York Times*, 25 April 2013.

28. Brown, *Walled States*, p. 34; RT News, "'We did what we had to do': Putin opens up on Crimea reunification plan," RT News, 10 March 2015.
29. Russian Public Opinion Research Center, "Krym: dva goda vmeste s Rossiej," Russian Public Opinion Research Center, 17 March 2016; Sergei Glazyev, "Predotvratit' vojnu—pobedit' v vojne," Izborsky Club, 30 September 2014.
30. Mark Adomanis, "Putin's poll numbers are skyrocketing, but they aren't going to last," Center on Global Interests, 10 April 2014.
31. The Official Internet Portal of Legal Information of the Russian Federation, presidential decree by Vladimir Putin, "Ukaz Prezidenta Rossijskoj Federacii ot 28.05.2015 No. 273 'O vnesenii izmenenij v perechen' svedenij, otnesennyh k gosudarstvennoj tajne, utverzhdennyj Ukazom Prezidenta Rossijskoj Federacii ot 30 nojabrja 1995 g. No. 1203,'" The Official Internet Portal of Legal Information of the Russian Federation, 28 May 2015.
32. BBC News, "Putin reveals secrets of Russia's Crimea takeover plot," BBC News, 9 March 2015.
33. Paul Roderick Gregory, "Russia May Have Inadvertently Posted Its Casualties in Ukraine: 2000 Deaths, 3200 Disabled," *Forbes*, 25 August 2015; Sergei Goriashko, "Rossijanam ne nravitsja evropejskij' vybor Ukrainy," *Kommersant* No. 227 (10 December 2015), p. 8; Snyder, *The Road to Unfreedom*, p. 178.
34. RT News, "Two-thirds of Russians declare readiness to vote in 2018 presidential polls," RT News, 24 March 2017. Coincidentally, most supporters of the Crimean seizure—that is, most Russian nationals—do not question the absurdly high figure that 96.77 percent of the Crimean population that voted (cited at 83.1 percent) chose to support separation from Ukraine. Of course, neither did they question the official statement that 99.8 percent of voters in Chechnya chose to reelect Vladimir Putin as president in 2012, even after all the war, death, and repression he instigated there in his previous terms. This ignorance and unwillingness to think beyond the Kremlin's version of events is further indicative of a society well indoctrinated under Putinism and engrossed in the "successes" of nationalist foreign policy. Snyder, *The Road to Unfreedom*, p. 49.
35. Schoen, *Putin's Master Plan*, pp. 23-25.
36. Dan Smith, "Whither peace?" Stockholm International Peace Research Institute, 21 September 2016; McFaul, *From Cold War to Hot Peace*, pp. 330-331.
37. William E. Pomeranz, "Conclusion," in *Roots of Russia's War in Ukraine*, eds. Elizabeth A. Wood, William E. Pomeranz, E. Wayne Merry, and Maxim Trudolybov (Washington, DC: Woodrow Wilson Center Press, 2016), p. 133.

38. The United Nations, "STATEMENT by H.E. Mr. Vladimir V. PUTIN, President of the Russian Federation, at the 70th session of the UN General Assembly," The United Nations, 28 September 2015.
39. Official Internet Resources of the President of Russia, "Vstrecha s Sergeem Lavrovym i Sergeem Shojgu" [Meeting with Sergey Lavrov and Sergey Shoygu], Official Internet Resources of the President of Russia, 14 March 2016.
40. Helene Cooper, Michael R. Gordon, and Neil MacFarquhar, "Russians Strike Targets in Syria, but Not ISIS Areas," *New York Times*, 1 October 2015.
41. Maksymilian Czuperski, John Herbst, Eliot Higgins, Frederic Hof, and Ben Nimmo, *Distract, Deceive, Destroy: Putin at War in Syria* (Washington, DC: The Atlantic Council, April 2016), p. 3.
42. Czuperski et al., *Distract, Deceive, Destroy*, p. 12.
43. Levada Center, "Syria," Levada Center: Yuri Levada Analytical Center, 6 October 2016.
44. Francesca Borri, *Syrian Dust: Reporting from the Heart of the War*, trans. Anne Milano Appel (New York: Seven Stories Press, 2016).
45. Mikhail Zygar, *All the Kremlin's Men: Inside the Court of Vladimir Putin* (New York: Public Affairs, 2016), p. 331.
46. "Syria conflict: Aid convoy attack was air strike, UN expert says," BBC News, 5 October 2016; Zygar, *All the Kremlin's Men*, p. 333.
47. Laura Mills, "Putin Says West Unfairly Blaming Russia for Syria Cease-Fire Failure," *The Wall Street Journal*, 12 October 2016.
48. Human Rights Watch, "Russia/Syria. Daily Cluster Munition Attacks: Increased Use of Widely Banned Weapon," Human Rights Watch, 8 February 2016.
49. Sergey Lavrov, "Istoricheskaja perspektiva vneshnej politiki Rossii" [A historical perspective of Russia's foreign policy], *Russia in Global Politics*, 3 March 2016.
50. Lavrov, "Istoricheskaja perspektiva."
51. Agamben, *State of Exception*, p. 87.
52. Leon Aron, "The Putin Doctrine: Russia's Quest to Rebuild the Soviet State," *Foreign Affairs*, 8 March 2013.
53. Keith Gessen, "What's the Matter With Russia? Putin and the Soviet Legacy," *Foreign Affairs*, Vol. 93, No. 4 (July/August 2014); Keith Gessen, "Killer, kleptocrat, genius, spy: the many myths of Vladimir Putin," *The Guardian*, 22 February 2017.
54. Agamben, *State of Exception*, p. 69; Elena Barabantseva, "How do people come to identify with nations?" in *Global Politics: A New Introduction*, 2nd ed., eds. Jenny Edkins and Maja Zehfuss (New York: Routledge, 2008), p. 258.

55. Aron, "Putinism After Crimea," p. 79.
56. Agamben, *State of Exception*, pp. 16 and 67–73; Emile Durkheim, *Suicide: A Study in Sociology*, ed. George Simpson, trans. John A. Spaulding and George Simpson (New York: The Free Press, 1951), p. 252.
57. Hannah Arendt, *Origins of Totalitarianism* (New York: Meridian Books, 1958), p. 141.
58. Molly McKew, "Putin's real long-game," *Politico*, 1 January 2017.
59. David E. Hoffman, *The Oligarchs: Wealth and Power in the New Russia* (New York: PublicAffairs, 2011), p. 174; Lucas, *The New Cold War*, p. 12.
60. Priyanka Boghani, "Putin's Legal Crackdown on Civil Society," *PBS Frontline*, 13 January 2015.
61. Radio Free Europe/Radio Liberty. "10 Laws Putin's Foes Say Russia Needs To Scrap," Radio Free Europe/Radio Liberty, 23 December 2015; Boghani, "Putin's Legal Crackdown"; Graeme Robertson, "Managing Society: Protests, Civil Society, and Regime in Putin's Russia," *Slavic Review*, Vol. 68, No. 3 (Fall 2009), pp. 540 and 541.
62. Hoffman, *The Oligarchs*, pp. 125 and 175.
63. Marc Bennetts, *Kicking the Kremlin: Russia's New Dissident and the Battle to Topple Putin* (London: Oneworld Publications, 2014), p. 198.
64. Lucas, *The New Cold War*, p. 1.
65. Peter Pomerantsev, *Nothing is True and Everything is Possible: The Surreal Heart of the New Russia* (New York: PublicAffairs, 2014), p. 78.
66. Arendt, *Origins of Totalitarianism*, p. xxxvi.
67. Tom Balmforth, "Putin's New Security Force Seen As 'Praetorian Guard,'" Radio Free Europe/Radio Liberty, 6 April 2016.
68. Vadim Volkov (roundtable at the Association for Slavic, Eastern European, and Eurasian Studies' 2016 Convention, Washington, DC, 17–20 November 2016).
69. Carl Schmitt, *Political Theology: Four Chapters on the Concept of Sovereignty* (Chicago: University of Chicago Press, 2006), p. 12; see also Jan-Werner Müller, *A Dangerous Mind: Carl Schmitt in Post-War European Thought* (New Haven: Yale University Press, 2003).
70. Giorgio Agamben, *Means Without End: Notes on Politics*, trans. Vincenzo Benetti and Cesar Casarino (Minneapolis: University of Minnesota Press, 2000), pp. 104, 121, and 122; Franz Kafka, *The Trial* (New York: Penguin Classics, 2000).
71. Alain Besançon, interview by Marius Stan and Vladimir Tismaneanu, "I'm for the Cold War!" *Contributors.ro*, 28 June 2015; Alain Besançon, "La pensée Poutine," *Commentaire*, No. 149 (2015), pp. 15–22.

REFERENCES

Adomanis, Mark. 2014. *Putin's Poll Numbers Are Skyrocketing, but They Aren't Going to Last*. Center on Global Interests, April 10. Accessed 28 January 2017 at http://www.globalinterests.org/2014/04/10/putins-poll-numbers-are-skyrocketing-but-they-arent-going-to-last/

Agamben, Giorgio. 2000. *Means Without End: Notes on Politics*. Trans. Vincenzo Benetti and Cesar Casarino. Minneapolis: University of Minnesota Press.

———. 2005. *State of Exception*. Chicago: University of Chicago Press.

Arendt, Hannah. 1958. *Origins of Totalitarianism*. New York: Meridian Books.

Aron, Leon. 2013. The Putin Doctrine: Russia's Quest to Rebuild the Soviet State. *Foreign Affairs*, March 8. Accessed 2 September 2016 at https://www.foreignaffairs.com/articles/russian-federation/2013-03-08/putin-doctrine

———. 2016. *Drivers of Putin's Foreign Policy*. American Enterprise Institute, June 14. Accessed 8 October 2016 at https://www.aei.org/publication/drivers-of-putins-foreign-policy/

———. 2017. The Kremlin Emboldened: Putinism After Crimea. *Journal of Democracy* 28 (4): 76–79.

Balmforth, Tom. 2016. Putin's New Security Force Seen As 'Praetorian Guard'. *Radio Free Europe/Radio Liberty*, April 6. Accessed 6 April 2016 at http://www.rferl.org/a/russia-national-guard-or-praetorian-guard/27658769.html

Barabantseva, Elena. 2008. How Do People Come to Identify with Nations? In *Global Politics: A New Introduction*, ed. Jenny Edkins and Maja Zehfuss, 2nd ed., 245–268. New York: Routledge.

BBC News. 2015. Putin Reveals Secrets of Russia's Crimea Takeover Plot. *BBC News*, March 9. Accessed 9 January 2017 at http://www.bbc.com/news/world-europe-31796226

———. 2016. Syria Conflict: Aid Convoy Attack Was Air Strike, UN Expert Says. *BBC News*, October 5. Accessed 5 October 2016 at http://www.bbc.com/news/world-middle-east-37561755

———. 2018. Russian Spy: What Happened to Sergei and Yulia Skripal? *BBC News*, September 27. Accessed 15 March 2019 at https://www.bbc.com/news/uk-43643025

Bennetts, Marc. 2014. *Kicking the Kremlin: Russia's New Dissident and the Battle to Topple Putin*. London: Oneworld Publications.

Besançon, Alain. 2015a. "I'm for the Cold War!" Interview by Marius Stan and Vladimir Tismaneanu. *Contributors.ro*, June 28. Transcript available at http://www.contributors.ro/cultura/%E2%80%9Csunt-pentru-razboiul-rece%E2%80%9D-un-dialog-cu-alain-besanc%CC%A7on-realizat-de-marius-stan-%C8%99i-vladimir-tismaneanu-paris-28-iunie-2015/

———. 2015b. La pensée Poutine. *Commentaire* 149: 15–22.

Blow, Charles M. 2013. The Political Uses of Paranoia. *New York Times*, April 25. Accessed 5 October 2018 at https://www.nytimes.com/2013/04/25/opinion/blow-politics-of-paranoia.html

Boghani, Priyanka. 2015. Putin's Legal Crackdown on Civil Society. *PBS Frontline*, January 13. Accessed 2 February 2017 at http://www.pbs.org/wgbh/frontline/article/putins-legal-crackdown-on-civil-society/

Borri, Francesca. 2016. *Syrian Dust: Reporting from the Heart of the War*. Trans. Anne Milano Appel. New York: Seven Stories Press.

Brown, Wendy. 2010. *Walled States, Waning Sovereignty*. New York: Zone Books.

Cooper, Helene, Michael R. Gordon, and Neil MacFarquhar. 2015. Russians Strike Targets in Syria, but Not ISIS Areas. *New York Times*, October 1. Accessed 3 October 2016 at https://www.nytimes.com/2015/10/01/world/europe/russia-airstrikes-syria.html

Czuperski, Maksymilian, John Herbst, Eliot Higgins, Frederic Hof, and Ben Nimmo. 2016. *Distract, Deceive, Destroy: Putin at War in Syria*. Washington, DC: The Atlantic Council, April.

Durkheim, Emile. 1951. *Suicide: A Study in Sociology*. Ed. George Simpson and Trans. John A. Spaulding and George Simpson. New York: The Free Press.

Fish, M.Steven. 2018. What Has Russia Become? *Comparative Politics* 50 (3): 327–346.

Gessen, Keith. 2014. What's the Matter with Russia? Putin and the Soviet Legacy. *Foreign Affairs* 93 (4): 182–189.

———. 2017a. Killer, Kleptocrat, Genius, Spy: The Many Myths of Vladimir Putin. *The Guardian*, February 22. Accessed 1 July 2018 at https://www.theguardian.com/world/2017/feb/22/vladimir-putin-killer-genius-kleptocrat-spy-myths

Gessen, Masha. 2017b. *The Future Is History: How Totalitarianism Reclaimed Russia*. New York: Riverhead Books.

Glazyev, Sergei. 2014. Predotvratit' vojnu—pobedit' v vojne [To Prevent War, Win the War]. *Izborsky Club*, September 30. Accessed 10 July 2018 at http://dynacon.ru/content/articles/3963/#a5

Gorbachev, Mikhail. 2016. *The New Russia*. Cambridge: Polity Press.

Goriashko, Sergei. 2015. Rossijanam ne nravitsja evropejskij' vybor Ukrainy [Russians Do Not Like Ukraine's Choice of Europe]. *Kommersant* 227 (December 10).

Gregory, Derek. 2004. *The Colonial Present*. Malden: Blackwell Publishing.

Gregory, Paul Roderick. 2015. Russia May Have Inadvertently Posted Its Casualties In Ukraine: 2000 Deaths, 3200 Disabled. *Forbes*, August 25. Accessed 29 January 2017 at http://www.forbes.com/sites/paulroderickgregory/2015/08/25/kremlin-censors-rush-to-erase-inadvertent-release-of-russian-casualties-in-east-ukraine/#115bbcf05b26

Herszenhorn, David M. 2014. *Putin Vows to 'Actively Defend' Russians Living Abroad*. The Atlantic Council, July 2. Accessed 29 January 2017 at http://www.atlanticcouncil.org/blogs/natosource/putin-vows-to-actively-defend-russians-living-abroad

Hoffman, David E. 2011. *The Oligarchs: Wealth and Power in the New Russia*. New York: PublicAffairs.

Human Rights Watch. 2016. Russia/Syria. Daily Cluster Munition Attacks: Increased Use of Widely Banned Weapon. *Human Rights Watch*, February 8. Accessed 8 February 2016 at https://www.hrw.org/news/2016/02/08/russia/syria-daily-cluster-munition-attacks

Inozemstev, Vladislav. 2017. The Kremlin Emboldened: Why Putinism Arose. *Journal of Democracy* 28 (4): 80–85.

Kafka, Franz. 2000. *The Trial*. 1925. New York: Penguin Classics.

Lavrov, Sergey. 2016. Istoricheskaja perspektiva vneshnej politiki Rossii [A Historical Perspective of Russia's Foreign Policy]. *Russia in Global Politics*, March 3. Accessed 20 January 2017 at https://www.globalaffairs.ru/global-processes/Istoricheskaya-perspektiva-vneshnei-politiki-Rossii-18017

Levada Center. 2016. *Syria*. Levada Center: Yuri Levada Analytical Center, October 6. Accessed 12 January 2017 at http://www.levada.ru/en/2016/06/10/syria-2/

Lucas, Edward. 2014. *The New Cold War: Putin's Russia and the Threat to the West*. New York: St. Martin's Press.

Mardell, Mark. 2016. Does Hitler's Legacy Still Cast Shadow over the World? *BBC News*, October 21. Accessed 21 October 2016 at http://www.bbc.com/news/world-europe-37703416

Marson, James. 2009. Putin to the West: Hands Off Ukraine. *TIME*, May 25. Accessed 11 October 2016 at http://content.time.com/time/world/article/0,8599,1900838,00.html

McFaul, Michael. 2018. *From Cold War to Hot Peace: An American Ambassador in Putin's Russia*. New York: Houghton Mifflin Harcourt Publishing Company.

McKew, Molly K. 2017. Putin's Real Long-Game. *Politico*, January 1. Accessed 2 January 2017 at http://www.politico.eu/article/putin-trump-sanctions-news-hacking-analysis/

Mills, Laura. 2016. Putin Says West Unfairly Blaming Russia for Syria Cease-Fire Failure. *The Wall Street Journal*, October 12. Accessed 12 October 2016 at https://www.wsj.com/articles/putin-says-west-unfairly-blaming-russia-for-syria-cease-fire-failure-1476280317

Müller, Jan-Werner. 2003. *A Dangerous Mind: Carl Schmitt in Post-War European Thought*. New Haven: Yale University Press.

Official Internet Portal of Legal Information of the Russian Federation. 2015. Presidential decree by Vladimir Putin. *Ukaz Prezidenta Rossijskoj Federacii ot 28.05.2015 No. 273 'O vnesenii izmenenij v perechen' svedenij, otnesennyh k gosu-*

darstvennoj tajne, utverzhdennyj Ukazom Prezidenta Rossijskoj Federacii ot 30 nojabrja 1995 g. No. 1203' [Presidential Decree of 28.05.2015 No. 273 "On Amendments to the List of Information Classified as State Secrets, Approved by Presidential Decree of 30 November 1995 No. 1203"]. The Official Internet Portal of Legal Information of the Russian Federation, May 28. Accessed 29 January 2017 at http://publication.pravo.gov.ru/Document/View/0001201 505280001?index=0andrangeSize=1

Official Internet Resources of the President of Russia. 2007. Speech by Vladimir Putin. *Vystuplenie i diskussija na Mjunhenskoj konferencii po voprosam politiki bezopasnosti* [Speech and the Following Discussion at the Munich Conference on Security Policy]. 2007 Munich Conference on Security Policy, February 10. Accessed 7 January 2017 at http://en.kremlin.ru/events/president/transcripts/24034

———. 2014. Speech by Vladimir Putin. *Konferencija rossijskih poslov i postojannyh predstavitelej* [Conference of Russian Ambassadors and Permanent Representatives]. Official Internet Resources of the President of Russia, July 1. Accessed 12 September 2016 at http://en.kremlin.ru/events/president/news/46131

———. 2016. *Vstrecha s Sergeem Lavrovym i Sergeem Shojgu* [Meeting with Sergey Lavrov and Sergey Shoygu]. Official Internet Resources of the President of Russia, March 14. Accessed 10 February 2017 at http://kremlin.ru/events/president/news/51511

Ogarkova, Tetyana. 2018. *The Truth Behind Ukraine's Language Policy*. The Atlantic Council, March 12. Accessed 5 October 2018 at http://www.atlanticcouncil.org/blogs/ukrainealert/the-truth-behind-ukraine-s-language-policy

Passerini, Luisa. 2006. Memories Between Silence and Oblivion. In *Memory, History, Nation: Contested Pasts*, ed. Katharine Hodgkin and Susannah Radstone, 238–254. New Brunswick: Transaction Publishers.

Plokhy, Serhii. 2015. *The Last Empire: The Final Days of the Soviet Union*. London: Oneworld Publications.

Pomerantsev, Peter. 2014. *Nothing Is True and Everything Is Possible: The Surreal Heart of the New Russia*. New York: PublicAffairs.

Pomeranz, William E. 2016. Conclusion. In *Roots of Russia's War in Ukraine*, ed. Elizabeth A. Wood, William E. Pomeranz, E. Wayne Merry, and Maxim Trudolybov, 131–136. Washington, DC: Woodrow Wilson Center Press.

Porębski, Czesław. 2018. General Introduction: Political Philosophy, Philosophy of History, Russian History. *Russian Thought on Europe*. Class lecture at Jagiellonian University, Kraków, Poland, October 3.

Radio Free Europe/Radio Liberty. 2015. 10 Laws Putin's Foes Say Russia Needs To Scrap. *Radio Free Europe/Radio Liberty*, December 23. Accessed 3 February 2017 at http://www.rferl.org/a/russia-10-laws-that-must-go/27445573.htm

———. 2018. Report: Third Alleged Russian Agent Involved in Skripal Mission Identified. *Radio Free Europe/Radio Liberty*, September 28. Accessed 15 March 2019 at https://www.rferl.org/a/report-third-russian-agent-involved-in-skripal-mission-identified-/29514321.html

Robertson, Graeme B. 2009. Managing Society: Protests, Civil Society, and Regime in Putin's Russia. *Slavic Review* 68 (3, Fall): 528–547.

RT News. 2015. 'We Did What We Had to Do': Putin Opens Up on Crimea Reunification Plan. *RT News*, March 10. Accessed 29 August 2016 at https://www.rt.com/news/239197-putin-crimea-referendum-decision/

———. 2017. Two-Thirds of Russians Declare Readiness to Vote in 2018 Presidential Polls. *RT News*, March 24. Accessed 30 March 2017 at https://www.rt.com/politics/382153-two-thirds-of-russians-declare/

Russian Public Opinion Research Center. 2016. *Krym: dva goda vmeste s Rossiej* [Crimea: Two Years Together with Russia]. Russian Public Opinion Research Center, March 17. Accessed 28 January 2017 at http://wciom.com/index.php?id=61anduid=1249

Schmitt, Carl. 2006a. *Dictatorship: From the Beginning of the Modern Concept of Sovereignty to the Proletarian Class-Struggle*. 7th ed. Berlin: Duncker and Humblot.

———. 2006b. *Political Theology: Four Chapters on the Concept of Sovereignty*. Chicago: University of Chicago Press.

Schoen, Douglas E. with Evan Roth Smith. 2016. *Putin's Master Plan: To Destroy Europe, Divide NATO, and Restore Russian Power and Global Influence*. New York: Encounter Books.

Shore, Marci. 2017. The Poet Laureate of Hybrid War. *Foreign Policy*, October 26. Accessed 26 October 2017 at https://foreignpolicy.com/2017/10/26/the-poet-laureate-of-hybrid-war/

Smith, Dan. 2016. *Whither Peace?* Stockholm International Peace Research Institute, September 21. Accessed 30 September 2016 at https://www.sipri.org/commentary/blog/2016/whither-peace

Snyder, Timothy. 2014. Fascism, Russia, and Ukraine. *The New York Review*, March 20. Accessed 9 September 2016 at http://www.nybooks.com/articles/2014/03/20/fascism-russia-and-ukraine

———. 2015. *Black Earth: The Holocaust as History and Warning*. New York: Tim Duggan Books.

———. 2018. *The Road to Unfreedom: Russia, Europe, America*. New York: Tim Duggan Books.

Snyder, Timothy, and Thomas Carothers. 2018. *The Road to Unfreedom*. Presentation at Carnegie Endowment for International Peace, Washington, DC, May 18.

The United Nations. 2015. STATEMENT by H.E. Mr. Vladimir V. PUTIN, President of the Russian Federation, at the 70th session of the UN General Assembly. The United Nations, September 28. Accessed 4 October 2016 at https://gadebate.un.org/sites/default/files/gastatements/70/70_RU_EN.pdf

van Prooijen, Jan-Willem, and Paul A.M. van Lange. 2014. Power, Politics, and Paranoia: An Introduction. In *Power, Politics, and Paranoia: Why People Are Suspicious of Their Leaders*, ed. Jan-Willem van Prooijen and Paul A.M. van Lange, 1–14. Cambridge: Cambridge University Press.

Volkov, Vadim. 2016. Roundtable at the *Association for Slavic, Eastern European, and Eurasian Studies' 2016 Convention*, Washington, DC, November 17–20.

Zygar, Mikhail. 2016. *All the Kremlin's Men: Inside the Court of Vladimir Putin*. New York: Public Affairs.

CHAPTER 8

The New Dark Times

Bitches always hate decent people.
—Boris Nemtsov

Putinism thrives not simply because Vladimir Vladimirovich Putin's personality commands it, but because the majority of Russia's population also wills it. This does not change or lessen the fact that President Putin is an authoritarian; however, the social dimension should be understood because it means that he is a *creative* authoritarian at that. The Kremlin's power game is more than just a form of repression: it is a constant source of production for Russia's national narrative and identity. The Russian government actively seeks to recruit the population through inclusive methods meant to ensure allegiance to the state. This requires an exploitation of historical autocratic tendencies, popular desire for paternalistic authoritarianism, and a flaming nationalist ideology. Thus, it cannot be assumed that Putin has taken power by himself, against the whim of the citizenry: there is an undeniable social construction at play in sustaining the "Putin Phenomenon" that involves ideology, history, and popular consent. Without recognizing these dynamics, Russia's behaviors, policies, and goals will never be properly analyzed. As American historian Stephen Kotkin so aptly stated, "This is not your grandfather's authoritarianism."[1]

Authoritarianism is not defined just by the lack of democratic values. It is coordinated, planned by the ruling elites, demands obedience, and pays no heed to human rights, diversity, or tolerance. It grounds itself in the notion that there exists a single exclusive truth to the world that only authoritarian leaders and their followers are intelligent enough to understand.[2] At the most basic level, the Russian state has declared war on whatever it deems to be foreign to Russian culture. Its priority is to ensure the security of the nation from foreign, unknown elements that may (or *will*, in the likely opinion of a Kremlin official or nationalist) upset the regime's order.

Russian ideology, defined by a unified, superior "us" versus a Western, hostile "other," reflects this xenophobic fear. Russian domestic law further inculcates anguish within the citizenry to prevent autonomous opinions from gathering momentum and potentially challenging the government's grip on power. This ideology is reproduced through an obsession with national security, a history emphasizing a long trend of autocracy as a legitimate response to internal and external enemies, a nostalgia for the Soviet imaginary, extreme nationalism, and a desire for global power. It is the primary yet most-overlooked factor in explaining how Putin is able to exert so much control over the Russian population. Thus, the "Putin Phenomenon" cannot be chalked up to Putin's presumably charismatic leadership.

There are some who believe that Russia has fallen out of love with Putin, as journalist Ben Judah iterates.[3] But those in power now owe their current positions to Putin, as the late Karen Dawisha reminds readers in her outstanding book, *Putin's Kleptocracy: Who Owns Russia?* (2012). And they are not about to turn on the man who made them rich and warped society. Putin and the rest of the powerful people in Russia—all of whom he either created or helped to maintain the elite status of—are not about to risk the wealth, power, and influence that they have both seized by force and received voluntarily from a country whose laws and values allow for such bloodsucking. They will not reveal the lies they helped to disseminate across the population and throughout the media, the education system, the Russian Orthodox Church, and other societal mouthpieces. And even if ordinary Russians, those without elite statuses and hence no genuine access to platforms of political change, recognize the ills of their Russia, they stand no chance against Putinism as a national system. To fall out of love with Putin would be to destroy chances for success in an already dismal society with one of the worst wealth inequality levels in the world, where 87 percent of the country's wealth is owned by 10 percent of the population (compared to 76 percent in the United States).[4]

Putinism's structural and historical ties act as effective safeguards against reform-minded criticisms, and its ideological roots further prevent the already unlikely seeds of protest from cultivating in a sufficient segment of the population that might then generate unavoidable calls for change. For the most part, Russian citizens outwardly champion the Putinist system, quietly believe in Putinism, or doubt it yet remain silent.[5] Even without Putin, and even among the silent doubters, there is little probability (not to mention little historical precedent) for sudden metaphysical changes of hearts for such grossly ingrained habits, particularly when accompanied by a lack of action or access to political debate.

The effects of the Russian ideology examined in this book intertwine in an enduring chemistry meant to deprive the individual of self-reliance, self-esteem, and civic courage.[6] Instead, decisions are forced upon subjects of the Kremlin—except these "decisions" are predetermined for them, in part because the government shapes untruthfully narratives so as to evoke one xenophobic, nationalist response, and also because these subjects want to survive and avoid punishment themselves. It is as American historian Timothy Snyder observed in *The Road to Unfreedom* (2018),

> Fascism is the falsehood that the enemy chosen by a leader must be the enemy for all. Politics then begins from emotion and falsehood. Peace becomes unthinkable, since enmity abroad is necessary for control at home. A fascist says 'the people' and means 'some people,' those he favors at the moment.[7]

Essentially, the Russian people are forced to choose "between murder and murder" of certain categories of humans whom the government has placed outside the protection of the law and inside the category of "national threat": do we Russians want to kill ISIS, or do we want them to kill us? Do we want to kill Chechen terrorists, or do we want them to kill us? Do we want to kill Ukrainian fascists, or do we want them to kill us? Do we want to continue to beat our wives and children and deny them equal justice under the law, or do we want to betray our Russian conservative heritage?

To prove our point, let us look into a rather simple event in recent Russian politics: the amendment of assault and battery laws in February 2017 that should have provoked outcries from every woman and child (and man, in an ideal world; of course, not even Americans would not achieve this level of activism, demonstrating that the entire global population needs to step up when it comes to issues of women's rights and domestic violence, even if these atrocities are happening in countries other than our own). The legal amendment, backed by the Russian government, officially betrayed the rights of the nation's female population in worse ways than before.

Now, the Russian legal code has never included provisions regarding domestic abuse specifically, which should say something right out of the gate about the poor status of women's rights in the country. The closest category that an instance of wife beating could fall under was battery. Somehow, though, the legal adjustment of February 2017 worsened the already invisible issue of domestic abuse. It made it so any first-time instance of "battery of close persons [in the family] that resulted in physical pain but did not inflict harm or other consequences" is not punishable under criminal law. Instead, abusers are lightly slapped on the wrist with short detention stays of up to 15 days, a fine up to about $500, or up to ten hours of community work. And this is only if the perpetrator is found guilty, which is rare enough in Putin's Russia.[8]

The Russian Orthodox Church was one of the biggest proponents behind the most recent reduction of the protection of women and children, the usual demographic of domestic abuse victims. They protested that laws criminalizing battery in the family were unwarranted forms of government intervention in the private sphere and that there exists "no real reason to criminalize the reasonable and moderate use of physical force by loving parents" when disciplining their children.[9] Natalia Kozlova, a female journalist writing for *Rossiyskaya Gazeta*, stated that the legal change and the Church's perspective constituted the "right" thing to do, despite the fact that mere sentences before she had cited the damning statistics that in Russia (1) 40 percent of incidents of serious violence occur within the household, (2) 93 percent of domestic violence victims are women, and (3) about 36,000 women suffer from domestic abuse each day. She, like most Russians, admits that the reduction in severity might seem inappropriate at first glance but overall defends the law by reminding naysayers that repeat offenders can be tried under criminal law.[10]

This might be enough to ward off serious condemnation from an already pacified international community, but the principle remains nonetheless: Russia is a conservative, misogynist state that does not care to protect its females, and, to a larger extent, human rights. Its government is actively taking steps to limit access to justice. And it should (in an ideal world) go without saying that there is no such thing as a "one-time" domestic abuser, nor should any instance of violence be treated leniently even if it happens only once. It can take "just one" time to beat a woman or child to death or to deny them their dignity and human rights, after all. Yet the Duma voted in favor of the bill by an astounding 380 in favor to three against. This simple fact, combined with the evidence that the majority of Russian women like Kozlova (a journalist, at that) accept the change, should be treated as a major pillar of proof that there is, in fact, a cultural ideology at play in Russia that actively feeds the Putin regime and its reproductive institutions.

Thus Putin's Russia is more than just authoritarian. It is fascist (regardless of its fond nostalgia for the leftist Soviet movement) in the primordial sense discussed by Umberto Eco: Putinism thrives on classic fascist features outlined by Eco such as the cult of tradition, the rejection of modernism, machismo, ultranationalism, youth mobilization, repression, propaganda, imperialism and the ideas that disagreement is treasonous, that difference is dangerous and to be feared, that the enemy is simultaneously strong and weak, and that everyone can and should be a hero for the collective society.[11] While the exact definition of fascism could be a book in itself, traditional political theory might define it as an authoritarian political movement that subordinates the average human's well-being to that of the nation-state.[12] It would be prudent to add that fascism is not monolithic, static, or rigidly constituted: it is about achieving a particular goal at a certain time using whatever deceptive means will best ensure the desired result, which is yet another theme that has been particularly verified throughout this book's course as a pivotal element of Putin's Russia. When a government like Russia's has, in a particularly violent way, convinced its citizens that their needs are one in the same with the nation-state—and when a government's chief goal is expressed in terms of protecting the nation-state, rather than protecting the supposedly equal people—conditions might allow for the emergence of fascism.

The next necessary element that brings a population closer to fascism is a deceptive, exclusionary, and hateful ideology, one that is eager to distort history, reality, and even the future for nationalist gains. Hannah Arendt focuses fascism upon a particular kind of "sophistic victory at the expense of reality." Such political deception constitutes a "lying world order," where those in political power can fabricate ideas, transform these lies into a false reality, and then masquerade them as truth in the eyes of the population.[13] The insistence of Putin's Kremlin upon constantly distorting the nation's history and making it appear as though Russia is unjustly victimized by the supposedly dominant West functions in the same way. In such a manner, Putin's Kremlin infuses all its policies, statements, and actions with ideas that falsely idealize the image of the Russian state and its population. Most significantly, this image pits an innocent Russian state against the West. A Manichaean view of the world, like that espoused by the Kremlin, imposes a certain morality that forces Russian citizens down a single path of Russocentric thought—one that is already prescribed by Putin's fascist Kremlin.

It is at this point, when avenues of individual expression, thought, and encounter are obstructed, that fascism can cross the line into something even worse: the fascist government has won a terrible triumph characteristic of a totalitarian regime.[14] Most scholars refuse to call Russia a totalitarian state, complaining that "Putin is not Stalin or Hitler" and citing how the people are highly supportive of Putin's rule. But Stalin and Hitler are not the thresholds for totalitarianism. Rather, they are unprecedented examples of it, located at the extreme end of the spectrum. (And for that matter, we cannot forget other murderous totalitarians like the Khmer Rouge's Pol Pot, Communist China's Mao Zedong, the Japanese Empire's Hirohito, North Korea's Kim dynasty, Sudan's Omar al-Bashir, Iraq's Saddam Hussein, Syria's Hafez and Bashar al-Assad, Albania's Enver Hoxha, Romania's Nicolae Ceauşescu, Italy's Benito Mussolini, and others, although these names do not receive nearly enough attention in today's memory.) It would be a logical fallacy—and worse still, a great disservice to millions of people living under such authoritarian, fascist, and/or totalitarian rules—to immediately dismiss the claim that Putin belongs to the same general category as Stalin and Hitler merely because he has not systematically murdered several million people; in fact, it is also arguable that Putin has at least murdered the individuality and ability to freely think within a great percentage of the Russian population. That is no small injustice.

As with the term "fascism," the definition of "totalitarianism" is also beyond the scope of this text. In fact, it seems to defy categorization, considering its deeply confounded nature as a rather aberrant form of politics. Nevertheless its most useful conception, in terms of our research, adheres to Hannah Arendt's understandings of it, in which totalitarianism is presented as an overwhelming ideology that commands all aspects of life across an entire society that is governed by a limitless state authority. It is, in essence, fascism in power, bent on reordering society and ushering it toward a preordained end that seeks some sort of change in human nature.[15] Our book has argued that this is the case of Putin's Russia—but only in part.

The label of "totalitarian" is not descriptive enough because Putinism would not be nearly as successful as it is today were it not for a willing population, an element so pivotal to Russia's totalitarian functioning that it must be reflected in the label. For this reason we deem Putin's Russia to be a "totalitarian democracy." This term, coined by the late political scientist and author of *The Origins of Totalitarian Democracy* (1952) Jacob Talmon (1916–1980), signifies a totalitarian government that implements its means across a complicit population. In a totalitarian democracy, individuals become "the vehicle of uniformity" and thus "the distinction between active and passive citizens cease[s] to exist" because every decision made, and every thought allowed, reinforces the state's control. The choices of buying a Putin chocolate bar and speaking badly of protestors and watching Russian news channels, among thousands of other possible decisions that face each person each day, do more than just support the Kremlin's totalizing goals[16]; their approval and constant acceptance of the Kremlin's narratives and actions provide a pretense to further fuel the regime and expand its power beyond simple legal rules to the realm of the metaphysical, in which the Kremlin can attack morals, values, and humanity as a whole.

Because Russia is a totalitarian democracy, its likelihood of success and longevity, not to mention its array of means and potentially achievable ends, might be larger than those of simpler totalitarian systems. The popular element of Putin's totalitarian democracy is what unlocks so many possible avenues for totalitarian means and ends. To better explain why, we now bring up another significant feature of totalitarian regimes: the ability to abolish within subjects' minds the distinction between good and evil, or, in other words, the destruction of the people's individuality, morality, and values. French historian Alain Besançon offers an updated comprehension of this aspect of totalitarianism, one that is even more useful when considering Putin's Russia: he says that it is not the ability to abolish the distinction between good and evil but the ability to "falsify the good" that defines totalitarian regimes.[17] Such a regime can justify its actions in the name of one sacred mission for the entire nation's glory (no matter how ill-defined that mission's specific goals officially are, as is the case in Russia). Fascist and Communist governments of the twentieth century were particularly adept at this skill, allowing them to sanctify even the most barbaric of methods in the name of their utopian goals[18]; the falsification of good is a central tenet of totalitarianism that still thrives in the twenty-first century. In fact, it is what allows Putin's Kremlin to invade the sovereign nation of Ukraine and seize Crimea—a despicable act that murdered thousands upon thousands of innocent people and violated international law—yet be met with euphoric support from the Russian citizenry. And this is just a single example among many of how Putinism exploits its status as a totalitarian democracy and manipulates its subjects' morals and standards of human decency.

Of course, it must be discussed that a number of scholars refute the notion that Putin's Russia is totalitarian at all. Many of those who do so employ the argument that a regime cannot be categorized as totalitarian without a clearly recognizable telos, or end goal. For example, at the simplest level Hitler's telos can be identified as the rule of a perfect Aryan race, an objective apparent from his genocidal policies. It is true that we [KL and VT] cannot claim to know what Putin's end goal is, or if he even has a specific one in mind. But we argue that this ultimate end need not be exactly known in order to prove totalitarianism in every instance—after all, totalitarianism's terrifying power can be found in its determination to destroy the ability to think in ways not permitted by the state. Perhaps such a scenario could be a totalitarian leader's primary objective, anyway; an objective that once attained then opens the door for the fruition of a host of more detailed secondary desires. Thus, Putin's Russia should not be dismissed as non-totalitarian simply because its telos is unclear or vague, in contrast to what many academics have cautioned. Putinism, instead, should be recognized as a form of totalitarianism because it warps millions of Russians' moralities and controls information flows, destroying plurality and diversity as it strengthens. Putin's totalitarian democracy, then, is not just a means, but also an end in itself.[19] More alarmingly, totalitarian Putinist propaganda is spreading to populations beyond Russian borders and even beyond those of the post-Soviet space.

Furthermore, to say Putin could not be totalitarian because he is supported by an overwhelming majority of citizens is also illogical and altogether overlooks the conceptual significance of totalitarian democracy. This argument is ridiculous for a number of reasons, although the example of Nazi Germany serves as a case in point: Hitler was certainly a totalitarian leader, and he was elected democratically and generated a mass following—one so ideologically devoted that even decades later, a fair number of Germans still believe his National Socialist policies were inherently good. Likewise, in the words of Carl Schmitt, a political philosopher fascinated by tyrants, despots, and dictators, "Sovereignty emerges from a constitutive act of absolute power, made through the people." Thus, totalitarianism does not necessarily entail the domination of one person's unique beliefs over a completely unwilling population. This book has explained such an idea in regard to how the Russian nation-state can only exercise long-term authority if it has the consent of the governed, as well as to how the state can manipulate both ideology and information in a way that "naturally" leads its subjects into supporting its ends. In this typical fashion of totalitarian democracy, popular enthusiasm and belief in the Messianism of the nation-state are easily exploited by the ruling powers.[20] This ideological molding of the people constitutes the Putin Phenomenon, a popular desire for restrictive policies—enacted by a strong, autocratic sovereign—which citizens are duped into believing are in their best interests and will foster the growth of a superior Russian state.

If one is hesitant to call Putin a totalitarian leader, then one should examine the other aspects of a totalitarian government and how they match up to Putin's leadership. Late historian Tony Judt (1948–2010) wrote in his book, entitled *Reappraisals: Reflections on the Forgotten Twentieth Century* (2008), that "totalitarianism is always about sameness." Our book has documented the Kremlin's impulses toward such sameness, which seeks to confine the Russian population within one narrative and convince them that they are one in a united, superior nation.[21] It has analyzed how the Kremlin has cracked down on so much as *potential* avenues of divergent thought: the independent media have shriveled into silence, political opposition to Putin is strangled, public demonstrations are almost always dubbed illegal and therefore punished, and so on. Instead, ultranationalist state propaganda reigns, winning the hearts and minds of those exposed to it on a daily basis from various sources (education, religion, media, societal views, family, etc.) and unifying them to emotionally defend their superior nation-state. These chapters have attempted to prove the treachery of the Kremlin's extreme, flattening ideology, specifically the dangers of its fluidity and all-encompassing nature. Putinism is suited to broadcasting a seductive myth, which allows for the state to control the minds and actions of indoctrinated citizens and to prevent them from envisioning other possible futures.[22]

Another common counterargument against our classification of Putin's Russia is the line that Russia engages in regular elections and so it cannot be as totalitarian as we [KL and VT] make it out to be. Yes, we admit that elections are regularly held, but we also remind readers that the few international observers allowed consistently report voter fraud, ballot box stuffing, and bribery. Furthermore, it is difficult enough to get on the ballot in the first place as an opposition member. (True, Putin would likely get enough votes to stay in power even without this extra effort of keeping opponents off the ballot, but this is a further testament to the devious nature of his rule.) And then there is the additional matter that society is taught to view oppositionists as traitors, Putin as their strong leader, and Russia as a nation of traditional conservative values that must be defended from dangerous external forces. A combination of subliminal messages, explicit warnings, and distorted worldviews like this leads most indoctrinated citizens to a single "reasonable" conclusion: vote for Putin. How free, how genuine, could such an election be?

Still others might reject our book's thesis by claiming that Russia's economy is not at all a planned command one in the typical totalitarian sense. To this, we admit that Russia's economy is, technically speaking, a mixed one. But while Russia's economy is not planned in the sense of Communist centralization, we maintain that other forms of control are at play, namely in the sense that the flow of money is run by Putin's kleptocracy and profits are subject to state seizure and forced bribes.[23] It might be representative of a different kind of state planning than history and theory books usually cite, but it is a form of totalitarian control nonetheless.

Altogether, and at the heart of the issue, these elements and counterpoints culminate in the conclusion that Putin's regime manipulates the minds of the Russian citizenry and includes them into a national narrative that occults truth and prevents critical thinking. In the words of Hannah Arendt, "the ideal subject of totalitarian rule is not the convinced Nazi or the dedicated Communist, but people for whom the distinction between fact and fiction, true and false, no longer exists."[24] Indeed, Putin's Russia should be treated as a totalitarian system.

Putin rose to power in 2000 and has since sustained his influential position not because of his personality as a magnetizing figure, but because of his mass campaign of disinformation and mystification, which has been geared primarily toward inciting and weaponizing intolerant nationalist emotions and xenophobic fears within his electorate. In learning to call Putin's Russia what it is—a totalitarian democracy, a totalitarian state that relies upon the masses—perhaps the world can find new avenues of discussion regarding the extreme movements of the far Left and the far Right currently sweeping Europe, parts of Latin America, the United States, and elsewhere.

This phenomenon of emotional, myth-driven appeals to voters has been closely analyzed in our book with the intention of explaining how racist, ultranationalist, and authoritarian governments can thrive on popular support if they successfully convince their citizens of the need for security from threatening outsiders and continue to blame external factors for the world's woes. Russia, for example, continuously harangues the Nazis for brutally slaughtering millions of "their"[25] soldiers but stops short of admitting that Stalin sent plenty of soldiers to battle unarmed, or that the Soviet soldiers committed a terrifying amount of unnecessary rape, pillaging, and murder during World War II. On this note, just consider the coldblooded execution of 22,000 Polish officers at Katyn in the spring of 1940. The Katyn incident alone is powerful enough to demonstrate the hypocrisy of today's Russia and its refusal to admit its less-than-glorious sins of the past.[26]

The refusal of the Russian government to admit its own responsibility for injustices—whether they were committed in the present or in the Soviet history Russia so proudly claims to have inherited—is a crucial indicator of a country that rejects the rule of law, liberalism, tolerance, historical truths, and universal reality. Giorgio Agamben summed up the moral flaws of such a totalitarian system when he wrote in *Means Without End: Notes on Politics* (2000), "The totalitarian politics of the modern, rather, is the will to self-possession. ... The only human possibility is lost: that is, the possibility of taking possession of impropriety, of exposing in the face simply your *own proper* impropriety."[27] Such victimization and rejection of accountability fuels the imaginations of Russian citizens, further convincing them that Putin's Russia guarantees their protection from the wrongdoings of the rest of the world. This web of repression and obedience is so thick, so embedded in the fabric of Russian society, that it is hard to imagine any kind of cultural revolution taking hold in Russia any time soon; and without cultural revolution, there is no realistic hope that the totalitarian democracy will liberalize.[28]

At this moment, we choose to share a powerful excerpt from Soviet dissident Vladimir Voinovich's book *The Anti-Soviet Soviet Union* (1985). Though written in regard to the Soviet era, the following passage nonetheless offers an accurate diagnosis of Putin's Russia. It is emblematic of the deep-seated nature of the challenges that have been facing Russia and its people for decades (or centuries). Not only does it summarize the complex analyses discussed in our book, but it also suggests a possible way for the Russian population to begin to reconcile their ills and to move forward:

I fully agree with Leo Tolstoy when he said more or less the following: "People say it's shameful to change one's convictions. But I say: it's shameful not to."

To cling to convictions that have begun to run counter to one's experience of life or history is foolish, sometimes even criminal. Personally, I never trust any convictions that are not accompanied by doubts. And I do not believe that any single teaching can be acceptable to everyone.

My former friend thought otherwise. Passing from one belief to another, he thought he had changed. In fact, he was what he always had been; all he'd done was supplant one set of quotations with another. But he remained as militant as ever. Now he is operating with a new set of quotations, which he intends to use not only for his own satisfaction, not only to move toward a new goal, but also to drag others along with him. He and those who share his views keep parroting the old idea that Russia is a special country; the experience of other nations cannot be applied to Russia. It must go its own way (as if it hadn't). The creators of the new teaching do not find democracy suitable for Russia. They say that democratic societies are breaking down because of their unnecessary freedoms. They're weak, they give too much attention to human rights and too little to human obligations, and these societies are in fact ruled, not by outstanding men, but by mediocre bureaucracies. In place of democracy, they would offer authoritarianism.

I've asked many advocates of authoritarianism exactly what they mean by the term. What they tell me makes no sense at all. They say that authoritarian rule means rule by a wise individual whom everyone will recognize as the authority. But if in rejecting democracy we reject the practice, proven over the centuries, of democratically choosing trustworthy individuals for a limited period of time and with limited power by means of universal and free elections, then what method is there for determining what authority shall be in office and for what length of time? Won't that authority appoint himself to office? And, under his rule, won't society again be turned into a herd of frenzied followers brandishing quotations and machine guns? And weren't Lenin, Stalin, Hitler, and Mao genuine authorities for hundreds of millions of people? And isn't Khomeini an authoritative personality?

All this sophistry about enlightened authoritarian rule could well end in a new form of ideological madness. It is based neither on historical experience nor on reality. Where, in what country, is there even one wise authoritarian leader? In what way is he any better than leaders elected democratically and held in check by the "mediocre" majority? In what way are the authoritarian countries better than the democratic ones? ...

... Even now some of the advocates of authoritarianism say that they are the only true patriots (which, at the very least, is immodest) and declare all those who disagree with them slanderers and haters of Russia (just as the

Bolsheviks called their opponents enemies of the people). I find it quite easy to imagine how and against whom these people would use the police force of their authoritarian state were it ever to come into being.

Until that occurs, I'll risk saying that no serious problems can be solved without democracy. I do not in the least maintain that Russia is now ready for democratic change. All I know is that if an organism is afflicted with cancer, it's foolish to think it can recover without treatment, or with a treatment that does not correspond to disease.[29]

With this, Voinovich expresses how ideology, history, and social desires matter deeply when it comes to comprehending a state's behaviors and the machinations behind its authoritarianism (and beyond). Written policies and material or cooperative incentives are not the most important factors in Russia's deeply ideological choices. The emotions, irrationalities, and illusionary fantasies of the Russian totalitarian democracy—or of any ideological, human rights-defying society—are what make it so dangerous. Without studying these less tangible elements, no one will properly analyze or combat Putin's success.

Without that study, nor could anyone consider that Putin is paving the way for a modern update of what British historian Norman Cohn explored in his book, *Europe's Inner Demons: An Enquiry Inspired by the Great Witch-Hunt* (1975). Cohn's thesis held that the infamous witch-hunts of the Middle Ages were not instigated by the any actual existence of witches but by Europeans who built up stereotypes, feared the unfamiliar, desired a scapegoat for what they could not control or explain, and could not bring themselves to acknowledge their own faults. Thus, they allowed—urged, really—their bureaucracies to kill people with arbitrary traits en masse for no good reason.

Putting aside the now ridiculous topic of witches, it is not so far-fetched to illuminate the parallels between the hysterics of the Middle Ages and Putin's Russia. Swap the term "witches" for Ukrainian nationalists, gays, Muslims, the American media, the West, the threat of invasion, and so on. Recall that the forces of globalization and technology are changing daily life across the globe on what seems like an exponential scale, and that the ghosts of history moan louder the longer they go without reconciliation in the national consciousness. Keep in mind that if enough people believe in something, then even their subconscious thoughts and experiences can be deeply conditioned by the surrounding society.[30] Do this, and recognize that Cohn's message about inner demons glitters throughout a study of Putinism and its supporters.

Putinism does not just call upon its own inner demons. It has also been successful in reawakening the inner demons of Europe through its own domestic example and through its foreign instigations, as was discussed in the previous chapter. Such a trend can be seen in the swiftly rising movements of France's National Front, Greece's Golden Dawn and Syriza, Hungary's Fidesz and Jobbik parties, Poland's Law and Justice, Slovakia's Slovak National Party, Germany's Alternative for Germany, America's Trumpists, and many others. And even those of us who do not actively support any of these parties might still be guilty of remaining silent or of accepting them as wholly legitimate political contenders. Polish philosopher Leszek Kołakowski summarizes this dilemma about where to draw the line between healthy tolerance of diverse ideas versus unhealthy indifference of harmful ideas in his collection of essays entitled *Freedom, Fame, Lying and Betrayal: Essays on Everyday Life* (1999), writing,

> It is important to notice, however, that when tolerance is enjoined upon us nowadays, it is often in the sense of indifference: we are asked, in effect, to refrain from expressing—or indeed holding—any opinion, and sometimes even to condone every conceivable type of behavior or opinion in others. This kind of tolerance is something entirely different, and demanding it is part of our hedonistic culture, in which nothing really matters to us; it is a philosophy of life without responsibility and without beliefs. It is encouraged by a variety of philosophies in fashion today, which teach us that there is no such thing as truth in the traditional sense, and therefore that when we persist in our beliefs, even if we do so without aggression, we are *ipso facto* against tolerance.
>
> This is nonsense, and harmful nonsense. Contempt for truth harms our civilization no less than fanatical insistence on the truth. In addition, an indifferent majority clears the way for fanatics, of whom there will always be plenty around. Our civilization encourages the belief that everything should be just fun and games—as indeed it is in the infantile philosophies of the so-called "New Age." Their content is impossible to describe, for they mean anything one wants them to.[31]

As Kołakowski observed, indifference to actions and words that do serious harm to the human dignity of others cannot sustain a pluralistic or moral society. And indifference here does not only refer to literal feelings of ambivalence, but also to how someone fails to relate to the subject in question: if a Russian citizen thinks nothing of the Kremlin's decision to criminalize gay behavior, then that citizen is at best indifferent to the gay community's human dignity and rights, if not actively against them.

The Russian case is just one example out of many in this regard. The Kremlin capitalizes off of indifferent attitudes among the citizenry to demonize gays, the West, Ukrainians, Muslims, or whoever else sits in the Kremlin's purview at a particular moment. It can do so because few are likely to protest or to consider the rights another person or group deserves. As if indifference were not dangerous enough, it can also easily transform into intolerance. It already has been doing so in Russia, where Putin's government has been coercing its population (not to mention those outside its national borders who consume its state-approved media) to believe its narratives and to abandon alternative perspectives for almost two decades now. Intolerance of this kind essentially operates as a more aggressive, mobilizing form of indifference to which no free, healthy civil society should ever aspire.

A first and major step toward enlightening the world once again requires average human beings to drop their attitudes of "tolerant" indifference. In fact, they should realize that "tolerant" indifference is nothing but an oxymoron that certainly will not bring the world any more clarity than it has now. For this reason, there is a desperate need to disturb the "peace" and status quo of nationalism across the globe and to pledge allegiance to truth. To again quote Arendt, "legal textbooks don't prepare us for administrative mass murder"[32]: in other words, it is ridiculous to think one can comprehend the gravity of Putin's and Russia's crimes while remaining indifferent to their general motivations and consequences.

Hannah Arendt reminds us that it is a difficult task to pursue justice, particularly in an ideological nation-state. It requires an innovative, uncomfortable analysis of the capability of average citizens—including you, your child, your grandmother, your neighbor, and others—to believe in murderous tyrannical fantasies. Governments and activists throughout the world must look deeper into societies like Russia, especially those that claim to follow the rule of law or to be a democracy, yet all the while engage in state terror, and make an effort to delve into the national consciousness. Understanding just what ignorances and fears mobilize national populations to choose illiberalism and totalitarian practices is required if the world seeks to devise effective methods of sponsoring truly democratic politics that are all-inclusive and successfully combat the ideological traps found in Putin's Russia and beyond. To handle an ideological plague, as Cohn wrote, "one must refuse to take these lies and follies seriously and, when one meets them, expose their demonic origin."[33] If we take a moment to evaluate our world, and our positions in it as individual, active citizens, then we can at the very least prevent ourselves from becoming yet another ideological plague-carrier.[34]

Notes

1. Stephen Kotkin, "Comment: From Overlooking to Overestimating Russia's Authoritarianism?" *Slavic Review*, Vol. 68, No. 3 (Fall 2009), p. 549.
2. Jacob L. Talmon, *The Origins of Totalitarian Democracy* (London: Secker and Warburg, 1952), pp. 1–2.
3. Ben Judah, *Fragile Empire: How Russia Fell In and Out of Love with Vladimir Putin* (New Haven: Yale University Press, 2013), p. 325.
4. M. Steven Fish, "The Kremlin Emboldened: What is Putinism?" *Journal of Democracy*, Vol. 28, No. 4 (October 2017), p. 71.
5. Karen Dawisha, *Putin's Kleptocracy: Who Owns Russia?* (New York: Simon and Schuster Paperbacks, 2014), pp. 349–350.
6. Lev Gudkov and Eva Hartog, "The Evolution of Homo Sovieticus to Putin's Man," *The Moscow Times*, 13 October 2017.
7. Timothy Snyder, *The Road to Unfreedom: Russia, Europe, America* (New York: Tim Duggan Books, 2018), p. 278.
8. Nerses Isajanuan, "Russia: Decriminalization of Domestic Violence," *The Library of Congress*, June 2017; Yulia Gorbunova, "Law Not on Side of Russia's Domestic Violence Victims: One Year Since Legislative Changes Weakened Protections," Human Rights Watch, 14 February 2018.
9. The Patriarchate of Moscow, "Patriarshaja komissija po voprosam sem'i vyrazhaet obespokoennost' v svjazi s prinjatiem novoj redakcii stat'i 116 Ugolovnogo kodeksa," The Patriarchate of Moscow, 4 July 2016.
10. Natalya Kozlova, "*Ruku Opusti*," *Rossiiskaia Gazeta*, 9 February 2017.
11. Umberto Eco, "Ur-Fascism," *The New York Review of Books*, 22 June 1995; Jason Kottke, "Umberto Eco Makes a List of the 14 Common Features of Fascism," *Open Culture*, 22 November 2016.
12. Jeffrey T. Schnapp, "Fascinating Fascism," *Journal of Contemporary History*, Vol. 31, No. 2 (April 1996), p. 238. Alexander J. Motl, "Is Vladimir Putin a Fascist?" *Newsweek*, 27 April 2015.
13. Peg Birmingham, "A Lying World Order: Political Deception and the Threat of Totalitarianism," in *Thinking in Dark Times: Hannah Arendt on Ethics and Politics*, eds. Roger Berkowitz, Jeffrey Katz, and Thomas Keenan (New York: Fordham University, 2010), p. 74; Hannah Arendt, "The Seeds of a Fascist International," in *Essays in Understanding 1930–1954*, ed. Jerome Kohn (New York: Harcourt Brace, 1994), p. 145.
14. Hannah Arendt, *Origins of Totalitarianism* (New York: Meridian books, 1958), pp. 447 and 452.
15. Carl Schmitt, *The Concept of the Political* (Chicago: Chicago University Press, 1996), p. 22; Arendt, *Origins of Totalitarianism*, p. 380.
16. Talmon, *The Origins of Totalitarian Democracy*, pp. 45 and 79–80.
17. Alain Besançon, interview by Marius Stan and Vladimir Tismaneanu, "I'm for the Cold War!" *Contributors.ro*, 28 June 2015.

18. Vladimir Tismaneanu, *The Devil in History: Communism, Fascism, and Some Lessons of the Twentieth Century* (Berkeley and Los Angeles: University of California Press, 2012), p. 49.
19. Talmon, *The Origins of Totalitarian Democracy*, p. 230.
20. Talmon, *The Origins of Totalitarian Democracy*, pp. 8, 62, and 227.
21. Tony Judt, *Reappraisals: Reflections on the Forgotten Twentieth Century* (New York: Penguin Books, 2008), p. 261.
22. Timothy Snyder, *On Tyranny: Twenty Lessons from the Twentieth Century* (New York: Tim Duggan Books, 2017), p. 123; Yuri Burtin, "Zhivoe i Mertvoe," *Literaturnaya gazeta*, No. 34 (1990), p. 7.
23. Karen Dawisha, *Putin's Kleptocracy: Who Owns Russia?* (New York: Simon and Schuster Paperbacks, 2014). We again refer readers to Karen Dawisha's excellent examination of the shocking depth of corruption embedded within the Russian state at the behest of its top leaders.
24. Arendt, *Origins of Totalitarianism*, p. 474.
25. Again, this calls attention to modern Russia's invocation of a heroic, romanticized Soviet past. Russians today continue to ritualize worship for the Soviet soldiers who sacrificed their lives in World War II in the fight against fascism, but several million of them did not identify as Russian—a trait that heavily influences the culture of Putin's Russia. Grigori Krivosheyev *Rossija i SSSR v vojnah XX veka: poteri vooruzhennyh sil. Statisticheskoe issledovanie* (Moscow: Voennoe izdatelstvo, 1993).
26. Victor Zaslavsky, *Class Cleansing: The Massacre at Katyn* (Candor: Telos Press Publishing, 2008) and *Katyn*, DVD, dir. Andrzej Wajda (Warsaw: ITI Cinema, 2007).
27. Giorgio Agamben, *Means Without End: Notes on Politics*, trans. Vincenzo Benetti and Cesar Casarino (Minneapolis: University of Minnesota Press, 2000), pp. 97 and 98.
28. V. Fadeev, M. Rogozhnikov, A. Mekhanik, Yu. Polunin, and A. Smirnova, *Oppozitsii nashego vremeni: Doklad Instituta obshchestvennogo proyektirovaniya o sostoyanii i perspektivakh politicheskoy sistemy Rossii* (Moscow: Institut Obshchestvennogo Proyektirovaniya, 2011), p. 5.
29. Vladimir Voinovich, *The Anti-Soviet Soviet Union*, trans. Richard Lourie (San Diego, New York, and London: Harcourt Brace Jovanovich, 1985), pp. 312–314. While the authors were revising this manuscript, Vladimir Voinovich passed away on 27 July 2018. Vladimir Tismaneanu had earlier reviewed his book *The Anti-Soviet Soviet Union*; Tismaneanu reread—and Kate Langdon, having been born in 1995, read for the first time—Voinovich's book and found it enormously applicable to the culture of Putinism. The content of Voinovich's book offers the perfect diagnosis of Putinism and Russian society's larger ills, on the one hand; on the other hand, the later actions of the author—who accepted from Putin's Kremlin

both the State Prize of the Russian Federation in 2000 for his book *Monumental Propaganda* (about the Stalinist legacy's survival into modern Russia) and the Andrei Sakharov Prize for Writer's Civic Courage in 2002— reveal a continuation of the very contradictions expressed in *The Anti-Soviet Soviet Union*. It is difficult to reconcile Voinovich's acceptance of these awards under Putin's administration, the leader whom he did not stop criticizing until his recent death. It was obvious from the start of the Second Chechen War in 1999 that Putin's regime had been based on genocide and racism, and the Voinovich of 1985 would have viewed the decision to accept an award from that kind of government as the despicable choice of an indoctrinated believer. Even though he spent the next several years of his life calling out Putin's authoritarianism, Voinovich did not remedy his choice to accept the awards. The fact that such an otherwise outspoken person did not renounce the prizes is demonstrative of modern fascists' abilities to transform angst about authoritarianism into support for authoritarianism. In a way, the dichotomy between Voinovich's critical thoughts about authoritarianism and his acceptance of an authoritarian government's awards is an accurate depiction of Putinism's beguiling tactics and facades. Now that we are coming to the conclusion of our book and have explained the Voinovich conundrum to readers, we hope readers can remember this book as a dialogue informed by both Voinovich's courage and his behavioral dilemma.

30. Norman Cohn, *Europe's Inner Demons: An Enquiry Inspired by the Great Witch-Hunt* (New York: Basic Books, Inc., 1975), pp. 224 and 259.
31. Leszek Kołakowski. *Freedom, Fame, Lying and Betrayal: Essays on Everyday Life*, translated by Agnieszka Kołakowska (London and New York: The Penguin Group, 1999), pp. 36–37.
32. Hannah Arendt, *The Last Interview and Other Conversations* (Brooklyn and London: Melville House Publishing, 2013), p. 61; Walter Laqueur, *Putinism: Russia and Its Future with the West* (New York: Thomas Dunne Books, 2015).
33. Cohn, *Europe's Inner Demons*, p. 219.
34. Tony Judt, *The Burden of Responsibility: Blum, Camus, Aron, and the French Twentieth Century* (Chicago: University of Chicago Press, 1998), p. 126.

References

Agamben, Giorgio. 2000. *Means Without End: Notes on Politics*. Trans. Vincenzo Benetti and Cesar Casarino. Minneapolis: University of Minnesota Press.
Arendt, Hannah. 1958. *Origins of Totalitarianism*. New York: Meridian Books.
———. 1994. The Seeds of a Fascist International. In *Essays in Understanding 1930–1954*, ed. Jerome Kohn, 140–150. New York: Harcourt Brace.

———. 2013. *The Last Interview and Other Conversations*. Brooklyn/London: Melville House Publishing.
Besançon, Alain. 2015. "I'm for the Cold War!" Interview by Marius Stan and Vladimir Tismaneanu. *Contributors.ro*, June 28. Transcript available at http://www.contributors.ro/cultura/%E2%80%9Csunt-pentru-razboiul-rece%E2%80%9D-un-dialog-cu-alain-besanc%CC%A7on-realizat-de-marius-stan-%C8%99i-vladimir-tismaneanu-paris-28-iunie-2015/
Birmingham, Peg. 2010. A Lying World Order: Political Deception and the Threat of Totalitarianism. In *Thinking in Dark Times: Hannah Arendt on Ethics and Politics*, ed. Roger Berkowitz, Jeffrey Katz, and Thomas Keenan, 73–77. New York: Fordham University.
Burtin, Yuri. 1990. "Zhivoe i Mertvoe" [The Living and the Dead]. *Literaturnaya gazeta* 34.
Cohn, Norman. 1975. *Europe's Inner Demons: An Enquiry Inspired by the Great Witch-Hunt*. New York: Basic Books, Inc.
Dawisha, Karen. 2014. *Putin's Kleptocracy: Who Owns Russia*. New York: Simon and Schuster Paperbacks.
Eco, Umberto. 1995. Ur-Fascism. *The New York Review of Books*, June 22. Accessed 15 March 2019 at https://www.nybooks.com/articles/1995/06/22/ur-fascism/
Fadeev, V., M. Rogozhnikov, A. Mekhanik, Yu. Polunin, and A. Smirnova. 2011. *Oppozitsii nashego vremeni: Doklad Instituta obshchestvennogo proyektirovaniya o sostoyanii i perspektivakh politicheskoy sistemy Rossii* [Opposition of Our Time: Report by the Institute of Public Planning on the State and Prospects of Russia's Political System]. Moscow: Institut Obshchestvennogo Proyektirovaniya.
Fish, M. Steven. 2017. The Kremlin Emboldened: What Is Putinism? *Journal of Democracy* 28 (4): 61–75.
Gorbunova, Yulia. 2018. Law Not on Side of Russia's Domestic Violence Victims: One Year Since Legislative Changes Weakened Protections. *Human Rights Watch*, February 14. Accessed 13 July 2018 at https://www.hrw.org/news/2018/02/14/law-not-side-russias-domestic-violence-victims
Gudkov, Lev, and Eva Hartog. 2017. The Evolution of Homo Sovieticus to Putin's Man. *The Moscow Times*, October 13. Accessed 15 March 2019 at https://www.themoscowtimes.com/2017/10/13/the-evolution-of-homo-sovieticus-to-putins-man-a59189
Isajanuan, Nerses. 2017. Russia: Decriminalization of Domestic Violence. *The Library of Congress*, June. Accessed 13 July 2018 at https://www.loc.gov/law/help/domestic-violence/russia.php
Judt, Tony. 1998. *The Burden of Responsibility: Blum, Camus, Aron, and the French Twentieth Century*. Chicago: University of Chicago Press.
———. 2008. *Reappraisals: Reflections on the Forgotten Twentieth Century*. New York: Penguin Books.

Katyn. 2007. DVD. Directed by Andrzej Wajda. Warsaw: ITI Cinema.
Kołakowski, Leszek. 1999. *Freedom, Fame, Lying and Betrayal: Essays on Everyday Life*. Trans. Agnieszka Kołakowska. London/New York: The Penguin Group.
Kotkin, Stephen. 2009. Comment: From Overlooking to Overestimating Russia's Authoritarianism? *Slavic Review* 68 (3, Fall): 548–551.
Kottke, Jason. 2016. Umberto Eco Makes a List of the 14 Common Features of Fascism. *Open Culture*, November 22. Accessed 15 March 2019 at http://www.openculture.com/2016/11/umberto-eco-makes-a-list-of-the-14-common-features-of-fascism.html
Kozlova, Natalia. 2017. *Ruku Opusti* [Leave the Hands]. *Rossiiskaia Gazeta*, February 9. Accessed 13 July 2018 at https://rg.ru/2017/02/09/rg-publikuet-zakon-o-dekriminalizacii-domashnego-nasiliia.html
Krivosheyev, Grigori. 1993. *Rossija i SSSR v vojnah XX veka: poteri vooruzhennyh sil. Statisticheskoe issledovanie* [Russia and the USSR in the Wars of the 20th Century: Losses of the Armed Forces: A Statistical Study]. Moscow: Voennoe izdatelstvo.
Laqueur, Walter. 2015. *Putinism: Russia and Its Future with the West*. New York: Thomas Dunne Books.
Motl, Alexander J. 2015. Is Vladimir Putin a Fascist? *Newsweek*, April 27. Accessed 7 April 2017 at http://www.newsweek.com/vladimir-putin-fascist-325534
Schmitt, Carl. 1996. *The Concept of the Political*. Chicago: Chicago University Press.
Schnapp, Jeffrey T. 1996. Fascinating Fascism. *Journal of Contemporary History* 31 (2): 235–244.
Snyder, Timothy. 2017. *On Tyranny: Twenty Lessons from the Twentieth Century*. New York: Tim Duggan Books.
———. 2018. *The Road to Unfreedom: Russia, Europe, America*. New York: Tim Duggan Books.
Talmon, Jacob L. 1952. *The Origins of Totalitarian Democracy*. London: Secker and Warburg.
The Patriarchate of Moscow. 2016. Patriarshaja komissija po voprosam sem'i vyrazhaet obespokoennost' v svjazi s prinjatiem novoj redakcii stat'i 116 Ugolovnogo kodeksa [The Patriarchal Commission on Family Affairs is concerned about the adoption of a new version of Article 116 of the Criminal Code]. *The Patriarchate of Moscow*, July 4. Accessed 13 July 2018 at http://www.patriarchia.ru/db/text/4553320.html
Tismaneanu, Vladimir. 2012. *The Devil in History: Communism, Fascism, and Some Lessons of the Twentieth Century*. Berkeley/Los Angeles: University of California Press.
Voinovich, Vladimir. 1985. *The Anti-Soviet Soviet Union*. Trans. Richard Lourie. San Diego/New York/London: Harcourt Brace Jovanovich.
Zaslavsky, Victor. 2008. *Class Cleansing: The Massacre at Katyn*. Candor: Telos Press Publishing.

Index[1]

A
Apartment bombings of 1999, 63–65, 75n28, 116
Arendt, Hannah, 1, 17, 85, 96, 122, 168, 208, 230, 239
Al-Assad, Bashar, *see* Syria

B
Berezovsky, Boris, 30n47, 62
Berzin, Yan, 56, 72n2
Besançon, Alain, 211, 231

C
Cohn, Norman, 167, 237, 239

D
Dawisha, Karen, 7, 8, 226
Death of Stalin, The (2017 film), 160–161

Dugin, Aleksandr, 23, 93–95, 105n29, 105n30, 106n31, 106n32

E
Eurasian Economic Union, 120
Eurasianism, 23, 93, 95–98, 105n28, 107n35, 107n38

F
France
  Le Pen, Marine, 1
  National Front, 1, 194, 238
Fukuyama, Francis, 15, 16, 28n34, 45

G
Germany
  Alternative for Germany, 194, 238
Global authoritarian wave, 1, 24–25, 193–194, 234, 238

---

[1] Note: Page numbers followed by 'n' refer to notes.

Gorbachev, Mikhail, 3, 16, 28n34,
    43–44, 60, 67, 99, 128
Gorbachev Phenomenon, 2–3, 15, 18
Great Patriotic War, 125–127, 165,
    199, 235
Greece
    Golden Dawn, 238
    Syriza, 194, 238
Gusinsky, Vladimir, 62, 208, 209

H
Hitler, Adolf, 8, 67, 89, 95, 104n20,
    122, 125, 145n55, 155, 215n19,
    230, 232
Homo sovieticus, 84, 139–141, 147n82
Hungary
    Fidesz, 194, 238
    Jobbik, 238
    Orbán, Viktor, 1

I
Ideology, 8, 11, 72, 83–85, 87–90,
    96, 100, 104n20, 116, 153, 164,
    165, 167, 201, 213n3, 226
    definition of, 85–87
Ilyin, Ivan, 23, 90–94, 105n27,
    122, 136
Intelligentsia, 38, 47n12, 114

J
Judah, Ben, 2, 135, 226
Judt, Tony, 35, 233

K
Kara-Murza, Vladimir, 2, 4, 5, 30n47
Khodorkovsky, Mikhail, 62, 170, 209
Kołakowski, Leszek, 171, 238
Kyivan Rus, 35, 36, 190, 196, 212n3

L
Laqueur, Walter, 14, 15, 91
Lavrov, Sergey, 122, 202, 204
Lenin, Vladimir Ilyich, 8, 21, 41–43,
    45, 49n22, 68, 72n2, 95, 96, 99,
    139, 169
Leninism, *see* Lenin, Vladimir Ilyich
Lewin, Moshe, 3
Litvinenko, Alexander, 30n47

M
Maduro, Nicolás, *see* Venezuela
McFaul, Michael, 50n31, 75n22
Medvedev, Dmitry, 29n45, 71, 73n6

N
Navalny, Alexei, 17, 30n47
Nemtsov, Boris, 30n47, 74n22
Neo-Eurasianism, *see* Eurasianism
Nicaragua
    Ortega, Daniel, 1, 15

O
Obama, Barack, *see* United States
Orbán, Viktor, *see* Hungary

P
Perón, Juan, 100–102
Poland
    Jedwabne, 175, 183n81
    Katyn Massacre, 235
    Law and Justice party, 1, 18, 238
Politkovskaya, Anna, 30n47, 70, 176
Putin Phenomenon, 2–4, 35, 177,
    225, 226, 233
Putin, Vladimir Vladimirovich
    corruption of, 5, 61, 168–170
    in Dresden as KGB agent, 57–61

early life of, 56
international admiration for, 9, 11, 19–20, 27n25
rise to power of, 3, 61–70, 234
Putinism, 4, 7, 8, 22, 23, 72, 84, 86, 98, 113, 115, 139, 165, 172, 189, 194, 195, 208, 213n13, 216n34, 225–227, 229, 231–233, 237, 238, 241n29
comparisons with Peronism, 100–102
comparisons with Zhdanovism, 115
functioning of, 88–90, 113–137
intellectual origins of, 90–97
as a mobilizing force, 6, 69, 157, 165–177, 178n13

R
Russia
anti-Westernism in, 96, 121–125, 177, 204
biopolitics in, 131–137, 196
censorship in, 160–161, 175, 208–211, 230, 233–234
comparisons with Weimar Germany, 46, 129–130, 145n55, 146n57, 175–177
foreign policy of, 24, 189–195
homophobia in, 137, 199
religious and ethnic discrimination in, 64, 136
totalitarian democracy in, 17, 230–234
under Communism, 40–44, 117–121
under tsarism, 36–41, 48n13, 63
Russian exceptionalism, 23, 91, 96, 115, 116, 121, 191
Russian Orthodox Church, 23, 37, 38, 71, 146n67, 155, 161–163, 177, 226, 228

S
St. George's ribbon, 163–165, 167, 181n43, 205
Schmitt, Carl, 135, 169, 211, 232
Second Chechen War, 65–67, 117
Shevtsova, Lilia, 2, 5, 119, 120
Skripal, Sergei, 194, 213n13
Sobchak, Anatoly Aleksandrovich, 61, 62
Solzhenitsyn, Aleksandr, 9
Stalin, Josef, 18, 21, 42–43, 49n24, 49n29, 69, 89, 99, 115, 121, 125, 127–128, 143n25, 155, 160, 167, 230
Stalinism, *see* Stalin, Josef
Starovoitova, Galina, 30n47, 176, 183n83
Surkov, Vladislav, 162, 170
Syria, 10, 179n26
al-Assad, Bashar, 1, 15, 28n29, 48n14, 202, 203, 230
Russian interference in, 201–205

T
Third Rome, the, 95, 107n35
Trump, Donald, *see* United States
Tucker, Robert C., 14, 44, 114, 154, 155
Turgenev, Ivan, 39, 141–142n2

U
Ukraine, 9, 106n31, 123, 164, 181n45, 213n3, 214n18
Orange Revolution, 163, 181n44
Russian interference in, 12, 73n2, 94, 106n32, 123, 124, 127, 141, 147n84, 155, 159, 192, 195–201, 206, 215n18, 216n34, 232

United States, 6, 9, 11–13, 15, 20, 28n29, 84, 102, 108n45, 123, 154, 159, 161, 166, 198, 202, 204, 205
  Obama, Barack, 11, 28n29, 205
  Trump, Donald, 1, 5, 7–9, 13, 15, 20, 25, 101, 102n1, 105n30
  Trumpism, 8, 13, 16, 238
Utopianism, 2, 11, 12, 21, 41–44, 58, 59, 84, 98–99, 114, 118, 119, 125, 127, 139, 140, 145n55, 231

V
Venezuela
  Maduro, Nicolás, 1, 8, 28n28

Voinovich, Vladimir, 124, 129, 235–237, 241n29
Von Stirlitz, Max Otto, 56, 60, 73n4, 73n6

Y
Yeltsin, Boris, 22, 36, 45–46, 50n31, 62–63, 69, 70, 74n22, 123, 168, 169, 181n56

Z
Zhdanov, Andrei, 114
Zinovyev, Aleksandr, 45, 49n29, 139

Printed in Great Britain
by Amazon